D1616727

HEGEL'S POLITICAL PHILOSOPHY

HEGEL'S POLITICAL PHILOSOPHY

INTERPRETING THE PRACTICE OF
LEGAL PUNISHMENT

Mark Tunick

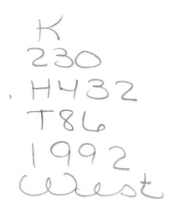
PRINCETON UNIVERSITY PRESS   PRINCETON, NEW JERSEY

Library of Congress Cataloging-in-Publication Data

Tunick, Mark.
Hegel's political philosophy : interpreting the practice of legal punishment /
Mark Tunick.
p.   cm.
Includes bibliographical references and index.
ISBN 0-691-07410-0 (CL)
1. Hegel, Georg Wilhelm Friedrich, 1770–1831—Views on punishment.
2. Hegel, Georg Wilhelm Friedrich, 1770–1831—Political and social views.   I. Title.
K230.H432T86   1992
320'.01—dc20   92-4108   CIP

This book has been composed in Linotron Sabon

Princeton University Press books are printed on acid-free paper
and meet the guidelines for permanence and durability of the
Committee on Production Guidelines for Book Longevity of the
Council on Library Resources

Printed in the United States of America

10   9   8   7   6   5   4   3   2   1

Contents

Preface   vii

Acknowledgments   xiii

List of Abbreviations   xv

One
Introduction to Hegel's Political Philosophy   3

   1.1   *Why Hegel?*   3

   1.2   *The Texts of Hegel's Philosophy of Right: The Lecture
Notes and the* Philosophy of Right   5

   1.3   *Hegel's Political Philosophy: Metaphysical or Political?*   12

Two
Hegel's Theory of Legal Punishment: An Overview   24

   2.1   *What Crime Is*   25

   2.2   *The Split Will*   29

   2.3   *The Significance of Punishment*   34

   2.4   *Hegel's Key Claim about Punishment*   35

Three
Hegel's Conception of Freedom   37

   3.1   *Paragraphs 5–7 of the* Philosophy of Right: *The
Concept of Will in General*   38

   3.2   *The Rest of the Introduction: The Appropriate Content
of the Free Will*   55

   3.3   *Subjective and Objective Justifications*   61

Four
Recht-an-sich and the Power That Punishes   76

   4.1   *The Power That Punishes*   77

   4.2   *The Early Vision of Ethical Substance*   81

   4.3   Recht-an-sich *in the* Rechtsphilosophie   91

Five
Hegel's Immanent Criticism of the Practice of Legal Punishment   108

   5.1   *Ideals in Practice*   108

   5.2   *Lawmaking: What Should Be Made Criminal?*   110

5.3   *Clutching: Hegel on Political Crime*   113

5.4   *Determination of Guilt*   120

5.5   *Sentencing*   131

5.6   *Infliction of Punishment*   133

5.7   *Hegel as Practical Theorist*   137

Appendix: Translation of Passage from Rph III on Political Crime   140

Six

Theory and Practice   142

6.1   *The Power of Theory: Kierkegaard vs. Marx*   142

6.2   *"The Actual Is the Rational"*   152

6.3   *Hegel and the Activity of Justifying Practices*   167

6.4   *Immanent vs. Radical Criticism*   172

Bibliography   175

Index   185

Preface

I BELIEVE that if political theory is to be more than intellectual edification it must bear on our practices. Georg Wilhelm Friedrich Hegel is one of the most important and influential political philosophers by most accounts of Western intellectual history, but he is virtually ignored by politicians and practitioners, who, busy enough just coping with the problems of everyday life, are unlikely to make the effort to master Hegel's exceedingly difficult terminology and grapple with a speculative philosophy that seems so far removed from their immediate concerns. In this book I aim to show how Hegel deserves his place among the great political and legal theorists precisely because of what he has to teach us about our practices.[1]

In this book I challenge many of the accepted assumptions about Hegel, assumptions that have led many students of political and legal theory readily to dismiss Hegel, students who share in my concern that theory be not an esoteric and arcane academic exercise, but relevant to the politics and practices of our times. Leaving aside his well-earned reputation for obscurity, Hegel is said to be an "Idealist," like Kant, of the sort who sticks to ideas and principles about what's right, indifferent to what counts as right in the world; someone who "takes refuge in a dialectical fiction."[2] To some, Hegel's idealism, his view that "what is actual is rational" and that "Reason" is in history, results not in an innocent escapism, but a nefarious conservatism that supports the "Powers that Be."[3] To others, Hegel is not necessarily dangerous; he is simply irrelevant: "Hegel's system does not generate correct suggestions for legal or political change. . . . In fact, Hegel structured his theory in a way that makes it impossible

---

[1] Some might argue that Hegel can teach *us* nothing about *our* practices because he wrote about *his* Prussia, whose practices were very different from our own. For the theoretical underpinnings for such an argument, see Quentin Skinner, "Meaning and Understanding in the History of Ideas." I have two responses. First, even if Hegel's discussions about legal punishment were about a practice very different from our own, the strategy I shall argue Hegel adopts, of immanent criticism, is very relevant to those of us who think about any of *our* practices. Second, the practice of legal punishment about which Hegel theorizes is in many respects similar to our own practice.

[2] Ossip Flechtheim, "Die Funktion der Strafe in der Rechtstheorie Hegels," p. 9.

[3] "Like those who invoke God's will and wisdom in history, the exact equivalence of *die List der Vernunft* [the cunning of reason], [Hegel] is always wise after the event. Until then he is on the side of the 'Powers that Be' " (Sidney Hook, "Hegel Rehabilitated?" p. 65). For others who understand Hegel's views to be conservative and potentially dangerous, see note 17, below.

to derive definitive answers to political or legal questions from it."[4] Karl Marx, while at times acknowledging his intellectual indebtedness to Hegel, also casts him as a politically irrelevant metaphysician, calling Hegel's philosophy "logical, pantheistic mysticism," "sophistical," and "magical."[5] To Marx, Hegel is blinded by his speculative philosophy from adequately assessing and criticizing the world about him; Hegel shapes reality to fit his own system of logic.[6] Marx's Hegel is too much the outsider, dwelling in his "house of logic," to be political or to help us with our practices.

Students today aren't likely ever to read Hegel. Were Hegel the tedious, obscure, and irrelevant idealist who legitimates the powers that be, were he Marx's apolitical metaphysician, this would not trouble me. But the Hegel I know is not that. This book is my effort to introduce the Hegel I know: the profound and sweeping theorist and critic of social practices.[7]

It seems to me that the best way to show that Hegel is a practical theorist is to show him at work theorizing about one of our practices. One of the practices that most interested Hegel, and a practice that is one of the most divisive to us, is legal punishment. The practice of legal punishment raises not only a difficult philosophical question—how can one justify the state inflicting pain or suffering on a human being?—a question for which Hegel has an original and elaborate answer that draws us to the very core of his political philosophy, but also numerous issues that arise inside the practice: Given that we punish, how should we punish? For what actions should we punish? Should we punish a person who did not intend to commit a crime, perhaps because she lacked the capacity to know the nature of what she was doing? Should we use expedients such as plea bargaining, where the prosecutor offers a less severe sentence to a defendant in exchange for a plea of guilty? Should we extend the sentences of repeat offenders on the ground that they pose a probable threat to society and need to be incapacitated? Should we sentence certain criminals to die? Hegel not only offers what I find to be a persuasive answer to the philosophical question of why we do (and should) punish at all; he also uses his conception of why we punish to address these and other

---

[4] Richard Hyland, "Hegel: A User's Manual," p. 1735.

[5] Karl Marx, *Critique of Hegel's "Philosophy of Right,"* pp. 7, 20, 34. I discuss and criticize Marx's dismissal of Hegel as an apolitical metaphysician in my article "Hegel's Justification of Hereditary Monarchy."

[6] Karl Marx, *Critique of Hegel's "Philosophy of Right,"* p. 14: "[Hegel] does not develop his thought out of what is objective, but what is objective in accordance with a ready-made thought which has its origin in the abstract sphere of logic."

[7] But I am not uncritical of Hegel; and in chapter 5 we shall see that the claims I make for Hegel's theory of legal punishment are rather modest. But then, I think that if theorists are to gain an audience with practitioners they must concede that no theory of any of our complex practices is likely to resolve all of our problems with respect to these practices.

practical issues. In this book I discuss not only Hegel's answer to the philosophical question, but also the theoretically informed prescriptions he has to offer those working within the criminal justice system and needing to know how to proceed.

Hegel says we punish not because of the utility of doing so—we do not punish in order to deter future crimes or to reform or incapacitate a dangerous person—but, rather, we punish because a wrong was done that must be righted. We punish because it is right to punish, and because only by punishing do we establish the crime as wrong, and the law it violated as right.[8] Hegel claims also that the criminal has a right to punishment, and that only by being punished is the criminal respected as a free human being. Hegel gives a *retributive* theory of punishment. There are many distinct retributive theories; but all share in common a rejection of the utilitarian view that we punish in order to augment social utility, and that we *should* punish only when doing so augments social utility. Perhaps the best illustration of a retributivist position is Kant's: on an island where all the people were to leave the next day, forever dissolving and dispersing the community, the last murderer in jail would have to have his execution carried out before the diaspora—justice demands this.[9] Kant, and retributivists in general, takes justice seriously: "if justice goes under, there is no more value in man living on earth."[10] To a people familiar with the language of utility and philosophies of pragmatism, such a view may seem, depending on one's temper, to be impractical though worthy idealism or bizarre and dangerous fanaticism.

Hegel's view on punishment is often the object of scorn or ridicule. Hegel writes that punishment "makes null the crime,"[11] a claim one recent commentator dismisses as "obscure,"[12] and to which another responds:

[8] PR 99. A guide to the abbreviations I use in citing Hegel's works appears at the front of this book. In citing from a work published in English translation (see the Bibliography), I modify that translation only when I think there is good reason to do so. For citations from a work for which no English translation is listed in the Bibliography, translations are my own.

[9] Immanuel Kant, *Metaphysik der Sitten*, A199, B229. This passage is often cited to show how Kant's theory of punishment is "deontological," or oblivious to consequences. For reasons that I discuss elsewhere, Kant's theory of legal (as opposed to moral) punishment is not properly labeled deontological. See my *Punishment: Theory and Practice*, ch. 3, sec. 2.3.

[10] "Wenn die Gerechtigkeit untergeht, so hat es keinen Wert mehr, daß Menschen auf Erden leben" (Immanuel Kant, *Metaphysik der Sitten*, A196–197, B226–227). Kant's retributivism differs from Hegel's; I discuss the differences in my *Punishment: Theory and Practice*, ch. 3.

[11] PR 97, 99.

[12] David Dolinko, "Some Thoughts About Retributivism," p. 548.

This Hegelian theory is really excessively obscure . . . how the infliction of punishment which neither reverses the evil act nor necessarily reforms the evil will
can be said to negate the wrong done is surely beyond the comprehension of
any literally-minded person. Such an assertion is the kind of thing which causes
philosophy to be regarded as a species of poetry rather than of exact thinking.[13]

It is easy after being frustrated in reading Hegel to give up and call his
philosophy poetry or mysticism. In a casebook on criminal law we read
that "[o]ther formulations of the retributive theory are (like Kant's) intuitive, and occasionally they take on a somewhat mystical tinge, as with
Hegel's view that crime is a negation and punishment a negation of that
negation."[14] Unfortunately, such a view receives a wide audience when it
is published in a casebook used to educate future lawyers and law professors.

The more judicious avoid name-calling and confess they simply do not
understand Hegel's theory.[15] But all too often Hegel, whose theory of
punishment is often wrongly identified with Kant's, is the victim of a vin-
dictive pen: "Kant and Hegel built theories of punishment around [the
retributivist] concept which had no more connection with the day-to-day
realities of our criminal law than with the pieces on [a] chessboard."[16]

My purpose here is not merely to vindicate Hegel in the face of the
above criticism. I do intend to show that Hegel's theory of crime and
punishment can be stated without obscurity, in terms that will satisfy the
analytical mind, and without recourse to mysticism. But my more ambitious purpose is to show that if we take the effort required we shall find
in Hegel's theory of legal punishment both a persuasive account of why
we punish, an account that will shed light on problems facing practitioners within the criminal justice system, and also an outstanding example
of how Hegel welds the theoretical and the practical, an example I hope
stimulates greater interest in the practical aspects of Hegel's political and
legal philosophy as a whole. I shall argue that Hegel is a legal interpretivist who developed an elaborate and persuasive understanding of a vast
array of specific social practices, laws, and institutions, including our
practice of legal punishment, which he uses in articulating what he claims
to be the objective justifications of these practices. Hegel, moreover, and

---

[13] D. J. B. Hawkins, "Punishment and Moral Responsibility," p. 16.

[14] P. Brett, *An Inquiry into Criminal Guilt* (London: Sweet and Maxwell, 1963), p. 51;
cited in George Dix and Michael Sharlot, *Criminal Law: Cases and Materials*, 3rd ed., p.
74.

[15] A. C. Ewing, *The Morality of Punishment*, p. 22. Ewing argues that punishment cannot
really undo the past evil and that if this is a metaphor Hegel employs its meaning remains
unclear.

[16] Norval Morris and Thomas Buckle, "The Humanitarian Theory of Punishment," p.
315.

contrary to the views of many Hegel scholars both past and present, conceives of his theoretical understanding of these concrete social practices as a measure by which to judge and *criticize* these very practices. Hegel does not accommodate himself to bad or unjust laws or practices merely because they exist.[17] His political philosophy is critical theory. If I am successful, we shall have not only a persuasive interpretation of Hegel's political philosophy as practical theory that goes against the grain of so much that is written on Hegel, but an interpretation of our practice of legal punishment that we can use as a standard of justification, a critical edge, when we engage in practical political dialogue regarding that practice.

After an overview of Hegel's political philosophy, taken up in chapter 1, we shall, in chapter 2, consider Hegel's views on legal punishment. We shall see how Hegel claims that the criminal is made free in her punishment and that punishment is her right. In chapter 3 we shall see what Hegel means by "freedom," and in chapter 4, what he means by "right." In chapter 5 we shall return to Hegel's discussion of punishment, now concerning ourselves with the sorts of details with which practitioners—judges, lawyers, legislators—concern themselves. Here we shall see how Hegel makes concrete and relevant his theory of why we punish. In the final chapter we shall step back from Hegel's specific theory of legal punishment to reflect on his political philosophy as a whole.

[17] Hegel began to earn a reputation as a conservative philosopher and justifier of the Prussian state virtually as soon as his book appeared in 1820. For a collection of contemporary reviews of Hegel's *Philosophy of Right*, see Manfred Riedel, ed., *Materialen zu Hegels Rechtsphilosophie*, vol. 1. Advocates of the conservative reading of Hegel include Rudolf Haym (*Hegel und seine Zeit*); the extreme conservative group of "New Hegelians," who wrote in the decades preceding World War II, and many of whom identify with Hegel's philosophy and see it as a justification of an individual's obligation to the state but not a corresponding duty of the state to uphold individual rights (see Hubert R. Rottleuthner, "Die Substantialisierung des Formalrechts" for discussion and bibliography); and Marxists and Marxians, who criticize Hegel's philosophy as "bourgeois" and see it as a justification for existing unjust social and economic relations (see Karl Marx, "Capital Punishment," in the *New York Daily Tribune*, Feb. 18, 1853, in *Marx-Engels Gesamtausgabe* (MEGA), vol. 12, pp. 24–30; A. A. Piontkowski, *Hegels Lehre über Staat und Recht und Seine Strafrechtstheorie*; Herbert Schnädelbach, "Zum Verhältnis von Logik und Gesellschaftstheorie bei Hegel"; and Mitchell Franklin, "The Contribution of Hegel, Beccaria, Holbach and Livingston"). Recently another version of the "Prussian state philosopher" reading appeared, proving that this myth has yet to be laid to rest (see Ernst Topitsch, *Die Sozialphilosophie Hegels als Heilslehre und Herrschaftsideologie*).

Acknowledgments _____

HEGEL IS special to me because it was the excitement I experienced in reading his work when I was an undergraduate, and the contact I then had with three inspiring, caring, and dedicated teachers at M.I.T., that motivated me to undertake graduate studies in and eventually teach political theory. I begin these acknowledgments by expressing my gratitude to my former teachers—Suzanne Berger, Joshua Cohen, and Dr. Louis Menand III; I feel that in some sense they are as responsible for the coming to be of this book as those who actually read its parts. I want them to know that they made a difference to me.

Several people looked at some or all of the manuscript, originally part of my doctoral dissertation at Berkeley (hence the reference to the "Berkeley Hegelian" at the beginning of chapter 6). Thanks are due to Hanna Pitkin in particular, for asking very hard questions, and for getting me not only to say what I meant where I had not, but also to see that sometimes I had not known what I meant, as well as to Jeremy Waldron, Norman Jacobson, Paul Thomas, Alyson Cole, Dan Avnon, Elizabeth Collins, Emily Hauptmann, Patrizia Heckle, Dennis McEnnerney, Jackie Stevens, and Brian Wiener; to "The Eleven Hegelians," the students of my undergraduate Hegel seminar at Stanford in the autumn of 1991, for their well-informed and sanely pragmatic, yet encouraging and sympathetic criticisms of my efforts to defend some of what Hegel says; and finally to my parents, to whom I dedicate this book. It was not easy for them to watch their son choose Hegel over a law degree, but they came to understand, and were wonderfully supportive.

Suhrkamp Verlag has kindly granted permission to publish a translation from Dieter Henrich, ed., *Philosophie des Rechts: Die Vorlesung von 1819/20 in einer Nachschrift* (Frankfurt am Main: Suhrkamp Verlag, 1983).

List of Abbreviations _____

ALL WORKS listed below are by Hegel. Citations in the notes refer to page numbers, except as indicated here. Full citations appear in the Bibliography.

Enz   *Enzyklopädie der philosophischen Wissenschaften*; *Encyclopaedia of the Philosophical Sciences (1830)*; references are to numbered paragraphs. "Rem" means remark; "Z" means addition (*Zusatz*)

GLog   *Science of Logic*

HP   *Lectures on the History of Philosophy*; references are to volume and page

JR   *Jenaer Realphilosophie*

NL   *Natural Law*

PH   *Philosophy of History*; page numbers are given from the German (*Werke in zwanzig Bänden*, vol. 12) and English (Sibree, trans.) editions, respectively

PhdG   *Phenomenology of Spirit*; references are to numbered paragraphs

PR   *Philosophy of Right*; references are to numbered paragraphs. "Rem" means remark, "Z" means addition (*Zusatz*), "Bem" means Hegel's handwritten marginal notes (*Bemerkungen*), included in *Grundlinien der Philosophie des Rechts*

PRel   *Lectures on the Philosophy of Religion*

Prop   *Philosophische Propädeutik*

RH   *Reason in History*

Rph I   C. Becker et al., eds. *Vorlesungen über Naturrecht und Staatswissenschaft*. In citations from Rph I–VII, references are to volume, page, and line when needed

Rph II   Karl-Heinz Ilting, ed. *Vorlesungen über Rechtsphilosophie (1818–1831)*, vol. 1

Rph III   Dieter Henrich, ed. *Philosophie des Rechts: Die Vorlesung von 1819/20 in einer Nachschrift*

Rph V   Karl-Heinz Ilting, ed. *Vorlesungen über Rechtsphilosophie (1818–1831)*, vol. 3

Rph VI   Ibid., vol. 4

Rph VII   Ibid.

HEGEL'S POLITICAL PHILOSOPHY

One

Introduction to Hegel's Political Philosophy

1.1 Why Hegel?

Why take seriously a metaphysician notorious for his prolix writing? Hegel's writing is dense, obscure, always difficult, and sometimes impossible to understand. Even if we can wade through it, the promised land is either nightmare or deluded utopia to anyone with the modern sensibility: its world has an "absolute rational design";[1] it is governed by God ("the actual working of His government—the carrying out of His plan—is the history of the world");[2] and in this world "the state is absolutely rational."[3]

I should be clear about my intentions at the start. I share in the modern sensibility that rejects at least these first two claims. (The third claim, that the state is absolutely rational, is too cryptic to pass judgment on at this time.) Hegel makes many metaphysical claims that, taken literally, I find unacceptable. Hegel claims to have discerned the objective and absolute justifications for and meanings of our practices and institutions, calling his account of our practices "science." For those, like myself, who reject "foundationalism," or the position that social practices have noncontroversial explanations and justifications with which any right-thinking person is compelled to agree, Hegel's metaphysics and claims to science pose a serious obstacle to appropriating his philosophy.[4] To nonfoundationalists, committed to the position that practices like punishment possess not one fixed meaning but a whole synthesis of meanings all of which are a matter not of knowledge but of *interpretation*, Hegel, by claiming to discern with his metaphysical insight the definitive meanings of and ob-

---

[1] PH 25 (13). A guide to the abbreviations I use in citing Hegel's works appears at the front of this book.

[2] Ibid., 53 (36).

[3] PR 258.

[4] Foundationalism, or the view that practices have meanings or justifications that we need only discover, can be distinguished from nonfoundationalism, or the position that practices have no such fixed justification or meaning and, rather, that we impute meaning to them, that their meaning is fluid and subject to dispute. Nietzsche is the paradigmatic nonfoundationalist: see his *On the Genealogy of Morals*, bk. 2, sec. 13; my discussion in *Punishment: Theory and Practice*, ch. 2, sec. 2.1; and Don Herzog, *Without Foundations: Justification in Political Theory*.

jective justifications for our practices, forecloses debate and discussion about competing interpretations. But the obstacles presented by Hegel's foundationalism are not insurmountable. I believe we can leave aside the metaphysics and appropriate Hegel as a theorist who can help us think clearly about our practices and about problems regarding these practices that we face every day and must resolve in some way.

Hegel scholars disagree about whether it is legitimate to appropriate Hegel by bracketing the metaphysics. Z. A. Pelczynski argues that "Hegel's political thought can be read, understood, and appreciated without having to come to terms with his metaphysics."[5] Stanley Rosen takes the opposite view: "I venture to assert that none of [Hegel's] writings or lectures can be read in a proper manner without a grasp of the main tenets of his logic."[6] I take a middle road. I agree with Pelczynski but acknowledge Rosen's point, and pay due respect to the texts, by calling attention to the fact that the Hegel I appropriate is a nonfoundationalist, nonmetaphysical, that is, a rehabilitated Hegel.

The charge that Hegel is an obscure writer is perhaps the more serious, for no theorist or practitioner of legal punishment will have the patience to endure texts written in language that is so cryptic. I take this charge seriously.[7]

Some have defended Hegel, or at least rationalized his use of dense language, by pointing to certain historical circumstances pressuring Hegel and his contemporaries to be obscure. Robert Solomon suggests that Hegel's difficult language, and also his claims for doing "science," are a result of Hegel's professional ambitions:

> In 1799 Hegel's father died, leaving his son enough money to allow him to think for the first time about an ill-paid but prestigious career in the universities. . . . Unfortunately, to be a philosopher with professional ambitions, then as now, meant that one had to be profound, i.e. obscure and serious, i.e. humorless and extremely tedious, and so Hegel began to learn the jargon and elongate and qualify his sentences in the "speculative" style of Schelling.[8]

In this view, it is significant that Hegel's earliest work, written before these ambitions had surfaced, and some of his later work, written by an

---

[5] Z. A. Pelczynski, "Introduction," in Hegel, *Political Writings*, p. 136.

[6] Stanley Rosen, *G. W. F. Hegel*, p. xiii.

[7] Because I oppose obscurity and the use of jargon and believe that political theory should speak to the ordinary practitioner, I have strived to write this book so that it could be understood by those who are not familiar with Hegel's work but who are interested in political theory, law, or the criminal justice system, including undergraduates and students, scholars, and practitioners of law. I therefore make use of examples and write in a style intended to engage this audience.

[8] Robert Solomon, *In the Spirit of Hegel*, p. 141.

already established professor, are relatively less obscure, and sometimes even clear.[9] Karl-Heinz Ilting argues in a similar vein that, given the situation in Hegel's Prussia, Hegel used his notoriously difficult language as a means of camouflage.[10] Such arguments, while perhaps conducive to greater tolerance of Hegel's writing style, do not make understanding his philosophy any easier.

Hegel was not always an obscure or incomprehensible writer—he was capable even of great elegance. What is more important, he was not an obscure *lecturer*. Particularly with respect to his political philosophy, or, as I shall refer to it in this work, following German commentators, his *Rechtsphilosophie* (literally "philosophy of right"), Hegel lectured with clarity, precision, and a concern for making himself understood by his audience—his students. We are fortunate to have reliable transcripts of many of Hegel's lectures, though most have not been translated into English, and I shall refer to these lecture notes repeatedly. In my view, the charge of obscurantism loses much of its force once we take these lecture notes as a text of Hegel's *Rechtsphilosophie*. Since I have a great stake in the authenticity of these lecture notes, and in the legitimacy of using them as texts, I shall, in the next section, defend my use of them.

1.2 The Texts of Hegel's Philosophy of Right: The Lecture Notes and the *Philosophy of Right*

The student of Hegel faces an immediate problem in approaching his works: what should count as the texts? Some of Hegel's works were published as books, for the academic community in general (the *Science of Logic* and the *Phenomenology*). Others were published as teaching tools, or compendiums to help Hegel lecture to his students (the *Propädeutik*, *Encyclopaedia*, and *Philosophy of Right*). Other sources of his philosophy include materials never published by Hegel—student lecture notes (*History of Philosophy*, *Philosophy of History*, *Philosophy of Religion*, *Lectures on Aesthetics*). While our concern with Hegel's political philosophy makes virtually all of these texts relevant, the text most important to us is the *Philosophy of Right*. Hegel gave a course of lectures on this subject seven times, and we have available to us, in addition to the compendium he published under the title *Grundlinien der Philosophie des Rechts*, several sets of notes of these lectures. The issue we face is, how seriously should we take the lecture notes?

[9] See ibid., p. 119, on the clarity of Hegel's very first works.
[10] See Karl-Heinz Ilting, Introduction in Hegel, *Vorlesungen über Rechtsphilosophie (1818–1831)*, vol. 1.

In general we should be leery of accepting as an authentic and accurate source of a philosopher's ideas lecture notes taken by his students. Students might misunderstand, or be too rushed to be accurate transcribers, or consciously or unconsciously interpret what they hear before writing it down, so that the result is a distortion of the lecturer's intentions. But also, a philosopher who lectures might assume that what he says is "off the record," and so he understandably might pursue lines of thought without thinking through all of the consequences of what he says. When he publishes his ideas he commits himself in a way that he does not intend to do when lecturing. For these reasons, some have avoided or used only with hesitation the famous "Additions" to the *Philosophy of Right*, which are translations of selected passages from some of the lecture notes. In the case of Hegel, however, several important facts warrant, I think, a suspension of skepticism about the lecture notes.[11]

First, it is generally agreed that Hegel was simply better at lecturing than at writing:

> One gets the impression that Hegel was one-sidedly given over to abstractions, given the schematic picture we receive in the *Encyclopaedia*, and that he reduced the actual world to a pair of conceptual formulas through his logical constructions. His audience, who were told in his lectures of the wide scope of the phenomenal world and the empirical knowledge of his time with astounding command of the material, knew better.[12]

In addition, unlike many professors, Hegel spoke slowly when lecturing, so that exact transcripts could be taken.[13] From one student's account, Hegel lectured in front of notebooks, constantly hunting back and forth; he coughed repeatedly; he would begin faltering, make an effort to continue, start all over again, pause, speak, and reflect.[14] The editions of the lecture notes of the *Rechtsphilosophie* that we have recently received through the labors of Karl-Heinz Ilting, Dieter Henrich, Claudia Becker, and others indicate what was originally written down, crossed out, and revised, so that we can virtually see Hegel at work taking an initial stab,

[11] We might ask why it should matter what Hegel's true views are. If our concern is with political and legal issues, then what matters are the ideas in the lecture notes, not whether they genuinely reflect Hegel's opinions. While I conceive of my project as on the whole political theory and not intellectual history, at times I do lay claim to setting aright some issues of Hegel interpretation. I do have a stake in issues such as whether Hegel is critical or accommodating, liberal or conservative, for or against the French Revolution, and other issues regarding Hegel's political judgment. We must settle the question of the reliability of the lecture notes if we are to deal adequately with these issues.

[12] Georg Lasson, "Einleitung," in *Grundlinien der Philosophie des Rechts*, p. 1.

[13] See Peter C. Hodgson, ed., in Hegel, *Lectures on the Philosophy of Religion*, pp. 7–8.

[14] The account of the student, Hotho, is retold in Franz Wiedmann, *Hegel: An Illustrated Biography*, pp. 98–99.

pausing, rethinking, and correcting himself. This suggests both that when Hegel lectured he did so with care and reflection, and that the students whose lecture notes we have received were diligent transcribers. We know that Hegel himself used the transcripts of one of his students, Karl Gustav Julius von Griesheim, to help him in subsequent lectures.[15]

Many Hegel scholars disagree regarding the weight of another reason that with Hegel we have cause to take special interest in the lecture notes: that because of political pressures culminating in the Prussian Carlsbad censorship decrees, Hegel was not able to publish his genuine views about politics, and so it is *only* in his lectures that we can pierce the mask and reach the man. In this view, the authentic *Rechtsphilosophie* (Hegel's philosophy of right) is not in the published *Grundlinien der Philosophie des Rechts* (which English-speakers know as the *Philosophy of Right*), but in the lecture notes.[16]

In order to follow this contentious argument, we need to know some essential information about when Hegel lectured and when he published the *Philosophy of Right*. Hegel gave his first lecture on the *Rechtsphilosophie* in the winter semester at Heidelberg in 1817/18; recently the notes of one of his students, Peter Wannenmann, have been published in German, and they are referred to as Rph I.[17] Hegel gave his next set of lectures in Berlin, in the winter semester of 1818/19—this is referred to as Rph II, Carl Gustav Homeyer's transcription of which has been published by Ilting in the first volume of his four-volume edition of the *Rechtsphilosophie*. Hegel lectured the following year (winter 1819/20), and Dieter Henrich has published a set of notes of these lectures taken by an unknown author, notes he found at the University of Indiana library. They are known as Rph III. Rph III is considered especially important, as these lectures began just after the Carlsbad decrees were announced (August 1819) and immediately preceded publication of the *Philosophy of Right*. The *Philosophy of Right* was published, according to most scholars, in October 1820—though for various reasons that need not concern us here, the exact date remains a point of controversy among some. After a one-year pause, Hegel resumed lecturing on the *Rechtsphilosophie* in the win-

---

[15] Hegel used Griesheim's notes of his 1824 lectures on the philosophy of religion to help him lecture in 1827. See Peter C. Hodgson, ed., in Hegel, *Lectures on the Philosophy of Religion*, p. 201, note 2.

[16] I italicize *Rechtsphilosophie* as I do all foreign words. The reader should remember, though, that the *Rechtsphilosophie* refers not to the book *Philosophy of Right*, but to Hegel's philosophy of right—which may or may not accurately be articulated in the *Philosophy of Right*.

[17] One piece of evidence in support of the reliability of Wannenmann's text is that it matches word for word with a corresponding transcription from the same lectures made by another of Hegel's students, Friedrich Wilhelm Carove; see "Einleitung," in Claudia Becker et al., eds., Hegel, *Vorlesungen über Naturrecht und Staatswissenschaft*, p. xv.

ter semester of 1821/22; this set of lectures is called Rph IV, but no transcript of them is available at present. Hegel lectured again in the winter semesters of 1822/23 (Rph V—Gustav Heinrich Hotho's notes are published by Ilting in volume 3) and 1824/25 (Rph VI—Griesheim's notes are published by Ilting in volume 4). After a long pause, during which his student Eduard Gans took over the course, Hegel resumed lecturing on the *Rechtsphilosophie* in the winter semester of 1831/32 (Rph VII), but he died after only two meetings. We have a transcript of the two lectures he managed to give, taken by the famous Hegelian David Strauss, published by Ilting in volume 4 of his edition.[18]

The argument that there is an exoteric and an esoteric Hegel was advanced by Ilting.[19] He argues that we can see from the lecture notes that the 1820 *Philosophy of Right* is not an authentic representation of Hegel's political philosophy. The *Philosophy of Right* was published in exceptional circumstances—directly following the Carlsbad censorship decrees. Ilting argues that Hegel, concerned with his professional career, changed his outward political position between 1817 and 1820. Ilting focuses on two points in supporting his claim: discrepancies between the *Philosophy of Right* and the lectures regarding both Hegel's view on monarchy and the famous passage from the preface of the *Philosophy of Right* declaring that the "actual is the rational."

In his *Philosophy of Right* Hegel seems to take a royalist position, declaring that governmental power derives from the monarch and that the monarch is head and beginning of the whole; but, notes Ilting, in both Rph II and Rph V Hegel says the monarch merely dots the i's,[20] suggesting that Hegel sees in the monarch not the source of real authority, but a mere symbol of unity. Hegel was taken as a philosophical royalist, for example, by Franz Rosenzweig and Rudolf Haym, on the basis of the published *Philosophy of Right*, but, argues Ilting, really he is not: Hegel's real views are expressed in the lectures. Ilting concludes that Hegel's monarchist view in the *Philosophy of Right* is a response to censorship pressures imposed by the nonconstitutional monarchy of Prussia and does not reflect a genuine change of view.

[18] The information for this last paragraph comes from both Ilting's introduction to the first volume of his four-volume edition of Hegel's *Vorlesungen über Rechtsphilosophie (1818–1831)*, and Henrich's introduction to his edition of Rph III: *Philosophie des Rechts: Die Vorlesung von 1819/20*. In this section I shall also refer to two other pieces by Ilting: "Zur Genese der Hegelschen Rechtsphilosophie"; and "Der exoterische und der esoterische Hegel (1824–1831)."

[19] Ilting has done a great service to students of Hegel by publishing Rph II, V, VI, and VII—I could not have advanced many of my arguments in this work had I not had access to the sources he has provided. However, it is difficult to ignore the great stake he has in arguing for the importance of the lecture notes he edited and published. (Of course, Henrich, and the editors of Rph I, deserve similar praise.)

[20] Ilting, Introduction, *Vorlesungen*, vol. 1, pp. 28–29.

In the preface to the *Philosophy of Right* Hegel writes that "what is rational is actual and what is actual is rational," suggesting that the practices and laws of the existing Prussian monarchy are rational, and that proposals for liberal reforms are unnecessary or even dangerous. Again Ilting argues that what Hegel says in the lectures goes against the apparently conservative position he made public in his book. Ilting notes that in Rph II and Rph VI Hegel makes clear that irrational positive law can exist, contrary to what he writes in the preface or expresses elsewhere in the *Philosophy of Right*.[21] Ilting also notes that in Rph VII Hegel says: "What is actual, is rational; but not all that is actual is what exists. What is bad is something that is nothing in itself"; and from other passages in Rph VII Ilting concludes that Hegel's meaning in his final set of lectures is: "The rational *should* be actual"[22]—hardly the view of a conservative justifier of all status quo laws and practices.

With both examples Ilting accuses Hegel of publishing conservative opinions that he did not genuinely hold. Why would Hegel do this? Ilting points to the political circumstances of the time. On March 23, 1819, Karl Ludwig Sand, a Jena theology student and radical member of the liberal and nationalist student fraternities, murdered the writer Friedrich Kotzebue, an alleged Russian agent who opposed the French Revolution and liberal freedoms. Kotzebue was admired by Klemens von Metternich, who prevailed upon Prussia's Friedrich Wilhelm III to issue the Carlsbad decrees in August 1819. These decrees were just one of several measures the government took to end the liberal reforms it had begun and to begin the restoration. Hegel had been a spiritual leader of the fraternities with which Sand was identified. On February 9, 1819, Hegel had taken part in fraternity celebrations of Prussia's stand against Napoleon. Hegel knew he could be seen as a spiritual leader of the fraternities.[23] In September 1819, a colleague of Hegel's, Professor Wilhelm Martin Leberecht de Wette, was dismissed after discovery of a letter of his to Sand's mother that expressed support for her son. Hegel feared for himself and began to distance himself from the views of his colleague. On November 13, he declared that the state has the right to remove a teacher from the university's faculty, so long as the teacher is left his salary. Hegel's colleague Friedrich Schleiermacher called Hegel's action "wretched."[24]

Ilting argues that another way Hegel distanced himself from views that the Prussian government might regard as threatening was to rework his preface to the *Philosophy of Right* in order to attack viciously his former

---

[21] Ibid., p. 117. I discuss this passage in detail in sec. 6.2.

[22] Ibid., p. 119.

[23] A detailed account of all the reasons Hegel had to be fearful of being associated with "demagogues" like Sand, and with the liberal movement, is given by Jacques d'Hondt, *Hegel in His Time*, trans. John Burbridge et al.

[24] Ibid., p. 63.

colleague at Heidelberg, the philosopher Jacob Fries, who in many respects supported the politics of de Wette and Schleiermacher. Hegel was
so effective in his reworking, clearly going beyond the bounds of collegial
reserve, as when, for example, he refers to Fries's philosophy as "the
quintessence of shallow thinking," that he marked himself as the "royal
philosopher of Prussia."[25]

Ilting concludes that in the *Philosophy of Right* Hegel did take a royalist position, but that really he supports a liberal constitutional monarchy; and that as soon as the crisis period of 1819–1820 was over, Hegel
could again make his opinions publicly known.[26] The true Hegel was no
royalist, but a protestant, liberal, pro–French Revolution, pro–English
freedom constitutionalist.[27] Ilting notes that Hegel himself characterizes
his own philosophy as not conservative but revolutionary, but a philosophy that conceals its revolutionary character; as philosopher, Hegel is like
a mole: "Spirit often seems to have forgotten and lost itself, but inwardly
opposed to itself, it is inwardly working ever forward (as when Hamlet
says of the ghost of his father, 'Well [grubbed], old mole! canst work i'
the ground so fast?'), until grown strong in itself it bursts asunder the
crust of earth which divided it from the sun, its Concept, so that the earth
crumbles away."[28]

Ilting's view has not become consensus. Dieter Henrich takes issue with
Ilting's claim that Hegel's views on monarchy are the result of political
accommodation: "Hegel was a monarchist out of not political tendency
but theoretical duty."[29] Others object to Ilting's argument as a whole.
Rolf-Peter Horstmann, for example, objects to the claim that Hegel gives
two opposed standpoints—an exoteric and an esoteric—and says that
Hegel gives, rather, fundamentally the same position with different accen-
tuations, and that the tension is within the *Philosophy of Right*, not between it and the lectures. Horstmann objects to Ilting's too-illiberal reading of the *Philosophy of Right* and too-liberal reading of the lectures.[30]

For our purposes we need not choose sides. If Ilting is correct that we
can trust only the lecture notes and not Hegel's published texts, then there
is strong support for my own use of the lecture notes. But even if Ilting is
wrong—and I think that he tends to exaggerate the differences between

[25] Hegel criticized Fries not because Hegel opposed liberalism—Hegel held many liberal
views—but because he opposed the irrationalist arguments Fries advanced to support his
views. See my discussion, sec. 3.3.1.4.

[26] Ilting, Introduction, *Vorlesungen*, vol. 1, p. 114.

[27] Ibid., p. 56.

[28] HP 3:546–547.

[29] Henrich, "Vernunft in Verwirklichung," p. 31.

[30] Rolf-Peter Horstmann, "Ist Hegels *Rechtsphilosophie* das Produkt der Politischen Anpassung eines Liberalen?" See also Klaus Hartmann's "Review of Ilting" for a criticism of
those who "foist modern liberalism" on Hegel.

the lectures and the *Philosophy of Right*—my use of the lecture notes does not consequently become any less legitimate: what is at stake in the issue of whether there is an esoteric and an exoteric Hegel is the authenticity not of the lectures, but of what Hegel published.[31]

My own reason for relying heavily on the lecture notes is that they make clear and concrete a very difficult and at times obscure text—the *Philosophy of Right*.[32] Hegel himself noted in his preface that his remarks were to indicate "[i]deas akin to my argument or at variance with it, further inferences from it, and the like, i.e. *material which would receive its requisite elucidation in my lectures*."[33] Horstmann has also noted that the value of the lecture notes lies above all in the clarification and concretization they bring to the *Philosophy of Right*: "The material Ilting makes available contributes in the sense of clarifying the political content of Hegel's *Rechtsphilosophie*, making it clearer; whether it contributes to Ilting's claim that Hegel's position is liberal, remains questionable."[34]

Of all the commentators on Hegel's theory of legal punishment of whom I am aware, only two make use of the lecture notes, available since 1973. Only Igor Primoratz comments on whether they add anything to our understanding of what Hegel publishes in the *Philosophy of Right*, but he concludes that they do not.[35] In my view, the lecture notes do add substantially to our understanding of the *Philosophy of Right*, and to Hegel's *Rechtsphilosophie*. I agree essentially with Horstmann's point, with one reservation. Occasionally Hegel advances important arguments in his lectures that are absent from the published text. These arguments include justifications or criticisms of particular practices, and other political judgments. In this respect Hegel's political philosophy—his *Rechtsphilosophie*—is not entirely captured in the *Philosophy of Right*. The lecture notes, in my judgment, are simply indispensable.

[31] Consequently I am not, at present, arguing that there is an esoteric Hegel belying the exoteric. For further discussion of these two dimensions of Hegel's work, see Heinz Kimmerle, "Die Widersprüche des Verhältnisses von esoterischer und exoterischer Philosophie in Hegels Systemkonzeptionen"; and for a general and well-known discussion, see Leo Strauss, *Persecution and the Art of Writing*.

[32] The real danger in using the lecture notes, then, will be if they oversimplify or desynthesize the complex argument of the published text. As Hanna Pitkin has suggested to me, this is what Wittgenstein's *Blue and Brown Books* do in relation to the *Philosophical Investigations*. I think this danger less likely in Hegel's case. The *Philosophy of Right* was intended as an outline for Hegel to use when he lectured and as a compendium for his students. Hegel closely followed the outline of the book in all of the courses he gave.

[33] PR Preface, p. 1, my emphasis.

[34] Horstmann, "Ist Hegels *Rechtsphilosophie* das Produkt der Politischen Anpassung eines Liberalen?" p. 277.

[35] Igor Primoratz, *Banquos-Geist: Hegels Theorie der Strafe*, p. 28. The only other commentator on Hegel's theory of crime and punishment making use of the lecture notes is, so far as I know, Wolfgang Schild, in his two German-language articles.

1.3   Hegel's Political Philosophy: Metaphysical or Political?

While much of Hegel's obscurity is removed by consulting the lecture notes, the metaphysics remains. Some of his most troubling claims Hegel expressed in his lectures, for example, that history is the march of God on earth. The role God plays in Hegel's philosophy is less than clear: some Hegel scholars regard Hegel's philosophy as "strictly secular" and antitheological.[36] The left-Hegelian Ludwig Feuerbach seems to have seen it in this light: "I had listened [to Hegel] for barely six months when my head and heart had been put right by him; I knew what I wanted and should do; not theology but philosophy! Not to drivel and rave but to learn. Not believe but think."[37] But even if God does not play a central role in it, Hegel's philosophy remains in significant ways metaphysical.

Hegel claims repeatedly that the practices of a rational modern state that are right are justified by the Concept (*Begriff*)[38] or by the "necessity of the Idea."[39] This is a metaphysical claim, a foundationalist justification for these practices.[40] Hegel distinguishes Concept "in the speculative sense" from "what is ordinarily called a concept."[41] "In the logic of understanding, the concept is generally reckoned a mere form of thought . . . [in this view] a concept is something abstract, empty, dead. The case is really quite the reverse. The Concept is, on the contrary, the principle

---

[36] Robert Solomon, *In the Spirit of Hegel*, p. 5; cf. my discussion in sec. 4.3.1. But see Emil Fackenham, *The Religious Dimension of Hegel's Philosophy* (Bloomington: Indiana University Press, 1967); and J. H. Stirling, *The Secret of Hegel* (Edinburgh: Oliver and Boyd, 1898).

[37] Karl Grün, *Ludwig Feuerbach in seinem Briefwechsel und Nachlass*, vol. 1 (1874), p. 387. Cited in Walter Kaufmann, *Hegel: Reinterpretation, Texts, and Commentary*, p. 356.

[38] See, for example, PR 36 on the Concept as the basis for the system of abstract rights (abstract rights include the right to property and contract); PR 101 on the Concept as determining how much we should punish; and PR 280 Rem on the Concept as justification for hereditary monarchy. I capitalize "Concept" when Hegel gives *Begriff* a metaphysical sense; otherwise I do not. Similarly, I capitalize "Idea," "Reason," and "Spirit" only when they have the metaphysical sense Hegel gives to them.

[39] PR 279 Z; cf. PR 176 on marriage as an immediate actuality of the Idea.

[40] Recent interpreters, relying heavily on the *Phenomenology*'s collapsing of subject and object, have argued that Hegel criticizes traditional metaphysics and foundationalism—see, for example, David Stern, "The Immanence of Thought: Hegel's Critique of Foundationalism," pp. 19–21. I agree with the spirit of these interpretations, but I think it misleading to say Hegel is a nonfoundationalist in every sense of that word. Hegel claims (1) that we will be reconciled with existing practices because they are right, and (2) that the standard of right is immanent in these practices. The second claim makes Hegel a nonfoundationalist in one sense, because he rejects the view that there is an external ground or standard by which to judge a practice; but the first claim, that we will find complete satisfaction and be at home in existing practices, requires further justification, which Hegel's metaphysics provides—so in another sense Hegel *is* a foundationalist.

[41] Enz 9.

of all life. . . . The Concept is a form, but an infinite and creative form, which includes, but at the same time releases from itself, the fullness of all content."[42] Here Hegel describes the Concept as a creative form; it has ontological status, it inheres in the world. That it inheres in the world is the Idea, which Hegel defines as the "unity of existence and the Concept."[43] Hegel claims that human beings, by virtue of their having self-consciousness, partake in what he calls Spirit (*Geist*); human beings are Spirit implicitly, but they must become aware of this explicitly. The Idea is the development of our consciousness that we are Spirit: "The Idea and it alone is truth. Now it is essentially in the nature of the Idea to develop, and only through development to arrive at comprehension of itself, or to become what it is."[44] The Idea is that self-consciousness becomes what it is implicitly; when it does this it is free.[45] Hegel says that the subject of self-consciousness, Spirit, reaches "its goal when the Concept of Spirit has completely actualized itself, or, what is the same thing, when Spirit has attained to complete consciousness of its Concept. . . . The entire development of Spirit is nothing else but the raising of itself to its truth."[46] The development of Spirit according to the Idea proceeds by the dialectic, by the process of "determinate negation." Hegel refers to the growth of a tree as an example of this process where primitive stages of development are negated yet preserved as necessary antecedent determinants of a later stage: "The development of the tree is the negation of the germ, and the blossom that of the leaves, in so far as that they show that these do not form the highest and truest existence of the tree. Last of all, the blossom finds its negation in the fruit. Yet none of them can come into actual existence excepting as preceded by all the earlier stages."[47] Hegel generalizes from this example to a philosophy of development: "Our attitude to a philosophy must thus contain an affirmative side and a negative; when we take both of these into consideration, we do justice to a philosophy for the first time. We get to know the affirmative side later on both in life and in science."[48] Hegel sees the dialectic of determinate negation at work in the history of cultures as well as in natural history. Hegelian logic is a description of this process, and so, as has often been noted, it is "not a logic at all, but an ontology or an explanation of existence."[49]

---

[42] Ibid., 160 Rem.

[43] PR 1 Z.

[44] HP 1:20ff.

[45] Cf. PR 10 and Rem.

[46] Enz 379 Z.

[47] HP 1:37–38.

[48] Ibid.

[49] See, for example, the summary textbook account in David Ingersoll and Richard Matthews, *The Philosophic Roots of Modern Ideology*, 2nd ed., p. 117. On Hegel's logic as ontological, see also Charles Taylor, *Hegel*, pp. 226, 298–300.

In claiming that something is justified by the Concept or the necessity of the Idea, Hegel invokes his ontological logic, his claim that human beings are implicitly Spirit and will develop the consciousness of this, with the help of appropriate practices and institutions that will by necessity develop in history through a dialectical process. But at times Hegel uses the word "concept" without these metaphysical implications, to mean the idea of a thing, the principle underlying it. Hegel speaks of the concept of punishment as retribution not utility, meaning that the purpose or essential principle immanent in the practice is not deterrence or reform or incapacitation, but the vindication of right.[50] Hegel says that consanguineous marriages are opposed to the concept of marriage because the concept of marriage is to unite what is different.[51] In these examples, Hegel means by the concept of a thing its principle or purpose.[52]

In the following sections I shall argue that essentially what Hegel is up to as political philosopher is interpreting our social practices, ultimately so he can criticize them. Hegel looks at a practice he sees around him and develops an account of its purpose or rationale, an interpretation of the meaning the practice has, of its "concept," which he then uses to criticize manifestations of the actual practice that diverge from this purpose. Hegel casts his interpretations as truths by appealing to the metaphysics of the Concept and the Idea. He claims, not that his account of a practice's meaning is merely one of several possible accounts, but, rather, that his account establishes a practice's true meaning. In my view, those of us who reject the idea that a practice can have a true meaning can reject Hegel's foundationalism, his claim that practices have "absolutely valid justifications" based on the Concept,[53] yet still draw upon his interpretations of the purposes of and principles underlying our practices, his interpretations of their concepts. While Hegel's political philosophy is metaphysical, rehabilitated it can be political.[54]

1.3.1 Interpretivist

In the final part of his three-part *Encyclopaedia* Hegel defends his claim that history has an absolute end, or *telos*, against critics who think historians should not read into history any object or purpose. These critics

---

[50] PR 99 Rem.

[51] "Ist dem Begriffe zuwider" (ibid., 168). "Was schon vereint ist, gibt sich nicht" (ibid., 168 Bem).

[52] Cf. PR 2 Rem, p. 15.

[53] Ibid., 3 Rem.

[54] I discuss the reason for seeing metaphysics and politics as mutually exclusive in the next section.

insist that "there should be no prepossession in favour of an idea or opinion, just as a judge should have no special sympathy for one of the con-
tending parties. In the case of the judge it is at the same time assumed that
he would administer his office ill and foolishly, if he had not an interest,
and an exclusive interest in justice . . . or if he declined to judge at all."[55]
But, Hegel continues, these critics go wrong in failing to see a vital distinction between the judge and the historian. The judge is engaged in an
activity where the line between impartiality and partiality is sharply
drawn. Everyone would agree that the judge who takes a special interest
in one of the parties crosses that line. But the historian is engaged in a
different sort of activity, where the line between impartiality and partiality is not merely fuzzy, but inappropriate. Hegel says the critics of his own
philosophy of history fail to see this difference: "In speaking of the impartiality required from the historian, this self-satisfied insipid chatter lets
the distinction disappear. . . . It demands that the historian shall bring
with him no definite aim and view by which he may sort out, state, and
criticize events, but shall narrate them exactly in the casual mode he finds
them, in their incoherent and unintelligent particularity."[56] To Hegel, this
critic mistakes the judge's desire to be impartial, a virtue in the activity of
legal judging, for what, when applied to the historian, is a vice—the desire
to give a purely empirical understanding that refrains from reflecting
upon the object of history and subjecting history to critical examination.

Hegel understands the activity of the historian as essentially interpretation. The good historian aims at a narrative that makes sense of the
stuff of history and critically examines its comparative importance: "A
history without such aim and such criticism would be only an imbecile
mental divagation, not as good as a fairy tale, for even children expect a
motif [*Interesse*] in their stories, a purpose at least dimly surmiseable with
which events and actions are put in relation."[57]

Hegel's entire theoretical activity is devoted to interpretation. He reads
meaning into the social and intellectual history of the world. He engages
in a search for a compelling interpretation of reality that finds order in
apparent chaos. As Hugh Reyburn emphasizes, for Hegel, "reality is not
a datum of knowledge, but a complex interpretation of experience."[58]

Sometimes Hegel admits that his interpretation of history is a product
of what he brings to history. He says that if we come to history with the
Idea the world spirit reveals itself to us; but if we come with contingent
thoughts, we find only contingency.[59] Hegel admits without shame that

---

[55] Enz 549 Rem.
[56] Ibid.
[57] Ibid.
[58] Hugh A. Reyburn, *The Ethical Theory of Hegel*, p. 264.
[59] Rph III, 282,16–22.

as a philosopher of history and social institutions he is not detached or disinterested. He thinks we do philosophy ultimately to help us live our lives—to resolve the contradictions we face and to arrive at a state of self-knowledge and satisfaction (*Befriedigung*).[60] We take up philosophy, and the philosophy of history, because we are searching for self-knowledge, meaning, wholeness, integrity. We bring with us this aim, and it conditions the interpretation we give to history.

But Hegel calls his interpretations "objective truth." Hegel saw his philosophy of history not as just one possible interpretation of history, but as the final, complete, definitive account. He says he discerns the "essential connection" among seemingly chance events.[61] In the introduction to his *Philosophy of History* Hegel declares that history "has proceeded rationally, that it represents the rationally necessary course of the World Spirit," and he characterizes this claim not as a presupposition, but as a "result" that "happens to be known" to him because he already knows "the whole."[62] While sometimes Hegel seems to commit only to the weaker point that history is a value-laden activity, other times he makes the much stronger claim that history uncovers a teleological process, gives a metaphysical conception that is right. Hegel calls what he does "science," and he says that it yields "absolute knowledge." Hegel's science seeks out "the substantial and underlying essence, and not the trivialities of external existence and contingency."[63] Hegel says his task is "to apprehend in the show of the temporal and transient the substance which is immanent and the eternal which is present."[64]

If that *is* Hegel's task, it is hard to see how Hegel is political. For, as Benjamin Barber persuasively argues, politics in the modern world is about having to choose "when the grounds of choice are not given *a priori* or by fiat or by pure knowledge."[65] In Barber's compelling account of politics:

> Where there is certain knowledge, true science, or absolute right, there is no conflict that cannot be resolved by reference to the unity of truth, and thus there is no necessity for politics. . . . Where consensus stops, politics starts. . . . Politics is a rag and bone shop of the practical and concrete, the everyday and the ambiguous, the malleable and the evanescent. Politics is what men do when metaphysics fails.[66]

[60] On the significance of satisfaction in the *Phenomenology*, see chapter 3, note 74.
[61] HP 1:6.
[62] RH 12.
[63] Enz 549 Rem.
[64] PR Preface, p. 10.
[65] Benjamin Barber, *Strong Democracy: Participatory Politics for a New Age*, p. 121.
[66] Ibid., pp. 129–131.

Can Hegel, the metaphysician and truth bearer who says that "philosophy is not concerned with the tangle of particular interests," and who distinguishes philosophy from "microscopic investigations," on the grounds that philosophy regards "the substantial in the still space that is free from this or that interest,"[67] help us practice politics?

Barber sees politics as a "search for reasonable choices, which must be made in the face of conflict."[68] On this score, at least, Hegel agrees. Hegel recognizes the need for politics to be rational; he believes that in deliberating about choices over which there is conflict, we must give reasons to others for our choice. As we shall see in chapter 3, Hegel attacks both the ironists among the German romantics and those adhering to an ethics of conviction (*Überzeugungsethik*), because they deny the need to give reasons for their actions. The former go beyond the latter in declaring that even conviction is not worth much.[69] Both Hegel and Barber agree on the need for political discourse to be reasoned. But for Barber the search for reasonable choices takes place "in the absence of independent grounds for judgment"; "politics seeks choices that are something less than arbitrary even though they cannot be perfectly right or true or scientific."[70] Hegel's foundationalism, his commitment to his metaphysics, makes him seem, by Barber's standards, unpolitical and impractical. My suggestion is that we take Hegel as offering interpretations of the concepts of practices, and leave aside his metaphysical claim about the Concept, and, acknowledging that the nonmetaphysical philosophy we appropriate is a revised version of the foundationalist original, that we include Hegel's interpretation of our practices in our own political dialogues and, in particular, in our debates about legal punishment.

1.3.2 Legal Interpretivist

Hegel has already been recognized as an interpreter of history.[71] One commentator describes what Hegel practices as "a form of cultural hermeneutics."[72] What has not been emphasized is that Hegel is in particular a *legal* interpretivist.

In Hegel's view there is an idea of right, shared by a society and implicit in its practices and customs, that becomes formalized in law. Formalities,

---

[67] Rph III, 50.

[68] Barber, *Strong Democracy*, p. 127.

[69] PR 140 Rem and Z.

[70] Barber, *Strong Democracy*, p. 127.

[71] Among those who discuss Hegel as interpreter are Robert Solomon, *In the Spirit of Hegel*, and Charles Taylor, *Hegel*.

[72] Steven B. Smith, *Hegel's Critique of Liberalism: Rights in Context*, p. 11.

ceremonies, and usages are a practical necessity.[73] But Hegel insists that
we must not let some aspect of the form of law be taken as the thing itself.
If we take formalities too seriously we lose sight of the essence of the law.
Hegel blames the English for succumbing to the "empty formalism of the
letters," pointing as an example to how a Bartholomew Thompson
avoided punishment even though he had committed a crime, merely because his name was improperly written on the official complaint.[74] In
such a case, strict adherence to the letter or form of the law misses the
whole point of law—its substance. Hegel insists that we must sometimes
go beyond the letter of the law to its spirit, and that the judge has a duty
to stand up for what is "essential" or "substantial," against the distortions that surface by a rigid following of the law's letter.[75] Hegel's task as
legal interpretivist is to find the underlying principles or substance of the
law.

In Hegel's view, the legal interpretivist, having discovered or invented
the rational principle of law, lets us transform into a rational legal code
the mass of customary law that is the object of interpretation. In his day
Hegel was involved in a vocal debate with the historicist school of law,
led by F. C. von Savigny. Rather than codify customary law, the historicists attempted to describe it completely, through painstaking historical
study. Hegel thought the historicists were misguided: merely to describe
"what everybody does" yields an "unformed collection" of law lacking
underlying principles. For Hegel, the true task of a people is to codify
their law by recognizing "the determinate universality of existing legal
content."[76] Hegel criticizes England's common law because it remains a
mere unformed collection that leads to confusion; he turns for his model
of good law instead to the Napoleonic code.[77]

One problem Hegel sees in the historicist approach is that it so elevates
customary law as to enslave us to custom, even bad custom. Hegel argues
that "clearly" right began with customary law, but "man can become
accustomed to bad things, like slavery and serfdom."[78] For Hegel, law is
right, not because it is law, and not because of the wisdom of the original

[73] Hegel gives as examples of formalities that are essential if the concept of right, which
requires property ownership and contract, is to be posited and manifested in practical life,
boundary stones as signs, entries in property registers, and contractual forms (PR 217 Z;
Rph V, 3:658–659).
[74] Rph III, 175,21–27. Hegel was an avid reader of English newspapers and probably
learned about Thompson's case from his readings. See Michael J. Petry, "Hegel and 'The
Morning Chronicle.' "
[75] Rph III, 175,3–21.
[76] PR 211 Rem.
[77] Rph III, 170–173.
[78] Rph VI, 4:534,7–16.

lawmakers,[79] but because it accords with rational standards. "[Its] historical justification does not suffice to show the rationality of a law."[80] This is so not only for laws, but for practices and institutions as well. For Hegel, existing practices and institutions are justified not merely because they have come to exist in history, but because they are rational. What makes a practice rational may be wholly unconnected to the practice's historical cause or origin.[81] "The origin of a thing is completely beside the point. The question is only, is the thing true in and for itself."[82] Hegel criticizes those who think something is justified merely if a good historical reason can be found for it. To this view, which he identifies with "the Understanding," Hegel opposes his own, that what justifies a thing is its reason or rationality: "The Understanding has good grounds for everything, but this does not decide whether the thing is in fact rational."[83] Hegel argues that justifiers who turn to genealogy, to the origins of a law or practice, undermine their own justificatory project:

> When those who try to justify things on historical grounds confound an origin in external circumstances with one in the Concept, they unconsciously achieve the very opposite of what they intend. Once the origin of an institution has been shown to be wholly to the purpose and necessary in the circumstances of the time, the demands of history have been fulfilled. But if this is supposed to pass for a general justification of the thing itself, it turns out to be the opposite, because, since those circumstances are no longer present, the institution so far from being justified has by their disappearance lost its meaning [*Sinn*] and its right [*Recht*].[84]

Hegel gives the example of monasteries. Monasteries arose to cultivate and populate the wilderness and to transcribe manuscripts. If this is seen to be their justification, it follows that they are now superfluous and lack purpose.[85]

A particular law or a particular action of a practice might not be ratio-

---

[79] Hegel would, I think, oppose constitutional theorists who privilege original intent. Hegel might say that we live under the law, and so the intent that matters in applying the law is the intent we could have had we made the law.

[80] Rph VI, 4:89–90. Cf. PH 417 (345): "legitimacy comes from rational principles grounding law, not tradition or custom."

[81] PR 219 Rem.

[82] PH 400 (331).

[83] Rph VI, 4:91,8–9.

[84] PR 3 Rem.

[85] Ibid.; Rph VI, 4:89. In his lectures Hegel draws the conclusion that the monastery is an institution that is no longer rational—it has become unjust and harmful—whereas in the *Philosophy of Right* he concludes merely that *if* we took the historical justification as the rationale for monasteries *then* they would be superfluous. (Compare Rph VI, 4:89 with PR 3 Rem, pp. 17–18.)

nal. But, Hegel argues, on the whole laws and practices accord with rational standards. Laws and practices are right not because they exist, but
because they accord with these standards. As a legal interpretivist who
claims to discern these standards of rationality, Hegel offers us the pros-
pect of liberation from particular irrational laws. Hegel is committed to
finding principle in the law, so that where customary law is contradictory,
principle can guide us.

1.3.3 Immanent Criticism

Political theorists are often regarded as outsiders—prophets with visions,
architects designing utopias, moles burrowing through to the hidden deep
structures that shape appearances, philosophers leaving the cave to find
truth. Aristophanes painted a picture of a ridiculous Socrates, an intellectual housed in his "Thinkery," who rides in a basket up in the air and
"looks down upon the sun from a superior standpoint," rather than pur-
suing his inquiries "down there on the ground" ("The earth, you see,
pulls down the delicate essence of thought to its own gross level").[86]
Machiavelli joins in Alexander's laughter at Dinocrates, who showed Alexander how he could build a city on top of Mount Athos that would be
"a most marvelous and rare thing," worthy of Alexander's greatness; but
when asked by Alexander how its inhabitants would live in this city, an-
swered, "[I] had not thought about that."[87] It is their distance, necessary
to gain a critical perspective of their society, that has created a barrier
between theorists and the more practical-minded person concerned with
her existing commitments and duties, with the matter at hand. For it is
"inside," amid the world of "appearances," that we live, with our settled
ways, our habits, customs, well-established institutions and practices. It
is with this world that we must cope. Hegel achieves that precarious balance between, on the one hand, distancing himself from his society and
its practices in order to find ideals by which to judge and if need be criticize those practices; and, on the other hand, remaining connected to his
world, recognizing that we can not just build a society from scratch, as
Dinocrates tried.

Hegel thinks there are standards by which to judge social practices,
standards that are separable from those practices. But Hegel is no utopian: "Since philosophy is the exploration of the rational, it is for that
very reason the apprehension of the present and the actual, not the erection of a beyond, supposed to exist, god knows where, or rather, which

---

[86] Aristophanes, *The Clouds*, trans. William Arrowsmith, pp. 33–34.
[87] Niccolò Machiavelli, *The Discourses*, bk. 1, ch. 1.

exists, and we can perfectly well say where, namely in the error of a one-sided empty ratiocination."[88] Hegel insists the ideals by which we judge our practices are not external, nor merely subjective—not any ideals will do. For Hegel, ideals or standards are abstracted from the practices we already have, but the ideals stand apart: all aspects of the practice need not accord with the ideals. The ideals are taken from an interpretive account of the world and so are removed from that world; but they are not external, inasmuch as they derive from an interpretation *of* the world.[89]

While Hegel remains connected to this world, he is not uncritical of it. Hegel abstracts from a practice what he sees as its essential purpose or idea—its concept—and takes his theory of the practice as both a justification for it and a standard by which to criticize it. Hegel is an *immanent critic*.[90] He steps outside a practice in order to think about it, to adduce its purpose or concept, and then steps back inside the practice, using his account of the principle(s) immanent in the practice to criticize the actual practice should it diverge from the principled or idealized practice.[91] Hegel's task is essentially critical.

Slowly this is being realized. Jeremy Waldron, for example, observes that Hegel's theory of private property lends a critical edge to that institution. "Private property was an existent institution that Hegel saw in the world around him," and he took it upon himself to display the rationality inherent in this existent institution. "[I]f we are led to agree with Hegel that private property is a rational necessity, then we will be inclined to give a positive evaluation of some features of society . . . (of those that represent a progressive tendency towards private ownership) and a neg-

[88] PR Preface, p. 10.

[89] We might think Hegel is a "subjectivist" nevertheless, because for him standards derive merely from an interpretation, and interpretations can vary. At this point Hegel avoids the charge of subjectivism, and the related charge of relativism, by his metaphysical claim that his interpretation is not merely best but true.

[90] The idea of immanent criticism has been nicely articulated by Hanna Pitkin: "For whatever reasons, and with no deliberate, common purpose, men may gradually develop fixed ways of doing something—institutionalized behavior which has become habitual. From this patterned behavior they may begin to abstract express ideas about what it is for, how it is to be done, what principles and purposes underlie it. And, in due time, those principles may themselves come to be used as new aims for revising the institution, as critical standards for assessing the way in which it functions and improving it" (*The Concept of Representation*, p. 236). See also Michael Walzer, *Interpretation and Social Criticism*; Michael Walzer, *The Company of Critics*, on the idea of connected criticism; Steven Smith, *Hegel's Critique of Liberalism*, pp. 10, 13, 169–175; Steven Smith, "Hegel's Idea of a Critical Theory"; and Mark Tunick, *Punishment: Theory and Practice*, ch. 1, sec. 3.

[91] Cf. Tunick, *Punishment: Theory and Practice*, ch. 1, sec. 3: "Immanent criticism is possible because it's possible for us to have ideals that guide us, but for us occasionally (or even often) to act against those ideals."

ative evaluation . . . of others."[92] Hegel's discussion has a "critical edge,"
and Hegel uses his account as "a basis for some practical criticism and
evaluation."[93] Steven Smith also notes the critical power of Hegel's philosophy. In his view Hegel is "the great champion of a form of philosophical practice that I want to call immanent critique. By an immanent critique I mean a form of theorizing that seeks standards of rationality
within existing systems of thought and forms of life."[94]

But little has been said about how Hegel applies his strategy of immanent criticism to social practices. Smith, in his chapter on Hegel's idea of
a critical theory, argues that on epistemological issues Hegel maintains
that standards of cognitive acceptability "are already at hand within existing modes of cognition."[95] This is an important aspect of Hegel's critical theory, but Smith does not show the practical uses Hegel makes of his
strategy. Smith gives no indication of how Hegel criticizes actual social
practices by using as standards the principles he finds immanent in them.
To show this is one of the central tasks of this book. As immanent critic,
Hegel takes practices as he finds them and comprehends the standards
implicit in them. The act of comprehension is an act of interpretation,
although Hegel often speaks of it as an act of discovery.

The immanent critic situates herself in the difficult position between the
real and the ideal and tries to reconcile the two.[96] For Hegel, part of having an ideal is knowing what belongs to it—that is, knowing the "infinite
amount of miserable contingency" with which any ideal must be inter-
mingled if it is to be an actual ideal. Hegel criticizes Plato for not including the real in his ideal state—what remains is a wish or a dream.[97] The
theorist bearing reason must recognize the limits imposed on reason by
the finite material of the world. On the other hand, the theorist must be
able with her ideal to persevere in the face of facts in the world that contradict the ideal. Hegel goes back and forth between the real and the ideal
with his dialectic; he adjusts his ideal in light of the facts, and with his
ideal he perseveres in the face of nonideal aspects of reality.[98]

For Hegel, and for the immanent critic in general, our ideals, the principles we use to determine what ought to be, derive from existing practice,

[92] Jeremy Waldron, "Hegel's Discussion of Property," in *The Right to Private Property*,
pp. 345–347.
[93] Ibid.
[94] Smith, *Hegel's Critique of Liberalism*, p. 10.
[95] Ibid., p. 173.
[96] See Lasson, "Einleitung," pp. xxxiv–xxxv: "the ideal world is in general not to be separated from the ethical world. At the moment one arrives at the concept of the self-deter-
mining genuine and free will that wills the free will, one is on the ground of absolute reconciliation of the real and the ideal."
[97] Rph VI, 4:478,8–15.
[98] Cf. sec. 6.2.

from what is. Hegel is committed, on the whole, to existing practices, and to finding the rational principles immanent in them. Hegel is elusive about what makes these principled practices rational, as we shall see. His position seems to be that a law or practice is rational if it is integral to a whole system of laws and practices appropriate to the spirit of the people to which it belongs, a system in which this people can understand themselves to be free.

Those who regard existing practices as bad root and branch will not be satisfied using ideals derived from these practices to criticize the actual practice. Why should the standards we use for judging how we should live derive from the practices we have about us and not from some other practices we have yet to enjoy? What justifies existing practices? Ultimately Hegel justifies his strategy of immanent criticism by appealing to his metaphysics, his claim that the existing practices from which he derives his critical standards are the result of a rational process at work in history. If we reject this metaphysical justification, as I suggest we do, what is left to justify our appropriation of Hegel's immanent criticism? In the next several chapters we shall unpack Hegel's interpretation of the practice of legal punishment, and his immanent criticism of the actual practice. In the final chapter we shall have to return to this fundamental question.

Two

Hegel's Theory of Legal Punishment: An Overview

AMONG ALL our social practices, legal punishment is one of the most troubling to us. Some think punishment is institutionalized revenge, a barbaric practice we should now be above.[1] Others respond that punishment is our way of meting out just deserts: someone who is rightly condemned deserves to be punished, and failure to punish her is wrong.[2] To some, such justice is hypocritical, and punishment nothing but a "morality play."[3] Legal punishment is a practice troubling not only to those concerned with the "timeless" ethical questions of right and wrong, of justice and injustice, but to those who work within the criminal justice system and must confront issues such as: What should we criminalize (flag burning? abortion? consensual homosexual sodomy?)? Whom should we hold accountable (the negligent? the insane? children?)? Should we exclude evidence illegally obtained though it could help prove a wrong was committed? Should we use expediencies like plea bargaining to cope with our over burdened courts? Should we put more people into already overcrowded prisons? Hegel speaks to us about the broad moral issue of whether punishment is justified at all; but, unlike most philosophers who take up this general question, Hegel speaks also to practitioners about practical problems such as these. His reflections on the philosophical issue inform his reflections on the practical problems: his conception of why we punish at all informs his views on how in particular we should go about legally punishing.

With the discussion in chapter 1, we now have a general understanding of what Hegel is up to as political philosopher, and which sources can help us discern his views. With this background we can turn to Hegel's theory of crime and punishment, in order to describe it, not in the detail that we will uncover later, but in enough detail so that we may understand Hegel's broad interpretation of the practice—what he thinks is the purpose and significance of punishing people for committing crimes.

[1] See, for example, Karl Menninger, *The Crime of Punishment*.

[2] Robert Nozick notes how a state will nurse an ill inmate on death row so that he is healthy enough to receive the punishment he deserves (*Philosophical Explanations*, p. 370).

[3] Menninger, *The Crime of Punishment*, pp. 153–154.

2.1 What Crime Is

The state does not automatically reward people who do praiseworthy deeds; but the state does insist that people who commit crimes should in principle be punished. A first step in making sense of the practice of legal punishment is understanding what it is about certain actions that makes them crimes and sets in motion a whole series of responses to them.

What is it about certain actions that makes punishment of those actions appropriate? The answer to this question is a matter of considerable controversy. Some retributivists insist we punish to express social disapproval or condemnation of acts society regards as wrong, and so to them what makes an action a crime is that it violates the social morality.[4] Other retributivists argue that we punish to vindicate not *right*, understood as shared social values, but *rights*, which are held by individuals and violated by the criminal, who in usurping these rights has taken an "unfair advantage" of others.[5] Utilitarians such as Jeremy Bentham, though, interpret crimes not as affronts to a social morality, or even to individual rights, but merely as "mischiefs" that decrease total social happiness.[6] For Bentham, no action is intrinsically evil or wrong; an action is evil or wrong only if its consequences are to decrease pleasure or increase pain. Whereas some retributivists insist that a crime is distinct from civil offenses because it is an action that violates society as a whole, and for this reason is responded to by the state's prosecutorial power, Richard Posner argues that in principle there is no distinction between a crime and a tort.[7] Some see crimes as affronts to the social morality, others, as affronts to particular individuals, while Bentham does not see crime as an affront at all. Some positivists interpret crimes as simply whatever actions the criminal law proscribes.[8]

Hegel puts forth an interpretation of crime that emphasizes the retributivist view that crime is an affront to social morality, or right. Hegel

[4] See Henry M. Hart, Jr., "The Aims of the Criminal Law"; and Joel Feinberg, "The Expressive Function of Punishment," in his *Doing and Deserving.*

[5] See Herbert Morris, "Persons and Punishment," pp. 26, 29–30. Morris argues that crimes are wrongs because they are the taking of an unfair advantage of others and that punishment restores the equilibrium of benefits and burdens. The purpose of punishment is to "provide individuals with a sphere of interest immune from interference" (p. 27). Cf. Jean Hampton, "The Retributive Ideal."

[6] Jeremy Bentham, *An Introduction to the Principles of Morals and Legislation*, ch. 12.

[7] Richard Posner, "An Economic Theory of the Criminal Law," p. 1204: "In cases where tort remedies, including punitive damages, are an adequate deterrent because they do not strain the potential defendant's ability to pay, there is no need to invoke criminal penalties . . . criminal sanctions generally are reserved, as theory predicts, for cases where the tort remedy bumps up against a solvency limitation."

[8] Thomas Hobbes, *Leviathan*, ch. 15.

recognizes that crime is a social mischief that poses a threat to society, that crimes are violations of proscriptions written as law, and that many crimes are injuries to another individual, or to another's property. But the essence and genuine significance of crime, in Hegel's view, are that it is a violation of society's general will, of the society's conception of right.[9] To show this, Hegel draws a distinction among three sorts of wrongs, only one of which he calls "crime." Hegel's account is somewhat obscure because he invokes three categories from his *Logic* that beg for explanation. Unfortunately, every commentator I am aware of who has at least pointed out the important distinction among wrongs merely repeats Hegel's own account, neither acknowledging its obscurity nor attempting to make it clear.

The distinction Hegel draws in the *Philosophy of Right* is among nonmalicious wrongs, fraud, and crimes. Nonmalicious or civil wrongs correspond to the logical category of "simple negative judgment"; fraud corresponds to a "positive infinite judgment"; a crime is the ominous "negative infinite judgment."

A nonmalicious wrong is nothing more than a mistake. I take your jacket, thinking it is mine. The jacket is in fact yours, and my taking it by mistake violates your right to it. Nonmalicious wrong is a "simple negative judgment" because my "judgment," declaring the jacket is mine, negates not the principle of right, but only your particular claim. If I commit a nonmalicious wrong, I do not challenge the property law by which you are entitled to the jacket; I claim only that I think the jacket is mine. Another case of a simple negative judgment is the statement "the rose is not red." Here I negate only the particular—that the rose is red. I do not deny that the rose has some color.[10] Nonmalicious wrong is not crime, because it respects right in general. Similarly, to be wrong about the color of the rose is not to be wrong about the concept of rose—if the rose is not red, it is still a rose. Hegel calls this category a "simple" and not "infinite" judgment because I am claiming something about not all roses, only this rose; about not all property, only this jacket.

Hegel's account of fraud is more complicated. If I commit fraud, I do not respect the laws that are accepted as right—I take them as mere demands without weight. While I regard the universal will that law expresses as a "show," I do, however, respect the particular wills of those

---

[9] Peter Nicholson emphasizes that for Hegel a crime is defined as a social harm ("Hegel on Crime," p. 120).

[10] The rose example is Hegel's: "If I say 'a rose is not red', I still recognize that it has colour. Hence I do not deny the genus; all that I negate is the particular colour, red. Similarly, right is recognized here. Each of the parties wills the right and what is supposed to result to each is the right alone. The wrong of each consists simply in his holding that what he wants is right" (PR 86 Z; cf. Rph III, 84,12–27; Enz 172–173).

with whom I deal. I injure not the particular but the universal will. For example, suppose I commit an act of fraud on you: I get you to give me money for what you think is a genuine diamond but is really a fake. In fact I have injured you and violated laws against misrepresentation. But you do not know this, and as far as you are concerned, you have purchased a real diamond. I have injured not your particular will, only the universal will, or right. (Of course, this is true only as long as you remain deceived about your purchase. Once you find out, I have injured both your particular will and the universal will.)

A fraud is a "positive infinite judgment."[11] Another of Hegel's examples of a positive infinite judgment is: "the lion is the lion."[12] In a positive infinite judgment, I affirm something particular but really make no judgment at all. A judgment relates something particular to something universal (the lion is an animal). The corresponding judgment in our case of fraud is something like: "the amount you should give me for this diamond is the amount you are willing to give me for this diamond." Someone who recognizes the universal idea of right would say something else: "the amount you should give me for this diamond is the amount it is worth." But when I commit fraud, I am concerned with satisfying not the demands of right, but only your particular will. Hegel does not explain very well why this category of judgment is infinite and not simple. I believe the reason must be that in asserting a tautology I am implying that the particular is all there is. When I make the "simple" judgment that the rose is red, I mean it is red not pink, not that it is red not a lion; I accept that there are a finite number of appropriate possibilities for my judgment. When I say the rose is the rose, I mean that it is the rose not the lion, and that it is not anything else, either. I deny that the rose is anything else; similarly, in fraud I deny that there is any standard by which to act other than the particular will of the person with whom I deal.[13]

Unlike nonmalicious wrong, fraud is punishable. In Hegel's view we punish those who commit fraud because they injure right, even though they injure right only in the abstract, since the diamond purchaser does not know or feel that she is injured. But fraud, though punishable, is still

---

[11] PR 88.

[12] Enz 173.

[13] Hegel's sharp distinction between fraud and crime is not without its problems. If I commit fraud, I probably will speak of the person with whom I deal as my "victim"—in other words, I am probably aware that I flout not only right but the real will of my victim (who wants a genuine diamond, after all). It is not very convincing to say that the person committing fraud is no criminal because he at least respects the particular will of his victim—for really the victim's particular will is being violated. But the staunch Hegelian would respond: all that counts is that the victim is happily deluded; the judgment that genuine diamonds are somehow better is just another universal judgment that the person committing fraud rejects.

not crime. When I commit a crime, I respect neither the universal will nor
my victim's particular will. In committing fraud I still respect the right of
the particular will, and of the person with whom I deal, for she agrees to
what we do. In fraud, it is only *Recht-an-sich*[14] that comes forward to say
I injured my "victim."[15] But crime goes beyond fraud: "Crime is an infinite judgment which negates not only the particular right, but at the same
time also the universal sphere, right as right. Crime has its own truth in
that it is an actual action, but because it relates itself completely nega-
tively to ethical life [*Sittlichkeit*], which makes up its universal sphere, it
is nonsensical."[16]

When I commit a crime, not only do I deprive you of your particular
right (in the case of theft, to your particular piece of property), but I also
flout the principle that you have a right in general (to property in general).[17]

The difference between fraud and crime is not simply that fraud injures
only the universal sphere of right and not the particular will of the victim,
while crime injures both.[18] If this is what Hegel meant, he would be leaving out of consideration as crimes all victimless crimes, where no particular will is actually injured.[19] But Hegel does not think crimes consist only
in the injury of or setback of interests to a victim. To understand the
distinction I think Hegel does mean, we must make sense of his claim
that, unlike fraud, crime is an "infinite negative judgment" and that it is
"nonsensical." An example of an infinite negative judgment is "the rose
is no elephant."[20] Why is committing a crime like claiming the rose is no
elephant?

There is a difference between saying "the rose is not red" and "the rose
is no elephant." In the first case I do not express a complete ignorance of
the concept of rose, for I at least recognize a rose is the sort of thing that
has color. I might be color-blind and wrong, but I would not be wrong in

---

[14] *Recht-an-sich* is an important term that we shall discuss in detail in chapter 4. It means
"right-in-itself"; we can think of this as what, in a rational modern state, is objectively right,
which for Hegel is what his *Rechtsphilosophie* determines is right.

[15] Rph V, 3:299,17–29.

[16] GLog 325.

[17] Hegel therefore thinks that the criminal law is not reducible to civil law. He gives this
example: if I murder you, your friends might demand civil punishment; "but still there is
the intellectual side, the action must be annulled" (Rph I, 53,263–273).

[18] Those who understand Hegel's distinction between fraud and crime in this way include
Igor Primoratz, *Banquos-Geist*, p. 33.

[19] As indicated above, some contemporary retributivists do see the significance of crime
as the victimization of an individual, or the taking of unfair advantage of another (Jean
Hampton, "The Retributive Ideal"; and Herbert Morris, "Persons and Punishment," pp.
26, 29–30). Hegel offers a very different and, I believe, a more persuasive conception of
crime.

[20] GLog 325.

any serious or malicious sense. However, if I were to say "the rose is no elephant," and I were not joking or playing some game in which what I said had a special meaning, then I would be expressing a complete ignorance of the concept of rose. To say "the rose is no elephant" is in effect to say "the rose is no thing"—it is not even a rose. But the person who makes a negative infinite judgment is incapable even of claiming that "the rose is no rose" because she has no idea of what a rose is—she is utterly ignorant of what it is to be a rose. Similarly, the criminal in effect says "your right to your property is no right"; but really the criminal is so utterly ignorant of what a right is, flouts it to such an extreme, that he could not understand what it would mean to say something is not a right; he might just as well say "your right is no elephant."

We can now see the essential difference between fraud and crime. If I commit fraud, I flout right but nevertheless appear to my victim as if I respect right—I make a "show" or appearance of respecting right. To do this, I must have an understanding of the concept of right. The criminal lacks this understanding when he commits a crime. (As we shall see, really I think Hegel is saying that the criminal acts *as if* he lacked this understanding.)

The diligent Hegelian might try to point out the significance of there being three sorts of wrongs corresponding to the three sorts of judgments Hegel lays out in his *Logic*. Hegel himself does not comment on this significance; he apparently thinks that his discussion of the three sorts of judgments as an analogy for the three sorts of wrongs is useful, and it is only for the sake of clarifying this distinction that I have tried to make clear Hegel's analogy. Comparing a crime to the judgment "the rose is no elephant" is a clever (if bizarre) way of seeing just how radical a flouter of right the criminal is, in Hegel's conception.

2.2   The Split Will

In committing a crime the criminal violates right, or the universal will as expressed in the state's criminal law.[21] The crime is a positive manifestation of the criminal's particular will: "The existence of crime lies only in the particular will of the criminal, that is its only source."[22]

Hegel makes the further claim, central to his theory of crime and punishment, that in committing the crime the criminal is in contradiction with himself: by acting out his particular will in violating the universal

---

[21] At this point we should want to ask: "What do you mean that the criminal law articulates a universal will?" I discuss Hegel's claim in detail, and critically, in chapter 4.
[22] PR 99 Bem; cf. PR 99.

will, the criminal violates his own implicit will.[23] In committing the crime,
the criminal's will is split: his real, implicit will is to obey the law; but his
actual will goes against his real will. The criminal, in this respect, is like
the smoker who knows that smoking is bad, and who wants very badly
to quit, but who nevertheless continues to smoke and enjoys doing so.
This smoker's de facto will is to smoke, but his real will is not to smoke.

Hegel is making a strong claim of which we may be just as skeptical as
we are of the smoker who says that she really wants to quit, just as she
lights up again. Hegel claims that the criminal's real or implicit will is the
universal will. In this respect Hegel's argument resembles, and follows,
that of Rousseau, who says that the citizen who follows his particular will
against the general will is unfree and that by being punished he is "forced
to be free"—he will be brought to see that he is only truly free when he
wills according to the general will, which is his own implicit will.[24]

If the criminal's real will is not to commit the crime, then it follows,
Hegel argues, that the criminal wills his own punishment. Some commentators have criticized this view, noting that the criminal usually wants to
be treated as an exception, and not be punished.[25] Hegel does not mean,
of course, that the criminal is a masochist who eagerly awaits infliction
of pain:

> The criminal who is punished can of course wish [wünschen] that the punish-
> ment will be diverted; but the universal will brings forth the demand that the
> crime be punished. We must accept that the absolute will of the criminal also is
> that he be punished. Insofar as he is to be punished, the demand is present that
> he understands it is just that he be punished, and though he understands he can
> of course wish that he be liberated from punishment as from an external suffer-
> ing; but insofar as he admits that it is just that he be punished, his universal will
> is in agreement with the punishment.[26]

From the previous section we know that Hegel views the criminal act as
a "negative infinite judgment." We saw that this meant the criminal
shows a complete ignorance of the concept of right. Yet now we see that
Hegel thinks the criminal *does* know implicitly what is right. In the previous section we saw Hegel interpreting the criminal act as if the criminal
were completely disconnected from the universal will that articulates
right. But now we know Hegel is claiming not that the criminal in fact is
disconnected from this will, but rather that his crime was an act of irrationality and internal contradiction, and that the criminal himself is im-

[23] Ibid., 99 Bem; Rph VI, 4:283,2–23. On the idea of a split will, see Jon Elster, *Ulysses
and the Sirens: Studies in Rationality and Irrationality.*
[24] Jean-Jacques Rousseau, *The Social Contract,* bk. 1, ch. 7, quoted below.
[25] Ossip Flechtheim, *Hegels Strafrechtstheorie,* p. 102.
[26] Prop 225.

plicitly a rational creature who, when he reflects, will come to see that what he did was wrong. The criminal commits an irrational act, but he has a rational essence.[27]

Hegel seems to be arguing that the criminal act is an irrational act committed by someone who at the time did not recognize what he was doing. One commentator has argued that since to commit a wrong requires that one recognize the law and know its meaning, in Hegel's view there can be no crime.[28] What is wrong with this argument is that in Hegel's view one can be a rational being yet still act as if one were not rational: "The claim is made that the criminal in the moment of his action must have had a 'clear idea' of the wrong and its culpability before it can be imputed to him as a crime. At first sight, this claim seems to preserve the right of his subjectivity, but the truth is that it deprives him of his indwelling nature as intelligent."[29]

Hegel's view is subtle, and this subtlety has been missed by some, caught by others. Igor Primoratz has caught and captured this subtlety in a succinct statement: "The criminal act is opposed to the rational will, but it is the act of a rational being."[30] Hegel insists that we treat the criminal as not only essentially a rational being, but a rational being at the time of committing the crime. To take the action of the criminal as the action of a rational being means to universalize it. We say that in committing his crime the criminal meant to proclaim that this is how to act.[31] Hegel wrote, in the plain language he mostly used for his *Gymnasium* students: "If you rob someone, you rob yourself; if you kill someone, you kill yourself; the perpetrator may be subsumed under the manner of treatment he established. His action is a law that he set up and which he had recognized through his own action."[32] Rather than excuse the criminal's act as the work of a madman, or even as a burst of irrationality from an otherwise sane person gone temporarily mad, Hegel has us respond as if the act was rational, which, in this context, means we universalize it. We respect the humanity and rationality of the criminal by treating him by the same standard guiding him when he committed his crime.

Hegel seems to make the Kantian assumption here that it is not rational to will a set of rules for yourself that differs from the set of rules by which you would have others live. In Kant's view, a moral agent wills according to the categorical imperative, which demands that "I ought never to act

---

[27] Cf. Flechtheim, *Hegels Strafrechtstheorie*, p. 63.

[28] Michael Mitias, "Another Look at Hegel's Concept of Punishment," p. 177.

[29] PR 132 Rem.

[30] Primoratz, *Banquos-Geist*, p. 50.

[31] Rph V, 3:344,3–9; see Primoratz, *Banquos-Geist*, p. 52 ("the rational being wills the universal").

[32] Prop 244.

except in such a way that I can also will that my maxim should become a universal law."[33] But there is an important difference between the views of Kant and Hegel. For Hegel, the source of right lies not in the categorical imperative, in a deduction by reason, but in the ethical life or ethos of our community, which laws of right articulate.[34] In his early "Natural Law Essay" Hegel says of Kant's categorical imperative that it pronounces right by completely abstracting from all content of the will, for in Kant's view, "to introduce a content is to establish a heteronomy of choice."[35] But Hegel thinks this abstraction, this appeal to pure reason as opposed to existing social practices and norms, deflects us from "what is precisely of interest," namely, "to know *what* right and duty are."[36] Kant and his followers insist that duties such as keeping promises or respecting property arise "on the basis of general moral principles that do not refer to the existence of social practices."[37] Hegel disagrees. For Hegel, laws of right merely describe the customs and practices we share as an ethical community: "We have laws against theft only to formalize our practice of respecting the property of our fellow citizens."[38] Another way to characterize the distinction between Kant and Hegel here is to say that for Kant, at least as Hegel understands Kant, to violate right is to violate the categorical imperative, which is to act inconsistently or contradictorily;[39] while for Hegel, to violate right is to engage not merely in contradictory behavior, but in *self*-contradiction. For Hegel, when we violate right we are not merely being inconsistent; rather, we are going against our own (second) nature, against what Hegel calls our own ethical substance.[40] We are violating the practices of the ethical community that shaped us, that made us who we are; we are violating ourselves. Hegel invokes a substantive conception of rationality that sees as irrational not simply the violation of rules one establishes for oneself, but the violation of the standards of the community in which one has grown up and partakes.

[33] Immanuel Kant, *Groundwork of the Metaphysic of Morals*, trans. H. J. Paton, p. 70. Kant regards this principle as nonempirical and absolutely necessary: "We cannot do morality a worse service than by seeking to derive it from examples." "Morality cannot be abstracted from any empirical knowledge" (pp. 76, 79; cf. p. 57).

[34] Hegel claims that our community is an ethical substance with a shared sense of right. I discuss this claim in detail in chapter 4.

[35] NL 76.

[36] Ibid.

[37] Thomas Scanlon, "Promises and Practices," pp. 211, 220.

[38] Rph VI, 4:603,25–26.

[39] In his essay on natural law Hegel charges Kant with declaring the wrong merely of contradictory behavior: Kant shows only that "property, if property *is*, must be property." "But the aim is precisely to prove that property must be," and Hegel argues that the categorical imperative cannot prove this; it cannot justify practices (NL 78).

[40] On the idea of "second nature," see the discussion in sec. 3.1.6; on ethical substance, see sec. 4.2.

The idea that it is not rational to will rules that differ from those you would have others live by (Kant), or from those of your ethical community (Hegel), is probably troubling to some. Still, it has strong intuitive appeal. The thief who steals my watch because her particular will is to have it does not will that someone else in turn steals from her the watch she stole from me. In stealing, the thief in effect declares that property rights not be respected; but she does not really will this, insofar as she wants others to respect her right to property. In stealing, she contradicts her own true will.

Crime, then, is the result of a rational being willing irrationally—according to his particular, not universal, will. It is important to see that crime is not the sort of thing of which we could reasonably expect to be rid permanently. Crime, and irrational willing, are part of the world of contingency (*Zufall*),[41] and Hegel thinks that there will always be contingency in the world.[42] Hegel further suggests that crime is even necessary. The state exists in the sphere of *Willkür* (arbitrariness) and *Zufall* (contingency),[43] and man is inherently a creature of contradiction,[44] and so clashes between particular wills and the universal are inevitable;[45] but they are also necessary, since the possibility of willing according to our particular will is essential to our freedom. Commentators who criticize Hegel for not being utopian enough to anticipate a society without crime miss this point.[46] Nor does Hegel's insistence that there will always be crime disprove his supposed claim that the world is rational—a claim we shall take up later.[47] Hegel can claim with consistency both that the world is essentially rational and that it consists partly in contingent and irrational actions, just as he can claim that human beings are essentially rational, and should be treated as rational beings, even though some occasionally act against the rational will.[48]

Why punish the criminal with a split will? If crime is a self-contradiction, does it follow that we must punish self-contradictory behavior?[49]

[41] See Rph I, 162,657–660: "Crimes are to be seen as contingent actions [*zufällige*]."
[42] Enz 408 and Rem. Cf. Dieter Henrich, "Hegels Theorie über den Zufall."
[43] PR 258 Z.
[44] Rph VI, 4:118,7–20; 4:172–173; 4:147,25–31.
[45] Rph II, 1:270,15–17; PR 86 Z.
[46] Ossip Flechtheim, "Hegel and the Problem of Punishment," p. 306.
[47] Cf. Ossip Flechtheim, "Die Funktion der Strafe in der Rechtstheorie Hegels," in *Von Hegel zu Kelsen*, p. 20.
[48] Hegel's conception of rationality seems to contain within it the idea of fallibility. Steven Smith has recently argued that, for Hegel, to be rational means to give arguments about which we can be wrong; see his "Hegelianism and the Three Crises of Rationality," pp. 968ff.
[49] David Cooper poses a similar question in his article "Hegel's Theory of Punishment,"

2.3   The Significance of Punishment

We have seen that for Hegel crime is an act of the criminal's particular
will contrary to the universal will that is both implicit in him and explicit
in the criminal law of a rational modern state. Crime is an act of self-
contradiction, but it is also a flouting of right; and one of the reasons we
punish is, in Hegel's view, to vindicate the law: if crime is not negated, its
positive existence would remain and replace what is *Recht-an-sich*.[50] "To
leave crime unpunished would let it be seen as right."[51] "If crime goes
unpunished, it would count as valid."[52] "To leave it unpunished would
make crime seem justified to others."[53] We punish, then, because, unless
we make clear that the criminal's particular will is not the rational will, it
may come to be taken as the rational will.

Hegel's position is not merely that right must be vindicated; it is that
right must be "restored" (*wiederherstellen*).[54] Hegel speaks sometimes of
right as lying in wait until it is violated, upon which it turns against the
criminal. He uses the images of *Banquos-Geist*,[55] to suggest that the
criminal's own true self turns against him like a ghost, and of the Eumenides, who are asleep, awakened by the act of crime and drawn to restore
justice so they may return to their sleep: "Right is the Eumenides, the
well-disposed, which is protectorate of crime, and now completes what
necessarily lies in the matter—no individual arbitrary will [*Willkür*]
makes itself valid in crime."[56] Hegel suggests with these images that the
power that punishes is not just the state, but the power of justice—and
justice does not exist merely in the form of state punishment. Hegel says
the state is not a presupposition for justice.[57] We shall consider this difficult aspect of Hegel's view in chapter 4.

Hegel articulated his retributive position that we punish not to augment social utility but for the sake of justice or right in an oft-quoted and
apparently obscure passage from his lectures, where he calls punishment
the "negation of the negation."[58] Crime negates the rational will, and

---

p. 160. However, Cooper does not distinguish between inconsistent and self-contradictory
behavior.

[50] Rph V, 3:310,28–34.

[51] Ibid., 3:662,16–19.

[52] Rph VI, 4:549,4–6.

[53] Ibid., 4:549,16–18.

[54] PR 99.

[55] Ibid., 101 Z.

[56] Rph V, 3:670,30–671,5. Cf. PR 101 Bem; Rph V, 3:323,6–9; 3:320,34–321,3.

[57] PR 100 Rem, p. 191: "Der Staat ist nicht die bedingende Voraussetzung der Gerechtigkeit an sich."

[58] Ibid., 97 Z.

punishment negates this negation. Hegel's point is that if the state fails persistently to punish crimes its citizens are likely no longer to regard crimes as wrongs. Retributivist theories are often cast as backward-looking, while utilitarian theories are seen as forward-looking or consequentialist. Hegel's retributivism *is* forward-looking: we punish to avoid a future condition where crimes no longer are regarded as wrong. But it would be mistaken to conclude that Hegel's retributivism is a "disguised utilitarianism."[59] For Hegel, the reason we want to avoid having crimes no longer regarded as wrong is that we should want right upheld, because it is right, and not that by vindicating right we augment social utility. In Hegel's view, we must punish those who have committed a wrong.[60]

2.4   Hegel's Key Claim about Punishment

Hegel's conception of punishment is more complex than the previous section suggests. We punish not only to vindicate the law. We punish also to further the interests of the criminal:

> Objectively [punishment] is the reconciliation of the law with itself; by the annulment of the crime, the law [*Gesetz*] is restored and its validity is thereby actualized. Subjectively, it is the reconciliation of the criminal with himself, i.e. with the law known by him as his own and as valid for him and his protection; when this law is executed upon him, he himself finds in this process the satisfaction of justice and nothing save his own act.[61]

Hegel is saying that there are both "objective" and "subjective" reasons for punishing. The objective reason is that right must be vindicated. The subjective reason is that the criminal himself in effect authorizes and demands his own punishment. In committing the crime, the criminal acts against his own implicit will, and punishment respects his rationality by universalizing the part of his split will that went against his implicit will. The criminal, by satisfying his particular will, injures the rights of his victim (if his crime had a particular victim), and of society as a whole, and no rational agent would truly will to do this. Punishment lets the criminal feel the consequence of his own misguided act, by applying to him the principle on which he acted in committing the crime. The criminal finds in his punishment "nothing save his own act."

Hegel makes another key claim about punishment: the criminal has a

---

[59] Cf. C. K. Benn, "An Approach to the Problems of Punishment," p. 330.
[60] How much we punish them is a distinct question. Cf. sec. 5.5.
[61] PR 220.

right to be punished, and by being punished the criminal is made *free*.[62]
Hegel says that the power that punishes is not an alien power but comes
from the criminal's own will: "A criminal who is to be punished may
regard the punishment he faces as a limitation of his freedom; in fact
punishment is not an alien power to which he is subjected, but rather the
manifestation of his own act, and insofar as he recognizes this, he faces
the punishment as a free being."[63] Hegel's argument, that the criminal can
be understood to be free in his punishment, echoes Rousseau's argument
in *The Social Contract*. Rousseau writes that

> each individual, as a man, may have a particular will contrary or dissimilar to
> the general will which he has as a citizen. . . . In order then that the social
> compact may not be an empty formula, it tacitly includes the undertaking,
> which alone can give force to the rest, that whoever refuses to obey the general
> will shall be compelled to do so by the whole body. This means nothing less
> than that he will be forced to be free.[64]

To be punished is to be free. We should wonder what sort of freedom
this is. Like Rousseau's, Hegel's conception of freedom may strike us as
something very strange, almost the opposite of what we normally regard
as freedom. In the next chapter we shall consider in great detail Hegel's
claim that the criminal is free in his punishment, by exploring what Hegel
means by freedom. We shall see how Hegel's theory of legal punishment
takes us to the very core of his political philosophy.

[62] Hegel's claim that the criminal has a right to be punished is linked to his claim that the
criminal is made free in his punishment, because, for Hegel, right and freedom are inextri-
cably connected. We shall discuss this connection in the next chapter.

[63] Enz 158 Z.

[64] Rousseau, *The Social Contract*, bk. 1, ch. 7, my emphasis. Rousseau needn't be taken
to mean that someone shall be forced to have pain inflicted on him, or suffer some other
sort of punishment, only that someone should be forced to do something.

Three

Hegel's Conception of Freedom

FOR HEGEL, practices, institutions, and laws are right (*Recht*) if we can understand ourselves to be free by living in accord with them. "The system of right is the realm where freedom is realised."[1] Something is right if by willing it we are free: "Any existent that is an embodiment of the free will is right."[2] Hegel also claims that a criminal, who has violated the law by committing a wrong (*Unrecht*), has a right to punishment, and only by being punished is he respected as a free human being.[3] In this chapter I discuss what Hegel means by freedom.

It is often said that freedom is at the center of Hegel's whole philosophy. One commentator even suggests that "the freedom of human beings is the *only* theme of the Hegelian philosophy."[4] We are bound to be confused about this philosophy if we are confused by Hegel's conception of freedom. In a widely known textbook of political theory, George Sabine calls Hegel's conception of freedom a paradox. Sabine explains:

> [Hegel] repeatedly equated individual choice with mere caprice, sentimentality, and fanaticism. Again and again he branded the right of private judgment as a merely "superficial" thing. . . . Yet he certainly believed that, *in some sense*

[1] PR 4. *Recht* can be translated as right but also as law. On the broad sense Hegel gives to the term *Recht*, see Wolfgang Schild, "Der Strafrechtsdogmatische Begriff der Zurechnung in der Rechtsphilosophie Hegels," pp. 459–460; and his "Die Aktualität des Hegelschen Strafbegriffes," p. 202. Schild properly notes that for Hegel *Recht* refers not just to positive law, but to the embodiment of freedom. (See PR 29; Enz 486: "Right is to be taken not merely as the limited juristic *Recht* but as the embodiment of all determinations of freedom.") For this reason it is better to translate *Recht* as right not law. This is contrary to the position taken by, for example, A. V. Miller in his translation *The Philosophical Propaedeutic* (Oxford: Basil Blackwell, 1986).

[2] PR 29. In his lectures Hegel acknowledged that his equating right with freedom may seem strange, and he tried to get his students to put aside their ordinary understanding of right: "With right one often thinks of possession, satisfaction of desires, and regards these as fundamental . . . right is the protector of possessions, of satisfactions, a protection we buy only by giving up a part of our freedom, so that right serves to protect only those who gave up a part of their freedom. In this way right is set in opposition to freedom, at once the servant of satisfaction, possessions, but also a limitation on freedom. This representation is to be given up in favor of one which sees freedom and spirit, not as restricted by, but as receiving their existence through right" (Rph V, 3:102).

[3] PR 100. Cf. sec. 2.4.

[4] Bruno Liebruck, "Recht, Moralität und Sittlichkeit bei Hegel," p. 13, my emphasis.

which he could never make clear, the modern state succeeds better than the ancient in respecting the individual's independence and right of choice. . . . As an historian he was even inclined to admire the iconoclasts and he was quite aware that the man who defies society at the dictates of his own conscience may become the most valuable of social forces. *Hegel never explained* how this can be compatible with the opinion that the right of private judgment is mere caprice.[5]

Sabine is correct to say that Hegel equated the freedom of individual choice with caprice and fanaticism. He is also correct to say that Hegel values appealing to one's own conscience. In this Sabine sees a paradox Hegel "never explained." To suggest, as does Sabine, that Hegel's conception of freedom is confused and inadequately articulated is to make a serious indictment of Hegel's whole philosophy. In this chapter I aim to vindicate Hegel in the face of this charge by unraveling the complexities of Hegel's conception of freedom. I shall show how Hegel clearly, consistently, and without paradox at once denounces as not real freedom the freedom of an individual to choose capriciously or arbitrarily, and proclaims that an individual is really free in following the dictates of her society only when she determines for herself that it is right to follow these dictates. To unravel Hegel's conception of freedom requires a systematic discussion of the introduction to the *Philosophy of Right*. This discussion may seem at first to be an unwarranted digression from our concern with legal punishment. But as we shall eventually see, it is essential if we are fully to understand and feel the force of Hegel's claim that to be punished is to be free.

3.1   Paragraphs 5–7 of the *Philosophy of Right*: The Concept of Will in General

When Hegel speaks of freedom he usually refers to a property of some agent. For Hegel, the agent is "will"; freedom is its property. Of course for us the agent is usually a person having a will. Hegel speaks of a disembodied will because he wants to give an account of the logical structure of the free will, and such an account must not depend on particular or contingent features of agents. In paragraphs 5–7 of the *Philosophy of Right* Hegel discusses the concept of freedom by identifying the features of the free will. It is to these passages, the foundation of Hegel's conception of freedom, that we now turn.

---

[5] George Sabine, *A History of Political Theory*, pp. 639–640, my emphasis.

3.1.1 The Capacity to Abstract

One feature of the (free) will[6] is, in Hegel's language, the capacity to abstract (*abstrahieren*) absolutely from any of its objects or aims.[7] Hegel's use of the word *abstract* can easily confuse us. We often use *abstract* to mean something that is not concrete; the word is an adjective. But *abstrahieren* is a verb: when the will abstracts, it is acting in some sense. But how?

Hegel's concept of an abstracting will resembles at least two concepts familiar to us: *renunciation* (as when we resolve never to take another drink); and *detachment* (as when we cope with the loss of a loved one by no longer calling to mind our shared memories; or when we respond to our bitter disappointment over the loss suffered by our favorite sports team by saying to ourselves, "it's only a stupid game"). When we renounce or detach ourselves from a commitment or interest, in Hegel's language we abstract from it, and by doing this we are *free from* it. Abstract freedom is freedom from.

Hegel says the will can renounce or detach itself from any thing and all things; it can abstract *absolutely*: "I can give up everything . . . even my existence."[8] He calls the state of absolute abstraction "unrestricted infinity":[9] when my will abstracts from some content, it is no longer constrained by or dependent on that content and in that sense is not finite, not bounded. Everything that seems important to me—my life, friends, love, for example[10]—I can become chained to, but insofar as I can give up all of these things, I am free.[11]

Hegel often speaks of this capacity of the will to abstract as the capacity of thought: "In thinking, one is utterly independent; nothing else can intrude upon one's freedom—one relates only to oneself, and nothing else can have a claim upon one."[12] It is a capacity only of humans. Only man can commit suicide.[13] Suicide is the most striking manifestation of this capacity of will; others include giving up friends, giving up chocolate, distancing yourself from a work of yours that is poorly received. A fa-

---

[6] The features I am describing are features a free will has. But a will that is not free might have one or the other of these features, and so it is correct to say both the will and the free will have this feature.

[7] PR 5.

[8] Rph III, 59,4–5.

[9] PR 5.

[10] Ibid., 7 Z.

[11] Cf. Rph VI, 4:112,2–7.

[12] PRel 257; cf. Rph VI, 4:112,17–19.

[13] PRel 121; PR 5 Z; cf. Enz 468: "without thought there can be no will. . . . The animal . . . because it does not think, is also incapable of possessing a will."

mous example of this abstracting will is Charles Dickens's Harold Skimpole: "I covet nothing, possession is nothing to me."

Hegel's concept of abstraction contains the ambiguity that arises from the different senses usually conveyed by the words *renunciation* and *detachment*. I can detach myself from some interest of mine without anybody else knowing and without committing myself in the way that I usually commit myself when I publicly renounce an interest of mine. Renunciation implies a declaration to others that commits me to act in a certain way. Renunciation implies opposition. But detachment often consists of nothing more than my own laughing off of something, perhaps as a way of coping with a frustration or disappointment. (One function of the comic, or of a sense of humor, is to help us abstract, to see that what we think terribly important really is not.) Detachment implies not opposition but withdrawal.[14] This leaves us with this ambiguity when Hegel speaks of the abstracting will: Is the act of abstraction a mental or *theoretical* act of detachment, so that the freedom we derive from this act of abstraction might be called a passive or inner freedom?[15] Or does Hegel

---

[14] The Latin roots of *abstract* suggest precisely this: *abs* = off, *tractus* = to draw; the *Oxford English Dictionary* tells us that *abstract* came to mean "withdrawing in thought." There appears to be another sense of *abstraction* not captured by the concepts of detachment or renunciation: to choose otherwise. When we choose otherwise we sometimes do so by renouncing one or another possibility. But sometimes we choose otherwise without having renounced other possibilities, as when we choose arbitrarily. If I am indifferent between Coke and Pepsi, my choice of Coke over Pepsi is arbitrary (assuming there is no other reason for preferring Coke, such as lower price or better taste) and does not reflect my renunciation of Pepsi. When we arbitrarily choose otherwise we cannot be said to abstract from. We will see that for Hegel the arbitrary will, *Willkür*, is not really free (see section 3.2.2). Here we see one reason why: *Willkür* can never be said to abstract.

[15] What I mean by passive or inner freedom is the sort of withdrawal into thought engaged in by J. K. Huysmans's Des Esseintes in *Against the Grain*: Des Esseintes, about to embark on a train trip to London, pauses, recalling in his imagination his past travels: "Des Esseintes could not stir a limb; a soothing, enervating lassitude was creeping through every member, rendering him incapable of so much as lifting his hand to light a cigar. He kept telling himself: 'Come, come now, get up, we must be off'; but instantly objections occurred to him in contravention of these orders. What was the good of moving, when a man can travel so gloriously sitting in a chair? Was he not in London, whose odours and atmosphere, whose denizens and viands and table furniture were all about him? . . . He sat dreaming and let the minutes slip by, thus cutting off his retreat, telling himself: 'Now I should have to dash up to the barriers, hustle with the luggage; how tiresome, what a nuisance that would be!'—Then, harking back, he told himself over again: 'After all, I have felt and seen what I wanted to feel and see . . . it would be a fool's trick to go and lose these imperishable impressions by a clumsy change of locality' " (pp. 129–130). Des Esseintes, of course, did not board the train. His imagination, his thought, held him back from acting. His abstraction (his choosing not to board and go to London) freed him from the tiresome troubles of travel. The imagination that liberated Des Esseintes from the troubles of travel literally immobilized his limbs. Withdrawal replaced action. This is freedom?

mean by "abstract from" a physical or *practical* act of renunciation?[16] Can a slave be free merely by thinking himself to be free or by convincing himself that the coercion exercised upon him by his master doesn't really matter, for though the master can whip his body, he cannot reach his soul? Those inclined to view Hegel as an idealist philosopher who seeks solace in the clouds to avoid getting his hands dirty in practical politics may be surprised to find that when he speaks of abstraction Hegel mostly refers to practical acts. Hegel says that the slave can overcome the coercive circumstances that determine how he must live by abstracting, where by abstracting he means the ultimate renunciation: "the slave can die free."[17] "If a person is a slave it is his will, for he need not be, he can kill himself."[18] In his earlier essay on natural law Hegel explains his concept of freedom also by referring to the act of suicide: "by his ability to die the subject proves himself free and entirely above all coercion."[19] Of course, suicide is a very special practical act, special in the sense that the freedom achieved will seem to the critic as questionable as passive or inner freedom. Later we shall see that this practical act is for Hegel a last resort, hardly the sort of action we should want to have to take. Still, that we know we have this last resort is liberating: "But life, being weary of these worldly bars, Never lacks power to dismiss itself. If I know this, know all the world besides, That part of tyranny that I do bear I can shake off at pleasure."[20]

Sometimes by "abstracting from" Hegel *does* mean an act only of thought; "Spirit flees to its inwardness, it can't be coerced."[21] But it is a mistake to think Hegel advocates a passive or inner freedom consisting in withdrawal into thought as a replacement for action. Hegel opposes the view that thinking (a theoretical activity) is separate from willing (a practical activity).[22] He thinks that to act freely we must first think, but we cannot be really free merely by thinking. Hegel says that the slave does not know himself as essentially a free being because the slave does not

---

[16] Here I follow Hegel's own use of the terms *theoretical* and *practical*: "Theoretical consciousness leaves things as they are. Practical consciousness is active and brings forth changes" (Prop 212).

[17] PR 57 Bem: "Doch können sie als frei sterben."

[18] Rph V, 3:226,19–21.

[19] NL 91; cf. PR 5, 70: On "death" see PhdG 80, 363–364, 452, 784; and Charles Taylor, *Hegel*, p. 173.

[20] Spoken by Cassius in Shakespeare's *Julius Caesar*, act 1, scene 3.

[21] Rph III, 59,11–13.

[22] See PR 4 Z; Enz 445, 481; Karl Larenz, *Hegels Zurechnungslehre*, p. 39; Karl Larenz, "Hegels Dialektik des Willens und das Problem der Juristischen Persönlichkeit," pp. 202ff.; and G. H. R. Parkinson, "Hegel's Concept of Freedom," p. 163: "one must not draw a sharp line between reason as practical and reason as theorizing."

think.[23] But the slave who *does* think but instead of acting withdraws into a passive, inner freedom, or Stoic freedom,[24] is not really free, because he stops short of willing. The thinking slave is free not because he can withdraw into himself—such withdrawal, we might say, serves only to distract him from the pain of his chains. The slave is free, in Hegel's view, because he can declare himself free and go on to demand that his conditions be changed: "The slave, once he says he should be free, is from that moment free, and he owes no compensation to his master, *indeed can even demand provisions from the master.*"[25]

In Hegel's view, all human beings, by virtue of their ability to think and their capacity for self-consciousness, are free and need only will their freedom actually to be free: "If I was born a slave, and was raised and nurtured by a master, and if my parents and all my forefathers were slaves, still I am free the moment I will it, the moment that I come to the consciousness of my freedom."[26] Perhaps this is unconvincing—the chains still bind the thinking slave who, conscious of those chains, demands freedom. But Hegel believes that in the movement of history the slave's demand will be met, precisely through the force of will, of thoughtful action. For Hegel, the capacity to abstract makes us really free only if we could and, when appropriate, do renounce by deeds: we are free not merely by subjectively detaching ourselves from our interests; we are free insofar as this detachment in thought leads, when appropriate, to objective action. The alcoholic who says she can quit any time is hardly free from her dependence by *saying* she could quit. She must quit.

But sometimes I *am* free by detaching rather than renouncing. There are times when it is possible to abstract only in thought, when all we can

---

[23] PR 21 Rem.

[24] PhdG 198–199.

[25] Rph II, 1:264,20–23, my emphasis. The less attractive part of Hegel's argument on how thought is necessary for practical freedom is his justification of slavery in Africa: Hegel says slavery is not so bad for "African negroes," who have no regard for life (PR 132) and who do not think, being still like animals (PH 122[93]; cf. PRel 202, note 3: "while humanity is, of course, implicitly free, Africans and Asians are not, because they have not the consciousness of what constitutes the concept of humanity"). Slavery makes them more human (PR 135). The argument echoes John Stuart Mill's discussion of the Chinese in *On Liberty*, pp. 68–69, 137–138. Mill argues that coercion is justified as a means of raising barbarians to a level of civility at which they can then live as free thinking beings. Our practice of forcing children to go to school reflects this idea of justified pedagogical coercion. This argument should not distract us from acknowledging Hegel's view that slavery is absolutely wrong or unjust: "a slave has an absolute right to free himself" (PR 66 Z; cf. Rph V, 3:251; Rph VI, 4:538,10–11: "an sich ist die Sklaverei unrecht"). Laws that permit slavery are only positive laws and are opposed to absolute right (Prop 233). The reason Hegel thinks slavery is absolutely wrong or unjust is that right (*Recht*) embodies freedom, and since slavery is counter to freedom (Rph VI, 4:89) it is counter to right.

[26] Rph I, 32,545–549.

do is withdraw—and here withdrawal *is* liberating. Hegel is not denying this, but he gives *this* freedom another name. In an extraordinary passage from his *Aesthetics*, surprisingly neglected in the English (but not German) literature, Hegel describes the withdrawal consisting in our detaching ourselves from our interests not glowingly as genuine freedom, but somberly as a desperate fleeing to *subjective* freedom:

> Insofar as an unjust situation is, because of the power of the existing conditions, insurmountable, then this situation can bring only misfortune and something false in itself. For the rational being must submit to necessity, that is, must not react against it, so long as he lacks the power or the means to overcome; rather, he must peacefully let pass what is unavoidable. *He must give up the interest and need that lies at the bottom of the limitation he faces, and bear the insurmountable with the still courage of passivity and patience. Where a struggle does not help, the rational man gives up the idea of struggle, in order to at least be able to withdraw into formal independence and subjective freedom.* Then the power of wrong has no more power over him; when he sets himself against the insurmountable, he experiences his entire dependence. Of course neither this abstraction to a pure formal independence, nor a fruitless battle, is truly nice.[27]

Sometimes detachment is all we can do, and Hegel grudgingly accepts the subjective freedom it brings, perhaps as our solace. But when detachment is a replacement for appropriate action, then Hegel belittles the freedom we think we have attained, this passive, subjective freedom.

Recently Bernard Yack has suggested otherwise, arguing that Hegel thinks all we can do in the face of the vexations of modern life is withdraw into a realm of thought that is separate from the practical world of social interaction. Since my argument is that Hegel is a practical theorist whose ideas we can appropriate when we engage in criticism of our practices, it is worthwhile to take up this contrary position, especially as Yack advances some claims that are often advanced but are not consistent with the best interpretation I think we can give to Hegel's political philosophy. Yack criticizes Hegel's later conception of freedom, found in the *Rechtsphilosophie*, as too theoretical, and he criticizes the older Hegel for taming his earlier longing for a new freedom. Yack says the younger Hegel demanded the transformation of society into a "fully human community."[28] The Hegel of the *Rechtsphilosophie*, in Yack's view, instead asks us to "seek satisfaction in the realm of speculative knowledge" and makes bold claims yet "accepts the limitations of contemporary institutions."[29]

---

[27] *Ästhetik*, in Hegel, *Werke*, vol. 12, pp. 286–287, my translation and emphasis.
[28] Bernard Yack, *The Longing for Total Revolution*, pp. 186–187.
[29] Ibid., p. 187.

Yack sees the later Hegel as a passive owl, a theorist who is not practical, not interested in *changing* the world.[30]

The longing Yack thinks Hegel held but then later tamed remains an extremely vague longing, easily susceptible to the slings of hard-line analytic types: Yack describes this longing as a "goal of transforming modern society into a community in which man's humanity is fully realized in the external world."[31] But what does this mean? The young "left-Kantian" Hegel did express visions of the sort Yack describes, but are they the visions whose practicality we want to contrast favorably with the allegedly theoretically saturated and practically deprived arguments Yack suggests we find in the *Rechtsphilosophie*? The aesthetic vision of the left-Kantian Hegel is closer to the sort of imagined world into which Des Esseintes escapes than to a political world.[32]

In advancing his "owl" reading of the mature Hegel, Yack argues that "Hegel finds no source of dissatisfaction in the institutions and social practices which, he argues, realize freedom in the modern world."[33] Yack makes clear a few pages later that he does not mean Hegel is satisfied with every aspect of existing practices, but, rather, that Hegel thinks that by a theoretical act the frustration we face in our practical activity need no longer be a source of dissatisfaction, and that we can be at home and satisfied in a "community of self-knowledge" that is separate from "the community of social interaction."[34] Indeed, we flee to the former because "we are always going to be dissatisfied with the latter."[35] In supporting his view Yack cites this passage from the *Philosophy of Religion*: "Thus modern man easily develops a mood in which he loses heart for everything else, and does not even seek to reach ends which he could reach."[36] But we need not take Hegel to mean in this passage that we will always be dissatisfied with our social reality and so we should withdraw. The passage expresses a truth about us: sometimes we want to withdraw or abstract from our world and its commitments. But Hegel thinks that to

---

[30] Yack suggests a break between an "early Hegel" with an aesthetic political vision and a "later Hegel" who tames this vision. Dieter Henrich has also suggested such a break, in his "Contemporary Relevance of Hegel's Aesthetics." I discuss the relationship I see between the earlier and later works of Hegel in the next chapter.

[31] Yack, *The Longing for Total Revolution*, p. 209.

[32] See note 15 above for the reference to Des Esseintes. In chapter 4 I shall argue that Hegel did not leave aside the vision given in his early work, imaginative and brilliant but obscure, but he made it much more concrete and translated it into terms that allow this vision to serve as a practical theory, or a theory with which we can criticize and possibly reform existing practices.

[33] Yack, *The Longing for Total Revolution*, p. 210.

[34] Ibid., p. 215.

[35] Ibid., pp. 219–220.

[36] Ibid., p. 220.

do so—to escape—is the path not to true freedom, but to an ultimately unsatisfying passive or inner freedom. Yack suggests that the mature Hegel, resigned and frustrated, gives up all political battles and instead accommodates himself to whatever exists, presumably even to unjust laws and practices. It is true that Hegel seeks the positive in what exists; but Hegel does not think existence consists only in the good, or that we must accept what is not good, or withdraw into a contemplative, apolitical world. We shall see that rather than accept injustice, or withdraw, Hegel criticizes existing laws and practices. He does not reconcile himself to unjust laws merely because they exist.

Toward the end of his chapter on Hegel, Yack speaks of him as encouraging the belief that the fully human community that left-Kantians had longed for is "within our grasp."[37] In Yack's reading, for Hegel this realization comes through philosophical speculation alone and cannot be realized in the practical world of social interaction. But for Hegel the world of thought is not divorced from the world of practical action and of willing: there is no sharp separation between the "community of self-knowledge" and "the community of social interaction." I want to focus on the words *within our grasp*. Hegel designates the theoretical activity of comprehending our world by *begreifen*. This word, like its English equivalent—to grasp—means both to comprehend in thought and physically to take hold of. For Hegel, grasping is a theoretical *and* a practical activity. To grasp is not to flee into thought but to make a political return.

3.1.2 The Limits of the Conception of Freedom as Abstraction

Hegel's attitude toward abstracting is complicated: to him the capacity to abstract is essential to our freedom; it is liberating. It is something powerful, but there is something suspicious about it. Sometimes we call the activity of abstraction cowardly withdrawal. What is so attractive about a dead slave? Is Des Esseintes really free by fleeing into his thoughts to avoid the troubles of acting?[38]

Hegel repeatedly emphasizes the inadequacies of taking this conception of freedom as real freedom, of taking this capacity of will as sufficient to be a genuinely free will. Hegel, after all, calls the freedom of the powerless who must give up their interests and passively withdraw not real but subjective freedom. He is sympathetic to the critic of withdrawal: "a human who negates an enemy by fleeing (i.e. withdrawing, escaping) is not free before the enemy."[39] And to die in a struggle between master and slave is

---

[37] Ibid., p. 223.
[38] See note 15, above.
[39] Rph V, 3:113,17–19.

not what Hegel thinks a satisfying outcome.[40] Neither death nor withdrawal is the ticket to real freedom. For Hegel, these must remain last resorts.

The more famous criticism Hegel gives of the "negative freedom" of abstracting is his linkage of negative freedom both with everything bad about the French Revolution and with religious fanaticism.[41] Negative freedom is akin as a theoretical attitude to the "Hindu fanaticism of pure contemplation,"[42] and as a practical attitude to the fanaticism of destruction, which Hegel sees in the French Terror, a destruction that can will nothing particular, only an abstract idea.[43] To the men of the Revolution, any institution was contrary to the abstract standard of equality they took to be freedom;[44] nothing was left standing. In neither standpoint, total detachment or total renunciation, are we truly free.

What is decisively wrong with the negative freedom of the abstracting will is that taken in itself it self-destructs—as in the case of the suicide. It negates everything and is left with nothing,[45] just as Kierkegaard's Socrates undermines every moral position he finds and is left with nowhere to stand, he only hovers.[46] The absolute negativity of Kierkegaard's Socrates, and the abstraction from every particular determination by the "pure I,"[47] represent only one side of freedom and are meaningless, even destructive, without the other side—embodiment in some content. The corpse of the suicide and the terror of the French Revolution are harsh reminders of what is bad about negative freedom taken in the extreme as a state of total detachment or total renunciation. Hegel does not think it is wrong to detach or renounce: the capacity to do so is essential if we are to be free. But to take freedom as consisting in only the capacity to abstract is to hold a fatally incomplete conception of freedom.

[40] See PhdG 188, in the section "Master/Slave," on the obvious inadequacy of trial by death as a basis for gaining recognition.

[41] PR 5 Rem.

[42] Ibid. Elsewhere Hegel describes this state of pure detachment, with reference to Buddhism and Lamaism, as a "state of negation" where one "must immerse oneself in this nothing, in the eternal tranquillity of the nothing generally," in which "all determinations cease," where one strives "to will nothing, to want nothing, and to do nothing" (PRel 253–256). Hegel calls this "the theoretical moment" (PRel 254). The version in the 1831 lectures of the *Philosophy of Religion* reads, "its characteristic *is not to act in opposition to* what is objective, to mold it, but to let it be preserved so that this stillness is produced in it" (PRel 254, note 149, my emphasis). This passage illustrates the distinction between detachment (withdrawal from without opposition to) and renunciation (opposition to).

[43] PR 5 Rem.

[44] Ibid., 5 Z; cf. Rph III, 59; and PhdG 585–592, though this is very cryptic.

[45] Rph VI, 4:115,1–2.

[46] Søren Kierkegaard, *The Concept of Irony*, trans. Lee Capel, p. 180.

[47] PR 5.

3.1.3   Embodiment in a Particular Content and the Necessity of Being Committed

Hegel was aware that most people in his day mistook negative freedom for freedom. To Hegel, these people were misguided, for they failed to acknowledge the other essential criterion or moment of freedom, or essential feature of the truly free will: the directing of the will toward some aim or object, toward what Hegel calls a "content."[48] Socrates must not just negate the views of everyone he finds; he will be free only if he finds some standpoint he can adopt as his own. Hegel describes this aspect of willing as "positing oneself as something determinate" and "stepping into existence."[49] Only by choosing something, by making it or determining[50] it as mine, do I have an existence: "If I am merely in a state of longing or striving, then I am nothing actual. The striving must come into existence."[51] Whereas the will that abstracts is universal, which is to say it has no particular properties, no particular content, and in the language of German Idealism is "abstract universality," the will that determines itself in some existing embodiment wills itself as something particular,[52] and only when the will has a particular content to which it is committed can the will truly be free. To be free we must be free *in*.

By choosing to have these friends, that house, this job, many will say that I have limited and constrained myself[53]—just think of all the responsibilities I must now take on, all the alternatives I have given up. Hegel attacks those who think that when we take on responsibilities and duties we make ourselves unfree. To Hegel it is *necessary* to determine something as mine: we must not remain like that beautiful soul that does not want to be soiled by something limited and particular—such a soul lacks existence, actuality, is passive, powerless, and lacks freedom.[54] To be free the will *must* take on some embodiment.[55]

---

[48] Ibid., 6.

[49] Ibid., my translation.

[50] *Bestimmen* (ibid.).

[51] PRel 187. We can understand Hegel's claim that only by taking on a content do I exist in a weak sense: only then do I have a meaningful existence, do I count as somebody, will others recognize my existence. Or in a much stronger sense: only then do I exist. The stronger claim would be bizarre. I take Hegel to mean only the weaker claim.

[52] Rph VI, 4:115,4–8,21–31.

[53] PR 6 Bem.

[54] Rph VI, 4:117,9–17; cf. PR 12, 13 Z.

[55] This idea of the necessity of taking some embodiment has been called the principle of necessary embodiment (Charles Taylor, *Hegel*, p. 83). A good discussion of this idea with respect to the ethical demand Hegel sees in our each embodying our will in some property is Jeremy Waldron, "Hegel's Discussion of Property," ch. 10 in his *Right to Private Property*.

3.1.4 Levels of Commitment

This principle of necessary embodiment in effect declares the necessity, if
we are to be free, of our being committed to something. But as we shall
see, Hegel claims we are free only in certain commitments. In this section
I shall discuss how it is that we are committed more to one thing, less to
another. We shall return to this idea of "levels of commitment" in making
sense of Hegel's claim.

We have all sorts of relationships and levels of commitment to the
things we will. For example: (1) To some objects of my will I am barely if
at all committed. I selected them arbitrarily and will readily renounce
them, or next time choose otherwise, without requiring a good reason:
today I pick Coke, tomorrow Pepsi. (2) Some objects of my will I am
happy to have for now, but when I find out something bad about them I
no longer want them: the auto mechanic I currently rely on; a favorite
food I just found out may cause cancer. Here it takes a good but not
compelling reason for me to renounce the object. (3) To some objects of
my will I am strongly committed, and those I will give up only if I have a
compelling reason to do so: my neighborhood; a good friend. (4) Some
objects I want I will keep no matter what I find out later about them (my
children; my country)—I am really committed, though it is possible for
me to renounce even these objects of my will. (It would be strange to
speak of something I could not possibly renounce as an object of my free
will, or as an object to which I am committed.) Each of these four relationships reflects a different level of commitment. Of course the standards
in (2) and (3) are vague—what counts as a good or compelling reason to
justify breaking our commitment? Nor is it always easy to decide which
category adequately reflects our level of commitment to various things;
probably we will disagree with one another about this. But fuzzy distinc-
tions can still be useful, and they are commonly used in practice. In the
case of (1), no reason needs to be given, since our commitment is based
merely on our arbitrary will.

One way to read the *Philosophy of Right* is as an account of the various
sorts of objects we will, ordered according to the level of commitment
Hegel thinks these objects command.[56] Property, which is an object of
our will, is something we all need to have to be free, but our commitment
to any particular property need not be strong, and we readily get rid of

---

[56] The following two paragraphs presuppose some familiarity with the structure of the
Philosophy of Right. The uninitiated might examine its table of contents to see that Hegel's
discussion proceeds in the manner I describe: from property to contract to family to state. I
discuss the structure of Hegel's *Philosophy of Right* in "The Justification of Legal Punishment: Hegel's *Rechtsphilosophie* as Practical Theory," ch. 8.

or alienate our property. The relation in (1) above is adequate, for our purposes, in describing the sense of commitment Hegel thinks we have to at least some particular property.[57] When we enter into contracts, we have placed our will in something to which we have a stronger commitment. With property, we relate ourselves to an object, but with contract we connect up with another person;[58] I now hold a thing by virtue of both my subjective will *and* another person's will.[59] My will is now a common will,[60] which Hegel distinguishes from the universal will with which he thinks we identify in relating ourselves to the state: Hegel says the universality of ethical relations (such as our relation to our state) is entirely different from the commonality (*Gemeinsamkeit*) in contract, "for the identity in contract can be extinguished."[61] The commitment we have in contract is stronger than that we have to particular property, but it is not as strong as ethical commitments. Although contract is entered into by our arbitrary will,[62] we are bound to the contract not by our arbitrary will but by the concept of right that is implicit in our relations with others.[63] When we have placed our will in a contract, we therefore are subject to various formalities and rules that reflect a greater commitment to the object of our will than that we have to, say, the apple we pick off a tree on a desert island.[64] The relation in (2) above seems adequate in describing our commitment in contracts.[65]

Another object of our will is our spouse. Hegel thinks that commitment to our spouse is stronger than the commitment we have in contracts or to property. Hegel thinks divorce requires a compelling reason. His reason is that now when we will we do so not arbitrarily, as Hegel thinks is the case in our appropriation of particular property,[66] but according to ethical standards.[67] Still, if I find out something very bad about my wife, or if I fall out of love with her, I need not remain committed.[68] The relation in

[57] We do have property in our person, but Hegel thinks this property is inalienable (PR 66). Hegel develops much of his argument by assuming our particular property is the content of our arbitrary will; see his discussion of contract, PR 75. See also PR 49 Z: in abstract right (the sphere where Hegel treats property) one should be indifferent to particularity.

[58] Ibid., 40.

[59] Ibid., 71.

[60] Ibid.; Rph V, 3:263.

[61] Rph V, 3:268,10–14.

[62] PR 75.

[63] Rph VI, 4:263,12–18; cf. Rph I, 38,754–755.

[64] On the formalities and rules involved in contracts, see PR 78, 79.

[65] See Rph II, 1:270,7: "iron contracts are unjust."

[66] PR 162 and 162 Z.

[67] For Hegel, certain commitments are rational or ethical. They are necessary, not in the sense of physical necessity by which we say it is necessary that when a pebble is dropped it hits the ground, but in another sense of necessity, which I shall discuss later in this chapter.

[68] PR 163 Z. But what counts as an acceptable reason: that she is unfaithful to me? that

(3) above seems a fair description of the level of commitment Hegel expects in marriage. The level of commitment Hegel expects us to have to
our state is even stronger—how strong is a matter we shall consider later,
when we discuss the citizen's obligation to obey the criminal laws of the
state. The relation in (4) may be an adequate description of Hegel's judgment.

3.1.5   True Freedom: Abstraction and Embodiment

True freedom is the "unity" of abstracting and taking a particular embodiment.[69] To Hegel freedom is a contradiction that human beings bear
and resolve: the essential tension is that on the one hand the free will must
not be stuck in any particular commitment, or content; on the other hand,
it needs some commitment or else it is no will.[70]

All of us, I think, are familiar with this tension: we care about things
that are worthwhile to us, but if we care about them too much we may
experience them as chains. We are therefore left with a precarious balanc-
ing act. I used to take football seriously. When my favorite team was in a
tight game that went down to the wire, I got worked up, even screamed
and yelled. If my team lost in the last seconds I got so upset, so depressed,
that to regain myself I had to abstract—I usually said to myself, "it's only
a stupid game." This helped me cope with my sense of real frustration.
But if I detached myself too often, or too early, I would never experience
the excitement that commitment to my football team brought me. Commitment means taking the lows with the highs. And to be free, for Hegel,
we must be committed.

This example is in one respect misleading: there is no real ethical point
to commitment to my football team. In section 3.2 we shall see how for
Hegel only certain commitments are ethical or rational, are ones in which
we are free. Not every choice the will makes is a choice of a free will.
Some of our choices are arbitrary, and in them we are not free—but we
are not unfree for choosing these. I am still a free human being though on
occasion I choose something to which I am not ethically committed. But
only in certain commitments that Hegel calls ethical am I at home and
free.

The will is truly free only when it both determines itself as something
particular and is at home (*bei-sich*) in this content and does not see this
content as limiting itself. The free will knows its choice as a pure possi-

---

she has become an invalid? Who decides what's acceptable? Hegel is silent on these difficult
questions. Cf. my discussion on Hegel's theory of marriage in sec. 6.2.

[69] PR 7.
[70] Rph VI, 4:118,7–20.

bility, as something it is in and to which it is committed, only because it puts itself there.[71] The free will sees its determination as not confining it.[72] For a person who understands the content of her will to be one in which she is at home, to be a commitment worth the obligations it imposes, willing this content is an act of free will. In this sense freedom is the benefit we reap from an act of understanding or comprehending. We have already seen how Hegel's use of *begreifen* helps advance his point that willing is both a theoretical *and* a practical activity, involving both knowing and acting, thinking and willing what is known.[73] If I know an ethical content in which I place my will (my society, my wife, my job) as not limiting, then I am free in that content. I can abstract if I want, this is a possibility that I know; but I choose not to, for I am satisfied with this content.[74] I know I need some embodiment, and I have persuaded myself that this is for me. I am at home here. I am committed. This is freedom.

3.1.6   A Concrete Example: Laws Proscribing Incest

Some contents of my will, some of my commitments, I never really chose—my natal family, perhaps my state. Yet Hegel says I am free in these contents, in part because I could abstract from them. This is a difficult idea. How can I be free in something I never chose in the first place? What does it mean to say I am free in it because I could choose to abstract from it? What is it like to be free in and free from all at once? So far, Hegel has not been entirely clear. But he does have an answer, and the following example will be our bridge to it. Let us consider freedom in the face of incest laws.

Laws prohibiting incest might be understood to be a restriction on my freedom, a convention that though perhaps not arbitrary nevertheless has no necessity and therefore need not be obeyed except for the fact that the laws have been posited and therefore command my respect. But they might also be understood as not convention but natural laws, laws that do not restrict my freedom, for it is in my very nature to obey them. Incest laws are not like the law of gravity; they can be disobeyed. There is almost certainly no chemical in our bodies that, released when the thought of

[71] PR 7.

[72] Rph II, 1:243,5–6.

[73] PR 13 Rem and Z.

[74] Cf. Rph V, 3:121,1–4. The idea that freedom is a state of satisfaction (*Befriedigung*) is, I think, central in Hegel's *Phenomenology* and other of his works. Cf. ch. 4, note 17. In the *Rechtsphilosophie* lectures Hegel also speaks of self-consciousness actively seeking satisfaction: when it no longer finds itself in customs and laws, it seeks its satisfaction in itself (Rph II, 1:290,16–27).

being incestuous enters our minds, induces feelings of repulsion sufficient
to prevent us from acting on the thought.[75]

We *can* choose to disobey, or abstract from, incest laws. We cannot
abstract from natural laws, and this is why such laws do not restrict our
freedom, even though we sometimes say they do.[76] It would be strange to
claim, for example, that having to eat is a limitation of our freedom. Suppose the state makes a law establishing criminal liability for failure to eat.
The law makes no demands on us as to how much we eat, so dieters
would not be restricted; and it makes some sort of exception for fasters.
Such a law would not be taken seriously. In contrast, laws that tell us we
may not abort a fetus might outrage us because they declare to some that
they may not do something they otherwise would want or felt the need to
do. But nobody would be outraged by the eating law, except perhaps by
its absurdity, because this law does not tell us to do anything we would
otherwise not do. The law does not restrict our freedom, as does the anti-
abortion law, because it does not demand that we engage in actions we
could choose to avoid. In Hegel's language, the activity the law prescribes
is not the sort from which we could abstract, and we are not unfree by
complying with this law.

Incest laws are a particularly striking and valuable example, worth
considering even at the risk of offending, because the argument is commonly and persuasively made that these laws are not the sort of thing
from which we can abstract. In this view, the sense of repulsion a normal
human being experiences at the thought of violating these laws is an empirical fact, something that happens to us, something over which we have
no control. The problem with this view is that even in our society incest
happens,[77] and in other societies it may even be required. The view above
is plausible only if we understand it to be claiming incest is an act we

---

[75] Some will say that there is a basis for incest laws in natural selection—that biologically
inferior offspring are produced, creating a selective advantage for species that avoid incest.
Such a claim may be used by some to *explain* these laws, and some might be led to think we
have no choice about having these laws, that they are "forced upon us" in the same way the
law of gravity is. Compare the sociobiological explanations of incest avoidance discussed in
Pierre L. van den Berghe, "Incest and Exogamy: A Sociobiological Reconsideration," *Ethol-
ogy and Sociobiology* (1980): pp. 151–162. Even if incest laws *did* emerge for selective
reasons, this biological explanation of their origins could not account for why societies with
reliable contraception should continue to prohibit sexual activity between near kindred that
does not result in offspring. A law proscribing such activity reflects a judgment that this
activity is wrong—it is not a reminder to us that the actions it proscribes are physically
impossible or prohibited by evolutionary forces not subject to human will.

[76] Sometimes we say that the law of gravity restricts our freedom, which is true. We are
more immobile than we would be without this law (though without this law our form of
life would never have evolved). But it would be rather absurd to claim we are unfree under
such physical laws—hence the joke: "Speed limit, 186,000 m.p.s.: it's the law!"

[77] See, for example, Judith Herman and Lisa Hirschman, "Father-Daughter Incest."

could but will not engage in. Such a view seems convincing and on the whole true of our society. We might say that for most of the members of our society it has become "natural" to avoid incest. But societies can be very different from ours, and it is certainly conceivable that in some societies near kindred do engage in sex without feelings of guilt or of having committed a wrong. When we consider such a society—different from our own—we then see that our norm is a possibility, a convention. It is something from which we, in theory, could abstract—we could choose not to live with this norm. But many of us could not think of ourselves ever violating this norm, at least not knowingly, not willingly. The fact that we could unknowingly violate it, as did Oedipus, shows our obstacle is not physical impossibility.

Our discussion of incest laws has led us to Hegel's own account of how we can be free in and free from all at once: we are free by living with the institutions, practices, and laws that we have, not because at any moment we can simply choose not to live by them, but because they are a possibility in which we are at home. They are our "second nature."

Hegel often speaks of custom as our second nature.[78] He says we are shaped and educated (*gebildet*) to our second nature.[79] He speaks of the ethical spirit as what is living in a people, what has *become* nature.[80] We can think of the law against incest not as a natural law, that is, as a law describing natural necessities, such as the law of gravity, but rather as a law that describes a "necessity" of a people brought up or formed in a certain way: to a people accustomed to the tabu against incestuous relations, and brought up learning that such relations are wrong, the law on the books against incest in effect describes what is already part of their (second) nature. A theorist who reflects on the law will know that it can be renounced. But to renounce it in practice would be to act against ourselves: in doing so we would not be free. Still, the *possibility* of our renouncing the law is essential to our being free under this law. Though we never chose this law, we are still free living under it, so long as we can understand it to be rational. Then we will choose it, so to speak, after the fact.[81]

Living under laws that are our second nature is different from being hypnotized or indoctrinated or brainwashed to act a certain way: Hegel would say we are free only in the first case. The difference is—to anticipate the next sections—that, for the laws under which we are free, rational grounds can be given to justify our acting in accordance with them,

[78] PR 151.
[79] Rph III, 124,21–28.
[80] Ibid., 210,5–15.
[81] Cf. section 3.3.2.

and rational grounds are something the hypnotizer or brainwasher or indoctrinator does not offer.

Perhaps it is confusing that Hegel both speaks of laws under which we are free as our "second nature" and insists such laws have rational grounds. If I say that something is second nature to me, I may imply that I do it or am committed to it without being able to say or justify why. Hegel does not claim that every law we are obligated to obey is second nature to us, but he does think that every such law, including the ones that are second nature to us, must have rational grounds. Hegel's objection to consanguineous marriages, which nicely connects up with our discussion of incest laws, lets us see this point. Hegel thinks such marriages are wrong not because of the "dark feelings of repulsion" that underlie their proscription, but because consanguineous marriages are counter to the concept of marriage. For Hegel, marriage is a way of ethically binding together people of different stock, and consanguineous marriages defeat this essential purpose.[82] While feelings of repulsion reflect how these laws have become second nature to us, in themselves they do no justificatory work.[83]

There is no reason to think the contradiction is ever removed between feeling the need to be committed and feeling the need to abstract from or break our commitment so that it does not limit us. Both moments of the will are with us. Most of us live the tension that results; some of us are obsessed by it, being acutely aware that "it takes ridiculously little, an insignificant breeze, to make what a man would have put down his life for one minute seem an absurd void the next."[84] The failure to see that this tension is always with us is one of the problems with Yack's interpretation of Hegel. Yack suggests that Hegel thinks we will always be dissatisfied with our social reality and so our only recourse is flight into philosophical speculation. But Hegel does not want us to give up the struggle so easily; he expects us to live it. His philosophy offers us not a path of escape, but a practical theory that can help us both criticize and keep us at home in our world.

It is important to see that Hegel emphasizes the moment of willing described in paragraph 6, of being committed. Hegel knows well how powerful is the impulse to abstract—it is a power that separates us humans from other animals, and it is essential to freedom. It is also a dangerous power, and Hegel's philosophy can be seen as a momentous effort to tame

[82] PR 168 Rem, Z; cf. PR 168 Bem: "what is already bound need not be married." See also my discussion in sec. 6.2.

[83] Cf. PRel 141, 143–144.

[84] Milan Kundera, *The Book of Laughter and Forgetting*, trans. Michael Henry Heim, p. 217.

it, properly to channel the potential energy of this capacity. But what is proper?

3.2 The Rest of the Introduction: The Appropriate Content of the Free Will

I may know I must will a content and be committed, but why am I free in this content but not that? We have seen that for Hegel the will is genuinely free when it wills a content from which it could abstract and in which it is at home, so that it is free in and free from all at once. Contents in which the will is free share certain additional features. Two can be singled out from Hegel's discussion in the rest of the introduction to the *Philosophy of Right*. (1) The content cannot be simply given to me immediately by nature, without the mediation of my will; it must be mine. (2) The content cannot be the product of my arbitrary choice; I must have appropriate grounds for choosing it.

Not all contents of the free will need be contents in which the (free) will is free and so need not share in these special features.[85] For example, I like hot dogs. When I choose a hot dog I do so simply because I like hot dogs—I can give no further reason. Maybe I like hot dogs because I had my first one while having an especially good time and I unconsciously associate hot dogs with good things because of this. But this is not my reason (perhaps it is the cause)[86] for my choosing hot dogs—I just like them. The hot dog, though a content of my will, does not have the special features of contents in which the will is free, because hot dogs are a content of my arbitrary will, my *Willkür*.[87] There is nothing wrong about hot dogs because of this. Hegel thinks it is very important that we all have the opportunity to choose things we can give no rational reason for choosing. But when Hegel talks about commitments in which we are free,

[85] Technical point on the use of "free will": Hegel's view, as I understand it, is that a human being potentially has a free will but doesn't always use it. Sometimes we will in a way that is not free (as we shall see, sometimes we will with our natural will, or else with our *Willkür*). If the content of this will is not the sort in which we could be free, it would not be appropriate to say we are therefore unfree. But if we will a content in a way that is not free, that is, other than with our free will, and this content is the sort in which Hegel thinks we could be free, Hegel would say we are unfree.

[86] On the distinction between "reason" and "cause" see Ludwig Wittgenstein, "Remarks on Frazer's Golden Bough," pp. 69, 72; his *Blue and Brown Books*, p. 88; and his *Philosophical Grammar*, p. 101; Peter Winch, *The Idea of a Social Science*, pp. 45–46; Donald Davidson, "Actions, Reasons, and Causes"; and Hanna Pitkin, *Wittgenstein and Justice*, pp. 250–253.

[87] See section 3.2.2.

he does not mean our commitment to hot dogs. He is talking about non-arbitrary contents to which we have special commitments.

3.2.1 Beyond the Natural Will

My will is not free if its content remains what is given me by nature—impulses, desires, inclinations. Hegel calls such a will the immediate or natural will and says of it that it does not resolve but, rather, takes its content as given. It is not an actual will and is not free in the sense that an animal is not free for it cannot choose.[88] The immediate will is not a reflective will, and does not universalize its desires.[89] An example that gets at what Hegel means here is a person with the eating disorder bulimia. The bulimic has an uncontrollable urge to eat lots of food, which he or she (usually she) then releases, often by induced vomiting. The bulimic probably is aware that what she does is abnormal and unhealthy. But her powers of reflection and thought are overcome by her natural, given desires. She continues to do what she knows she upon reflection would not do. Her particular passion of the moment blinds her to her universal interest; natural will overcomes thinking will.[90] Hegel would say of such people that they are not really free. We say this as well, of bulimics, of drug addicts, of alcoholics, and of others. Hegel's criticism of the immediate will makes explicit what was implicit in his discussion in paragraphs 5–7: the free will must have as its content something it could have chosen not to have, something from which it could abstract—the free will must choose; it must be a will.[91] We might say that the alcoholic or bulimic or drug addict has no will, or perhaps has a "split" will.

3.2.2 Beyond Willkür

To be free, a will must choose, or, where it cannot literally choose, it must understand its content to be one to which it chooses to remain committed. But a will is free, in Hegel's sense of freedom, only if it chooses in a certain

[88] Of course, anyone who knows animals may think they choose. Not Hegel: "animals have no wills and must obey their impulses" (PR 11 Z).

[89] Rph VI, 4:130.

[90] The Greek word *acrasia* captures this idea: I choose Y though I know X to be better. See Gregory Vlastos, "Socrates on Acrasia."

[91] Dostoyevski's underground man refuses medical treatment out of spite. He chooses to act against conventional notions of what it is to act rationally. A person acting on the basis of a natural will is not choosing even in this sense. The natural will cannot renounce or detach—it cannot abstract.

way. The content I choose must be one not given to me immediately, but it also must be one I choose not arbitrarily.

In his important paragraph 15 Hegel describes the arbitrary will, called *Willkür*, as *zufällig* and therefore not really free. *Zufällig* is typically translated as arbitrary, accidental, or capricious, but it comes from *Zufall*, which can mean contingency (or chance, accident), and *zufällig* can also mean contingently. This is important because there are different ways to interpret Hegel's claim that *Willkür* is not free: one way is to take *zufällig* as contingent. In this reading *Willkür* must choose among contents each of which is given by nature, and so each of the possibilities of *Willkür*'s choice is contingent on this possible content having been given by nature. Therefore *Willkür*'s final choice will be contingent and not free.[92] There is a problem with this reading and a reason why we should translate *zufällig* by arbitrary here. If we say "my choosing to eat a hot dog was contingent (*zufällig*) on my needing to eat" and then claim that "my choice was therefore not really free," we have played a trick on our-

[92] T. M. Knox, whose translation of the *Philosophy of Right* is virtually the exclusive source in English for Hegel's *Rechtsphilosophie*, translates *Willkür* as "arbitrary will" (this is a standard translation found in most dictionaries) but translates *zufällig*, mostly, as "contingently" (as in PR 15). Knox is not consistent; at least once he translates *zufällig* as "irrational" (PR 258 Rem), in a passage where Hegel criticizes Herr Haller's doctrine of might makes right. Hegel says Haller means by might not right or justice but what is *zufällig*. Knox's translation of "irrational" is acceptable, though I prefer "arbitrary" here, because it lets us see a coherence in Hegel's thought, so I shall argue. My position is that "accident" and "arbitrary" and "random," and even "irrational" (though this involves us with the difficulties in the concept rationality), are adequate translations for *zufällig*, and "arbitrary" is best. My objection to "contingent" is that it can mean "dependent," and dependence is a different concept than arbitrariness (though it is related, and Hegel plays on this relatedness in PR 15 Z and elsewhere, as in PR 238, where Hegel does mean dependence).

Knox's translation of *zufällig* as contingent can potentially confuse us, as it did me a great deal. Hegel distinguishes the natural will, which is dependent on what is given it by nature, from *Willkür*, but to call *Willkür* contingent is to call to mind the natural will, blurring the distinction Hegel wants to make. Karl Larenz also blurs this distinction when he describes the problem with *Willkür* as that its content is still something given or determined by nature (*Hegels Zurechnungslehre*, p. 47). G. H. R. Parkinson also blurs the distinction between the immediate will and *Willkür*. Parkinson says that *Willkür* is contingent; the content of this will "comes to it from the outside" ("Hegel's Concept of Freedom," pp. 160–161). Parkinson's confusion is apparent when he says Hegel's discussion of happiness concerns a stage of freedom between freedom as arbitrariness and genuine freedom. Parkinson fails to see that happiness is based on *Willkür* and that *Willkür* is different from the natural will. Parkinson writes that Hegel clearly regards choosing to be happy as "an advance over the arbitrary will" (p. 161). But Hegel thinks a choice for the sake of happiness is a choice that ultimately is arbitrary—see my discussion in section 3.3.1. Patrick Riley also blurs the distinction between the natural and the arbitrary will: "[Hegel] defined freedom, and goodness, and virtue in terms of the reconciliation of 'natural' will (impulse, caprice) with the real or rational will" (*Will and Political Legitimacy*, p. 167). So too does Steven Smith, in his *Hegel's Critique of Liberalism*, p. 108.

selves. If we really meant "choosing" in the first sentence, we must have meant something like "my choice of hot dog over hamburger"—otherwise we would have to be understood to have said something like "I chose to eat because I had to eat," and we would probably be taken as making a joke. Moreover, Hegel does think that there is freedom in necessity; he does think that I can be free in satisfying the desires, needs, and inclinations given me by nature—and so if by *zufällig* he meant "contingent on the will's content having been given to it by nature," he would not claim outright that *Willkür* is not free.[93]

Another interpretation makes better sense of Hegel's claim that *Willkür* is not really free. In this view *zufällig* means arbitrary and Hegel is claiming that when we arbitrarily choose our content we are not really free. I think this is Hegel's claim, and that it is one of the most important he advances in the *Rechtsphilosophie*.

If our will is *Willkür* there is no ground for deciding between our possibilities; our decision is arbitrary. Any of our choices is possible, none is necessary.[94] Hegel claims that insofar as my choice is arbitrary, or not necessary, I am not free in choosing it. We can think of Hegel's claim as an elucidation of how we sometimes use the word *freedom*. Some years ago a chain of convenience stores, 7-Eleven, ran an advertising campaign that aired commercials showing such symbols of freedom as the American flag, the message being that 7-Eleven provides "freedom." The ads apparently referred to the selection of goods these stores offer. I expect that many people found these advertisements to trivialize what freedom means. Hegel's claim that *Willkür* is not really free can help us see why. Hegel's point can be thought of in this way: if my choosing a Coke over a Pepsi is arbitrary, if I have no good reason why I chose the Coke, then

---

[93] "One must not reduce natural life to a chain, rather it is an essential moment of rationality; what is higher is to make these natural, found needs and desires products of oneself" (Rph V, 3:385,14–29, corresponding to PR 123). Hegel does not see freedom as renouncing our natural impulses but rather as comprehending them: "Freedom lies in not fleeing from natural desires, but having insight into their necessity and bringing them in accord with our will" (Prop 261). Cf. PR 19; and Karl Larenz, *Hegels Zurechnungslehre*, pp. 43–45.

[94] PR 15 Bem: something is arbitrary "because it is only possible, it can be or not be." Knox cites this in his footnote to PR 15 (PR, p. 314, note 52). Hegel is not merely giving the definition of *zufällig* as "possibility"; he is arguing that something that is *zufällig* is merely possible, and so there is no reason for it to exist (or be chosen) other than that it is possible. To see *zufällig* here as meaning contingent (as does Knox) is to conflate these separate propositions: (1) If I am given two possibilities between which I have no rational basis for choosing, my choice will be arbitrary. (2) If I am given two possibilities between which to choose, my choice will be contingent on the fact that these possibilities are given to me. In neither case is our choice an act of free will. By translating *zufällig* as contingent here, Knox ignores the first proposition, which I think lies at the heart of Hegel's discussion of *Willkür*, whereas the second proposition relates to his discussion of the natural will.

my choice of Coke over Pepsi was not an act of free will. In this respect I am no more free shopping at 7-Eleven, which has both, than in a store in Prague that has only Coke, so long as I am indifferent between Coke and Pepsi. Maybe I waste more time at 7-Eleven trying to decide what I have no basis for deciding, so that I might be less free shopping there. Rather than being more free in having more possibilities from which to choose, perhaps I am only more confused.[95]

Hegel says the genuinely free will is the will that wills not what is arbitrary or contingent merely on my particular will, but what is rational and necessary.[96] Here the two possible senses of *zufällig* meet: *Willkür* is arbitrary, and so what it chooses merely reflects its particularity. Its choice—from our observer's standpoint—is contingent on its having its particular features (i.e., that it prefers hot dogs to hamburgers), and these particular features are not rational or necessary.[97] When we do what is rational we do what is necessary or essential for us; we do what is grounded in essential facts about us; we will in a way that is true to ourselves: "For the will to be truly or absolutely free, what it wills, or its content, can be nothing other than itself."[98] Only when we do this are we at home.

There is no reason to think we must be at home in all of our commitments. We have many commitments that are barely commitments. These do not reflect who we essentially are, and it is not in them that we attain our freedom. Hegel's conception of freedom is intricately connected with a conception of identity—of who we are and what commitments make us who we are. If I gave up hot dogs I would no longer be "the one who is crazy about hot dogs," but I would still be me. Hegel would say that hot dogs are different from other commitments or contents of my will, such as family, profession, religion, state. It is only in the commitments that make us who we are that we are free. For Hegel, these commitments, which constitute our very identity, have rational grounds.[99] Acting according to the demands of these commitments is being not forced but free.

Hegel's claim that the will is free only when it can give rational grounds for its choice or commitments links up with our discussion earlier of the

[95] Consider this quote from an East German who fled to the West in the mass exodus of October 1989: "I didn't leave for better shopping possibilities" (*New York Times*, Oct. 9, 1989, p. A4).

[96] PR 15 Z.

[97] In his lectures Hegel describes *Willkür* as limited in that it has no rational basis to will (Rph V, 3:132–133).

[98] Prop 207.

[99] That they constitute our identity contributes to their being rational. See the discussion of what Hegel means by "rational" in sec. 6.2.

will in paragraphs 5–7, where we first saw Hegel's use of "being at home" as a metaphor for freedom. Another metaphor Hegel gives us is "being on firm ground." Hegel says that at the standpoint of *Willkür* there is no fixed ground, only that which I hold to as a matter of will,[100] and this remains subjective.[101] Hegel also says that none of the contents chosen by *Willkür* contains itself.[102] Part of freedom is to be able to abstract from our content, but what is just as essential is that we have a content that is so much a part of us that, though we could shed it, to do so would be to lose ourselves, shake the ground on which we stand, become homeless. With his discussion of *Willkür* Hegel has also given us a more analytic way of thinking about freedom: I am free in a particular content if it is *justified*.[103]

Our next step in unpacking what Hegel means by freedom is to answer the question naturally arising from this last point: What is justified? What, for Hegel, is the standard for justification by which an observer would judge that a will's grounds for choice were not arbitrary? We know from our preceding discussion that for Hegel something is justified only if there are good grounds, or nonarbitrary reasons, for it. His insistence on this point sets Hegel in opposition to "atomistic liberals," to whom a thing is justified solely by virtue of an individual's consent to it, even though this consent might be granted arbitrarily.[104] Hegel is not an atomistic liberal, because to him a justification that a free will would upon reflection accept is something "objective." It is a justification a rational will would, and must, accept. Here we can see one reason why Hegel usually avoids speaking of wills as being of individuals. To speak of the will as being of the individual is to give the impression that whatever the individual thinks is justified is justified. But Hegel thinks a justification is objective, and we must see what this means.

[100] Rph VI, 4:132,1–13.

[101] Rph V, 3:135,11–12; see section 3.3.1, below, and PR 8.

[102] Rph V, 3:133.

[103] Ibid., 3:134,28–32: "Zufälligkeit . . . hat die Bestimmung, daß dies Verhältnis ein wirkliches, aber andre ebensogut und ebensoviel berechtigt sind, es ist also ebensogut wenn ein andres, statt dieses wäre" ("Zufälligkeit . . . has the feature that this relation is an actual one, but is just as good and just as justified as if another existed instead"). Also, see the discussion below on subjective and objective justifications.

[104] Liberals might also agree to the claim that I am free only when what I have chosen is justified to me. Atomistic liberalism is a characterization of liberalism (Hegel's is one of the more famous) that is untrue to most classical liberals. Atomistic liberalism holds that the consent of the individual is the sole basis for determining whether a law or practice is justified. Even John Stuart Mill allows that an action may be rightfully limited by a law apart from my consent to that law: there is an objective principle that can be pointed to as evidence that an individual objecting to this law is wrong (for Mill this is the harm principle).

3.3   Subjective and Objective Justifications

In paragraphs 17–24 of his introduction to the *Philosophy of Right*, Hegel considers different grounds or justifications for choosing a particular content. First he suggests something sounding like utilitarianism,[105] which he calls the "Understanding." At this point Hegel criticizes without argument a hierarchical system of ordering, such as ranking by utility, as a basis for willing.[106] Before seeing why Hegel dismisses such a system it is important to see why Hegel considers it at all in connection with his search for a truly free will. If I have a rational system of ordering desires and needs, these needs and desires no longer are immediate, for they have become channeled into a rational system of satisfaction where my choice determines the actions I take to achieve satisfaction. The content of my will is no longer immediately given or imposed on me; it is mediated by my thinking and reflecting. From our discussion in section 3.2.1 we know this feature of willing to satisfy an essential condition of willing freely. In this respect utilitarian calculation is a plausible method for the free will to adopt as its basis for willing.

3.3.1   *The Limits of a Merely Subjective Justification*

What is defective about this method? What is unfree about ordering needs and desires into a rational system of satisfaction—for example, ordering them so as to bring happiness (as when I refrain from eating that extra piece of chocolate cake, though I want to, because overall being thinner makes me happier; or when I refrain from "fooling around," though I want to, because overall I am happier in my steady marital relation)? Hegel says a system such as happiness is only a formal universality; it purifies impulses of their crudity,[107] but as a universal, it is contentless and indeterminate.[108] He says the content of happiness is rooted in subjective pleasure and particularity and so, though happiness offers the form of universality, form does not match content.[109] In his lectures Hegel says happiness claims to generalize, yet is based on natural and particular drives;[110] happiness therefore contradicts freedom in that "its natural

---

[105] PR 17.
[106] Ibid., 17 Z.
[107] Ibid., 20.
[108] Ibid., 20 Bem.
[109] Ibid., 20 Z; Rph V, 3:145.
[110] Rph VI, 4:137.

content opposes universality in the form of freedom."[111] When we will
our happiness, we will not "a universality that has its determinations
within itself," but a universality (happiness) that has its determinations in
nature (pleasures, likings).[112]

In these difficult passages Hegel emphasizes that, though happiness
provides a general principle and a universal form for our desires, the contents of the actions we take in accord with this principle remain rooted in
particularity, subjectivity, and nature. Hegel thinks the commitments,
and actions demanded by these commitments, that I justify by appealing
to pleasure or happiness are too "subjective," and that therefore I am not
free in such commitments or in taking such actions: "pleasure is a subjective feeling, something arbitrary [*zufällig*] . . . it is not the objective, universal, rational. It is therefore no criterion or rule for judging a thing."[113]

Hegel makes several points when criticizing happiness, and we must
separate them out. He says a commitment in which we are free must be
justified by principles that are (1) universal, (2) objective, and (3) rational.
Each of these three claims belongs to a separate line of argument Hegel
offers in criticizing subjective justifications, though here he has mixed
them together in discussing happiness. Each of these three claims is connected to a distinct conception of judgment, and ultimately of politics.
But before examining them, I shall look at still another, a fourth argument
Hegel makes against subjective justifications.

3.3.1.1   THE PROBLEM WITH LIKINGS: FLUCTUATION

Why doesn't Hegel think we are free in our commitments to the contents
we choose for the sake of happiness? One reading, which I think insufficient, is that Hegel thinks happiness inadequate because everything I
choose to fulfill my desires in a way that makes me happy is contingent,
or dependent on the desire having been given to me by nature, or on my
happening to have this desire.[114] We have already seen that Hegel does

---

[111] Ibid., 4:138.

[112] Ibid.

[113] Prop 254. Social (as opposed to hedonistic) utilitarians might argue that their choices
are rooted not in their own likings or happiness but in an objective determination of social
happiness. While Hegel never addresses such a claim, he might respond that social happiness
must reduce to a summation of individual happinesses and that any conception of happiness
is ultimately rooted in a content of subjectivity and particularity and nature (as opposed to
a universal content, such as a rational law). Cf. Wolfgang Schild, "Der Strafrechtsdogmatische Begriff der Zurechnung," p. 451; Rph VI, 4:134–136.

[114] Two possible arguments should be separated out here. One is that I am not free in
choosing to fulfill my desires in a way that leads to my happiness because my having the
capacity to fulfill my desires is contingent on my particular characteristics and situation.
This is how G. H. R. Parkinson understands Hegel's criticism of happiness: happiness lacks

think there can be freedom in necessity, and so there is no reason why the fact that certain of my wants are imposed on me would lead Hegel to the conclusion that in fulfilling these wants I am unfree.

I argued above that the *Zufälligkeit* of *Willkür* is best seen as arbitrariness, not contingency. In a crucial passage from the last complete set of lectures, Hegel says that in satisfying my need for the sake of happiness I "remain dependent," but he adds, "and in a condition of fluctuation."[115] Another, and I think more promising, reading of Hegel's criticism of happiness focuses on this last clause and understands Hegel to mean that choosing even according to the universalized system of happiness remains not just contingent but *arbitrary*, and leaves us in a state of flux. Happiness is a "formal universality" because I have given my choice only the *form* of nonarbitrariness and universality. But the ground remains subjective pleasure,[116] and this is not steady enough a ground to support a truly free will. In claiming that my choice of x is arbitrary even when I choose x because I like it, Hegel is using a sense of "arbitrary" we might think strange. If I like chocolate ice cream more than any other flavor, I will not arbitrarily choose when I order my next cone—I will choose chocolate *because* it is my favorite. Hegel is not denying that I have a reason for my choice. He is saying that I will not be able to justify my choice as objectively right or rational. To an observer my choice remains arbitrary. Hegel's point is that to say of something "I like it," or "I prefer it," or even "it makes me happy," is not to *justify* it.[117]

The commitments in which I am free must be justified by firm grounds, so that I am at home in what I will, and will not upon reflection have the need to renounce or abstract from my commitments and actions. This is one reason why my liking hot dogs is not sufficient justification for saying I am really free in choosing hot dogs. Likings change. I used to like hamburgers, now it is hot dogs, next week maybe it will be salads. Why must freedom now depend on my continuing to want x again later? Because, in Hegel's view, we are truly free only in genuine *commitments*. Hegel, in his criticism of happiness in paragraphs 19–20 of the *Philosophy of Right*, argues that a necessary condition for the justification of a choice of a truly free will is that the ground appealed to be not subjective but

---

self-determination ("Hegel's Concept of Freedom," p. 161). If Hegel means by *zufällig* "contingent" in any sense, I think it would be the other possibility: I am not free because my having these desires is contingent, in the sense that the basis of my action, and the justification I can give for my action, remain tied to the contingency that I happened to have this or that desire—an observer would say my action is arbitrary.

[115] Rph VI, 4:138,17–29.
[116] PR 20 Z.
[117] Of course in many contexts to say "x makes me happy" *is* to justify x. But "justify" in these contexts might mean something like "give an account of my reasons for choosing" rather than "show the justice or right of."

universal, objective, and rational. This makes most sense, with respect to happiness, if we understand Hegel's criticism to be that such subjective justifications can be short-lived. Likings lack the solidity of a rational ground that will and must always command our commitment, even when the temptation to abstract is great.

3.3.1.2   THE PROBLEM WITH REVENGE: PARTICULAR, NOT UNIVERSAL

A justification that appeals to happiness is only one of Hegel's examples of a subjective justification and therefore of an unsteady ground for the free will. Another example, one that is important to Hegel's conception of crime and punishment, is the justification of punishing for revenge. For Hegel, the desire to avenge is associated with the desire for right or justice, but to establish right by revenge is subjective: "If right is established through revenge, then this right has a subjective content; something arbitrary [*zufällig*] is actualized, namely the subjective feeling that wants to avenge itself. The right that presents itself here is not the right that embodies freedom [*das freie Recht*]."[118] When we act out of revenge we justify our action by appealing to our subjective feeling of hurt and desire for right. To act out of revenge is to submit to particular emotions, and so is not to act freely. To act freely we must appeal to something universal; Hegel calls this universal *Recht-an-sich*: we are free by acting according to objective determinations of right. These institutions, practices, and laws are (or ought to be) universal, known by all, and independent of subjective whim. Only by acting in accordance with them, only by legally punishing as opposed to privately seeking revenge, is the establishment of right assured and not made contingent on the judgment of the offended subject. David Pare summarizes Hegel's view: "Revenge is essentially subjective because it is carried out by an interested party whose status as a judge is arbitrary, especially to the criminal."[119]

John Locke, in the *Second Treatise*, gives a similar justification for legal or state punishment as against reliance on revenge justice. One of the reasons we leave the state of nature is its lack of an indifferent judge. Locke adds that another reason we leave the state of nature is that we lack a power to back and support sentencing and execution (*Second Treatise*, par. 126)—he who has right on his side does not have enough force in the state of nature to punish delinquents (par. 136). With this second point, that we lack the power or strength to punish outside the state, revenge justice is criticized as contingent on our capacity to mete out retribution. Above I argued that in the case of happiness Hegel is not saying,

---

[118] Rph V, 3:142,17–30; cf. Rph VI, 4:136,24–26.
[119] David Pare, "Hegel's Concept of Punishment," p. 71.

mainly, that happiness is defective because our attaining it is contingent on our capacities. Rather, happiness is defective because as a justification for action it remains subjective and arbitrary. Similarly, Hegel's argument with respect to revenge is I think best interpreted as claiming revenge justice is defective because its justification appeals only to something subjective—my sense of hurt and of being wronged—rather than to objective and universal laws of right. Hegel is not, mainly, arguing that revenge justice is defective because whether it is satisfied is contingent on the strength of the victim.[120]

In the case of happiness, where we ground our commitments and actions in likings, Hegel thinks our ground is too unsteady, that we remain in flux. But the feelings that motivate us to seek revenge are often persistent, maintaining their force through generations, as in the case of family feuds. Hegel's criticism of revenge thus rests on a separate argument than the one he gives in criticizing happiness. I am not free when I act out of revenge, not because my reasons for acting are unsteady, or fluctuate, thereby betraying the arbitrariness of my act; but because the action reflects particular, not universal, standards of right.

In the next section we shall see that Hegel thinks the reasons we give to justify our actions must, if we are to be free in them, be objective, or "out there." Hegel's point with revenge is different. The person seeking revenge sometimes acts on the basis of his feelings. But sometimes his reasons are grounded in a family code of honor. The avenger may be able to point to existing, objective principles to justify his actions, principles that are "out there." The reason revenge is subjective is not that it is not objective, but that the principles used to justify revenge are not universal principles.

Underlying Hegel's claim that I am not free in acting according to particular conceptions of right or justice is a conception of politics I shall call communitarian politics. The arguments Hegel thinks we must give in justifying our actions must, if we are to be really free, appeal to standards shared by our community. For Hegel, this community is more than our family, clan, or tribe; it is the modern state, which Hegel says is the universal.[121] Hegel thinks our particular conceptions of right will coincide with the conception of right articulated in our community, and he characterizes the modern state as our community, as the locus of our ethical life.[122] These claims we shall discuss critically in the next chapter.

---

[120] Cf. PR 220: with revenge no attention is given to the universal character of the injury; and with revenge right lacks the form of right, it lacks the form of universality; but see PR 103, where Hegel does suggest revenge is defective because whether it is satisfied is contingent on whether one has power.

[121] PR 260.

[122] Ibid., 260 Rem.

3.3.1.3   THE PROBLEM WITH INWARD COMMITMENTS: AN AIM
UNFULFILLED, NOT OBJECTIVE

In his lectures corresponding to paragraphs 25–31 of the *Philosophy of
Right*, Hegel discusses what he means by "subjective" and advances a
further criticism of subjective justifications. Hegel distinguishes three
senses of subjectivity: (1) self-certainty; (2) particularity of the will; and
(3) an unfulfilled aim, not yet objectified.[123] A content might have a subjective justification if it is chosen according to what counts as right for the
will, according to its self-certainty; in this case its choice reflects its own
particularity, so it remains an arbitrary will and is not really free—it only
feels free. What we have not yet seen from our two examples is (3): a
subjective will is not yet objectified. Hegel is now linking up his discussion
of subjective freedom with his earlier discussion in paragraphs 5–7 of the
features of the free will. When the subjective will fails to take some objective content, it violates the principle of necessary embodiment.[124] For Hegel, the free will is a will that commits itself, and it must be committed to
something that is actual, already fulfilled, and present: something that is
"out there."

   Hegel's insistence that we will something actual and objective underlies
both his criticism of Kantian morality as well as his own defense of the
duties that make up our concrete ethical life.[125] Hegel defends the principle of binding ethical duties, the duties we already have as members of an
ethical community who take on various commitments and share in certain practices. These duties, Hegel argues, are not really restrictions on
freedom, and they appear so only to the arbitrary will or to those who
think freedom is abstract freedom. Rather, it is in ethical duty that liberation and real freedom lie. "In duty we are no longer dependent on purely
natural desires, nor are we depressed [*Gedrücktheit*] after morally reflecting on what ought to be; *nor are we stuck with an indeterminate subjectivity which never steps into existence and objectively determines itself in
action, instead remaining within itself as something lacking actuality.*"[126]
If we have no actual content to which we are committed and which binds
us to act in certain ways, we are indeterminate and not free.

   One way to understand this line of argument is as a criticism of commitments that are only internal. Such commitments do not bind us, except
perhaps to ourselves. We break such internal commitments without having to renounce outwardly or take opposition to anything in the world.
Such inner commitments are suspiciously like commitments in thought

[123] Rph VI, 4:144–145; cf. PR 25.
[124] PR 6; cf. PR 8; and section 3.1.3, above.
[125] Cf. sec. 2.2.
[126] PR 149, my translation, emphasis.

that we saw lead to only a passive, inner freedom, a freedom Hegel distinguishes from real freedom.

Hegel's claim that we are free only in commitments that are actual, or objective, connects up with a conception of politics that I call practical politics. Hegel opposes utopian theorists who think they can be free in some ideal that might never be realized on earth.[127] Someone with an inner feeling or conviction may call us to a new home. But Hegel is telling us we already have a home. It provides us our grounds for acting. Our home may not be perfect, but we can fix it up. To discard it would be to give up ourselves. Our home, in Hegel's view, is already built on principles we can discern and understand and use to justify our staying.

There are two ways to construe Hegel's criticism of internal commitments, neither of which seems adequate. Sometimes Hegel appears to claim that we cannot really *know* why the person with her inner feelings and convictions is committed—there is nothing out there to which she can point to justify her commitments—and this is why she is not free in them (in which case the avenger who can point to a family code seems to be an example that argues against Hegel's claim). Other times Hegel appears to claim that this person is not free in the commitments she takes on on the basis of her inner feelings because she does not know where her true commitments lie. In the former view, Hegel does not commit himself to the dogmatic position that there are true and false commitments; but, as we have seen with the case of the avenger whose reasons we *can* know, this view does not offer a sharp enough edge to criticize all the positions Hegel does criticize. Hegel does claim that the commitments that emerge in the modern state will be rational, will be our true commitments; not just because they shape us and constitute who we are, but because, in Hegel's view, history has a *telos*. The latter view is unattractive precisely for its dogmatism, for its insistence that we can be right or wrong about which commitments we should have; it makes us wonder whether Hegel's conception of practical politics is at all political, if by politics we mean a continuous, open-ended deliberation and exchange of judgments that can aim at persuasion but not proof.

3.3.1.4   THE PROBLEM WITH PIETISTS AND PHILOSOPHERS OF CONVICTION: THE DEMAND FOR A RATIONAL POLITICS

The last criticism of subjective justifications Hegel gives is the one I think closest to his heart. It encompasses the previous two criticisms. We can approach this line of argument by asking a question Hegel has the burden of answering as a critic of subjective justifications: why isn't the person

---

[127] Ibid., p. 10.

committed to his God, or to his own convictions of right, free in his convictions? Hegel's objection to pietists and political protestors who appeal to their feelings or sentiments is, I shall argue, that they are unable to give, through rational discourse, adequate reasons justifying their actions and commitments. They do not play politics the way Hegel thinks politics should be played—as rational politics.

Among Hegel's primary targets in the *Philosophy of Right* are the philosophers of conviction and sentiment who say that truth cannot be known other than by consulting what rises out of one's heart and emotions. Hegel says of the "ringleader of these hosts of superficiality," who has been "subverting the young" with politicized speeches like one he gave at a famous festival in Wartburg, the philosopher Jacob Fries, that his ideas are

> the quintessence of shallow thinking, [and] base philosophic science not on the development of thought and the concept but on immediate sense-perception and the play of fancy; [they] take the rich inward articulation of ethical life, i.e. the state, the architectonic of that life's rationality . . . [they] take this structure and confound the completed fabric in the broth of "heart, friendship, and inspiration." According to a view of this kind, the world of ethics . . . should be given over—as in fact of course it is not—to the subjective accident of opinion and caprice."[128]

Hegel's vitriolic attack on Fries in his preface to the *Philosophy of Right* has done much damage to Hegel's reputation. Fries was a leading representative of German liberalism and a target of the government in its persecution of "demagogues," or students and professors who challenged a Prussia still in many ways feudal and still lacking a written constitution. Hegel's attack is often pointed to as evidence that he was opposed to liberalism and had a reactionary streak. Jacques d'Hondt, in his book *Hegel in His Time*, emphasizes that Hegel was attacking Fries not for his liberalism but for his philosophy of subjectivism.[129] Although the liberalism of Fries was a confused liberalism that incorporated elements of xenophobia and anti-Semitism, elements D'Hondt persuasively shows Hegel renounced, Hegel's objection was in the main about form, not substance: rationalism against confused sentimentalism.[130]

Hegel opposed the use of irrational means in attaining one's political goals, such as the use of violence by the student Karl Sand. Sand, a mem-

---

[128] PR Preface, pp. 6–7.
[129] Jacques d'Hondt, *Hegel in His Time*, trans. John Burbridge et al., pp. 90–91. This is one of the finest secondary works on Hegel, although it pays virtually no attention to the texts, considering instead only Hegel's practical actions as a professor and as a citizen of Prussia.
[130] Ibid., p. 97.

ber of the *Burschenschaften* (fraternities), murdered a reactionary jour-
nalist, Kotzebue, to further the cause of his version of liberalism, then
prevailing in Germany.[131] The incident was used by the reactionary elements in Prussia as an excuse for clamping down on the "demagogues."
D'Hondt argues convincingly that "Hegel seems to have reproached Sand
primarily for having used crime, in a purely individual decision and in a
rash manner."[132] For Hegel, one task of the political philosopher is to
moderate the strong feelings aroused in protests like the Wartburgfest at
which Fries spoke. In their place Hegel insists we provide genuine, disci-
plined, rational social criticism.[133] Hegel was not opposed to many of the
important liberal principles that guided the "demagogues." D'Hondt tells
us that Hegel even expressed political solidarity with the liberals opposing the reactionary actions of the government by contributing clandes-
tinely to a year's salary for one of his colleagues, Professor de Wette, who
was suspended for sending a letter to Sand's mother that, while not ap-
proving of Sand's act, absolved the actor.[134] But Hegel could not condone
means of the sort Sand used. D'Hondt writes: "Hegel kept a watch on the
'demagogues,' on occasion passing a severe but justified judgment on
their escapades. But he also tried to guide them by offering advice and *by
discussing the principles of their action with them*. He often mingled with
them, in their festivities and their debates."[135]

Hegel opposes not only political protestors who appeal to subjective
feelings rather than rational reasons in demanding change, but also pietists, but pietists *of the wrong sort*:

> With godliness and the Bible, however, [piety] has arrogated to itself the highest
> of justifications for despising the ethical order and the objectivity of law, since
> it is piety too which envelops in the simpler intuition of feeling the truth which
> is articulated in the world into an organic realm. *But if it is piety of the right
> sort*, it sheds the form of this emotional region so soon as it leaves the inner life,
> enters upon the daylight of the Idea's development and revealed riches, and

---

[131] One of the reasons Kotzebue was a target of the liberals was his reputation for being
a spy of the tsar, and thus an opponent of those with nationalist leanings. We must remember that "Germanization" (*Deutschtum*) was an element of some of the liberalism of the
Burschenschaften. Hegel's attitude was that *Deutschtum* was *Deutschdumm* (Hegel, *Letters*, p. 312, cited in d'Hondt, *Hegel in His Time*, p. 105).

[132] D'Hondt, *Hegel in His Time*, p. 110.

[133] See Nicolas Haines, "Politics and Protest: Hegel and Social Criticism." In the final
chapter I criticize Haines's conclusion, that Hegel criticizes irrationalism (this is true) but
deserts us when we need public criticism (this is not true).

[134] D'Hondt, *Hegel in His Time*, pp. 111–112. As we have seen, though, outwardly Hegel
criticized de Wette. See sec. 1.2.

[135] Ibid., p. 114, my emphasis.

brings with it, out of its inner worship of God, reverence for law and for an absolute truth exalted above the subjective form of feeling.[136]

What Hegel has against pietists of the wrong sort is that they take for truth in matters of ethics merely what their intuition and feeling of the truth is, failing to see that reflection would lead them to see the truth in the ethical laws "out there." Hegel is saying that intuition and feelings do not justify our acting in this way or that; really Hegel is arguing that they should not count as justifications. Hegel is well aware that many in his day did justify their actions by appealing to intuition and feelings: "Is then something true or legitimate because it is in my feeling? Is feeling the verification, or must the content be just, true, or ethical in and for itself? These days we often find the former contention advanced."[137] Hegel is taking his stand against these "subjectivists":

> We have means enough in our consciousness for evaluating this contention. In our consciousness we know very well that, in order to know that a content is of the right kind, we must look about for grounds of decision other than those of feeling. For it is true that every content is capable of being in feeling: religion, right, ethics, crime, passions. Each content has a place in feeling. If feeling is the justifying element, then the distinction between good and evil comes to naught, for evil with all its shadings and qualifications is in feeling just as much as the good. Everything evil, all crime, base passions, hatred and wrath, it all has its root in feeling. The murderer feels that he must do what he does.[138]

Hegel does not think every law or institution or practice "out there" is right,[139] but for those we think wrong he insists our protest take the form of rational discourse, which means giving an objective account of the grounds of our commitments, that is, an account based not on feelings, preferences, and intuitions, but on principled reasons. As we have seen, Hegel thinks that only when we can give such an account are we really free. The Athenians, in Hegel's view, were not free because they could not give such an account when Socrates questioned them.[140]

This idea of rational politics for Hegel incorporates all of the preceding conceptions of politics. Rational politics is practical politics, in appealing to what is objective, or "out there." Rational politics is community politics, in pointing as a guide for action to the universal, shared standards of right. Hegel's conception of rational politics has within it all the tensions of the other conceptions, and it carries their burdens. Is Hegel's version

[136] PR Preface, p. 6, my emphasis.
[137] PRel 144–145.
[138] Ibid.
[139] In the final chapter we shall consider in great detail Hegel's criticisms of existing laws and practices.
[140] PR 147 Bem.

of practical politics political? Why am I free only by acting in accordance
with what is already "out there"? Why are community standards rational? If not all the laws and institutions of our community—our modern
state—are rational, how does Hegel tell which really are? Does Hegel
think these *are* rational, or only that they must be regarded as rational?
Does Hegel, by apparently insisting that feelings and sentiments be
banned from the political arena, sublimate politics and fill a space that
might otherwise be given to action? We cannot ignore these questions.
Hegel believes there are objective, absolutely valid grounds for, or essential purposes to, our practices. I think he is wrong. Indeed, I believe that
many of our practices are "essentially contested"—conflicting but equally
plausible reasons are immanent in them.[141] Yet Hegel's plea for a rational
politics and his criticism of subjective justifications can still have meaning
for us. We need not agree that there are core or essential justifications for
our practices to agree that discourse about practices should consist in appeal to reasons.

3.3.2   The Limits of Merely Objective Justifications

In the previous section "subjective justification" meant a justification that
appeals to subjective standards, such as feelings, likings, pleasure, happiness. Some commentators on Hegel take "subjective justification" to
mean something different: sometimes they express the view that a content
is subjectively justified if I, or any subject, hold it to be justified.[142] These
commentators, who rightly note, as did Sabine, cited at the very beginning of this chapter, that for Hegel we are free under laws or with practices only if it is our conviction or understanding that they are right, have
mistaken this *right of subjectivity*[143] for a claim Hegel supposedly makes
that all embodiments of right must *have* subjective justifications. We have
just seen that Hegel opposes the view that something is justified *because*
I believe it to be justified. Rather, it is justified if it accords with rational
principles: that which is right has an objective justification. But Hegel
goes on to claim that for me, and for any subject, such embodiments will
not appear to be justified—they won't be justified *to us*—unless it is our
conviction that they are justified. Only in the subjective will can freedom

[141] For example, both utility and retribution are principles immanent in the practice of
legal punishment. I develop the point that some of our practices are essentially contested in
my *Punishment: Theory and Practice*, ch. 5. For the notion that some of our *concepts* are
essentially contested, see W. B. Gallie, "Essentially Contested Concepts."
[142] Cf. Ossip Flechtheim, *Hegels Strafrechtstheorie*; and Igor Primoratz, *Banquos-Geist:
Hegels Theorie der Strafe.*
[143] PR 107, 118, 132, 260 Z.

be actual.[144] We saw in the passages above on pietism that Hegel does not condemn pietistic feelings or convictions. He only condemns pietism of the wrong sort. The pietist of the wrong sort takes his feelings or convictions as the standard for truth, as justificatory. The pietist of the right sort channels her feelings and passions into law, into the truth "out there"— she makes that truth her own truth.[145]

For Hegel, we are free in obeying a law only if we understand it to be right. Hegel praises Socrates because he believed Socrates inwardly reflected, subjected laws and practices to an inner determination of their right.[146] A merely ethical will that lacks subjectivity is like the will of a child or a slave, who, unable to abstract from his situation into his own subjectivity, merely obeys. If the will lacks the "infinite form of self-consciousness," it remains "sunk in its content"[147] and is unfree. Contents that are embodiments of right and freedom are not justified *by* my choosing them. Many of the contents in which we are free we never choose in a literal sense, for example, our natal family or our state. But we are free in these contents if we can understand them to be rational, if we are convinced it is right to act according to the demands entailed by commitment to these contents. We can abstract from these commitments in theory and see them as possibilities in which we are at home, and then return to them, choose them, so to speak, after the fact. Only then are we really free in these commitments.

3.3.3 *Justification as Subjective and Objective*

What must we do to will an objective, actual content that is already fulfilled and present? What must we do to be free? As we have just seen, Hegel cannot be claiming that to will freely I must will whatever objective content I face—this would violate the criterion he gives for freedom, that the content of my free will must be my own, and that I must see the reason for it. Hegel answers our question by saying that the free will must will the free will.[148] But what does this mean? In his lectures Hegel explains that freedom comes by willing according to the laws, practices, and institutions of the modern state. "Spirit comes to see the *reason* of the laws it at first sees as natural power or natural law, it sees the systematic ratio-

---

144 Ibid., 106.

145 Cf. Rph V, 3:388,1–8.

146 Rph VI, 4:301,15–25; cf. HP 1:407–425.

147 PR 26, my translation.

148 Ibid., 27: "In making freedom its object, mind's [*Geist*] purpose is to be explicitly, as Idea, what the will is implicitly. The definition of the concept of the will in abstraction from the Idea of the will is 'the free will which wills the free will.' "

nality of itself (i.e., of its own ethical life)."[149] To say that the free will wills itself by willing the laws of its state is to say that the will thinks or reflects upon the laws and institutions it finds, sees their rationality, and makes them its own. When it wills them Hegel says it wills itself;[150] it wills what is its own second nature. To take on commitments on the basis solely of one's convictions and without regard to objective (public, legal, institutional) duties and standards of right is not to be free. Similarly, to take on commitments and act in certain ways merely because this is "what is done," without seeing the reason or rationality of acting in this way, is not to be free—we might say it is not really to act, or will.

As we have seen, the free will does not always choose its content in the usual sense of "choose." Seldom do we actually choose our laws, institutions, and practices. But we can appropriate as our own content the laws of our ethical community by an act of understanding. When we do this, we are on firm ground when we act; the commitments that make us who we are are justified to us; we are at home in them; in willing them we are true to ourselves and free. The task of Hegel's political philosophy is to persuade us that this objective content is essentially rational, and that it is not only out there but also in us.[151] If his philosophy is successful, we will by Hegel's standards be free. If we comprehend the necessity of the institutions of the state, then we relate ourselves to these institutions as free beings.[152] By knowing these institutions to be necessary, it is rational for me to will in accord with them, and by doing so I am free.[153]

In a passage in his last set of complete lectures Hegel describes modern life as coping with the need both to withdraw from the ethical world before us and to be at home in this world. This is the essential tension we saw to be the subject of paragraphs 5 and 6 of the *Philosophy of Right*. Hegel says it is the aim of thought to bring ourselves not to an immediate identity with this world, as have children, slaves, or the Athenians in their happy state, but to a harmony based on reflective reconciliation.[154] There is I think no better illustration of what this reconciliation is like than the case of the criminal who sees and regrets his wrongdoing. Hegel says, "The criminal, for example, is punished according to laws, but he must also himself recognize that he has earned punishment, that he has damned

[149] Rph VI, 4:147,5–17.
[150] Ibid.
[151] Cf. Karl Larenz, *Hegels Zurechnungslehre*, p. 37: "The absolute is not outside of us, but rather it is in us as our self" ("Das Absolute ist nicht außer uns, sondern in uns als unser Selbst").
[152] Rph III, 243,25–29.
[153] PR 266; Rph VI, 4:640,4–14.
[154] Rph VI, 4:147,25–31; cf. 4:172–173; and PR 26.

himself."[155] The laws of the state are pointed to as the objective standard by which to judge the action of the criminal as wrong. Since we are free only by acting according to these standards, we can say that the criminal's act was not an act of a free will, just as the alcoholic's taking a drink, or the person with bulimia going on another binge, is not an act of a free will. If the criminal were to acknowledge this objective criterion as right, that is, appropriate it as his own criterion for right action, then he would understand his punishment as an act of right and he would see the act of his own punishment as an act of his own free will: "A criminal who is to be punished may see his punishment as a restriction of his freedom; in fact, in so far as he acknowledges that the punishment is not an alien force suppressing him but a manifestation of his own deed, then he comports himself as a free being."[156]

Pierre Riviere, the young Frenchman who in 1835 murdered three members of his family and became immortalized by his memoirs, stands as a symbol of the danger presented to the state by those who turn away from outward commitments and act by their own, subjective standards of right. Listen to the chilling words Pierre gives us in confessing his crime, the murder of not only his mother, whose cruelties to his father had so enraged Pierre, but also his sister, who sided with his mother against his father, and his brother, who loved his mother:

> I loved my father very much, his tribulations affected me sorely. . . . All my ideas were directed toward these things and settled upon them. I conceived the fearful design which I executed, I was meditating it for about a month before. I wholly forgot the principles which should have made me respect my mother and my sister and my brother. . . . I knew the rules of man and the rules of ordered society, but I deemed myself wiser than they, I regarded them as ignoble and shameful.[157]

Shortly after his trial, and like the criminal who is free in his punishment, Pierre repented for having "forgotten" the principles that would have restrained him and begged to die at the hands of the state. When the state refused, imprisoning him instead, he brought forth his own retribution by hanging himself.

I cannot help feeling that Hegel would have smiled (perhaps it would be a hesitant, ambivalent smile). Those of us who judge Pierre's act differently should be troubled. In the next chapter we shall consider Hegel's reasons for seeing in the laws, practices, and institutions of the modern

---

[155] Rph VI, 4:148,12–16.
[156] Enz 158.
[157] Michel Foucault, ed., *I, Pierre Riviere*, p. 105, my emphasis.

state the objective content of the free will. Being committed to its laws binds us to act in a certain way, but in these obligations we are free: "Only the will that obeys the laws is free, for it obeys itself and is at home [*bei sich selbst*] and free."[158] Not to obey, like Pierre, is to be unfree. To be brought back to commitment to the laws, as was Pierre through his punishment, is to be made free. But why does Hegel think that it is commitment to *this* content that makes us who we are, and that we are only really free by acting in accordance with the demands commitment to *this* content entails? We shall let Hegel speak for himself in trying to persuade those who would not share in his (perhaps hesitant, ambivalent) smile.[159]

[158] PH 57 (39).

[159] Later, when we discuss in detail Hegel's views on the practice of legal punishment, and his criticism of some laws and practices, we shall see why I think his smile might be hesitant and ambivalent.

Four

Recht-an-sich and the Power That Punishes

IN CHAPTER 2 we saw that Hegel claims there are both objective and subjective reasons for punishing a criminal. One objective reason is to vindicate right: if we do not punish the criminal, his action may come to be taken by society as right. Another objective reason, we said, is to restore right, or justice. We noted that Hegel speaks sometimes of right as lying in wait until it is violated, upon which it turns against the criminal. Hegel suggests that the power that punishes is not just the state but justice, which he sometimes depicts with the images of *Banquos-Geist* and the Eumenides.[1] In other words, the state is not a presupposition for justice.[2]

In chapter 3 we saw that Hegel maintains that the criminal, like all other citizens of the modern state, is free only by obeying the laws of her state and acting in accordance with the demands entailed by commitment to the modern state. It is this feature of the practices, institutions, and laws of the state—that by living in accord with them human beings can be understood to be free—that makes them right. In Hegel's view, the modern state is not a presupposition for justice, but its laws do articulate right, and the power that punishes those violating these laws is the power of right.[3]

The purposes of this chapter are to see what Hegel means in saying that (1) the power that punishes is not the state but right, and that (2) the modern state is the agent of right, and whether what Hegel says is plausible. In the process of explicating Hegel's view, itself no easy task, I shall

[1] PR 101 Z; Rph V, 3:670,30–671,5; PR 101 Bem; Rph V, 3:323,6–9; 3:320,34–321,3.

[2] PR 100 Rem.

[3] This note is for those troubled by my use of the term "power to punish" to refer to the right to punish. Of course we might say that anyone who is strong enough has the power to punish. John Locke argues that one reason we leave the state of nature is for lack of a sufficient power to back and support sentencing and execution (*Second Treatise*, par. 126). Locke holds that in a state of nature that is prior to the existence of the state with its administration of justice, we each in theory have the power, or God-given right, to punish, but in practice we might lack the physical strength to mete it out—we might be the victim of someone stronger than us. Locke argues that each of us consequently give up our single power of punishing and authorize the state to punish for us (pars. 87–88; 127–128; 130). In speaking of the power to punish as the right to punish, we are following Locke in equating power with right. Locke himself slips back to a different sense of "power" when he measures it by physical strength; but he typically means that to punish is to punish by right, and while to do this may require strength, one might have strength without right.

advance an argument about the development of Hegel's philosophy that is not entirely peripheral to the project of understanding and evaluating his *Rechtsphilosophie*. The argument is that in his early writings (for my purposes these are the works Hegel wrote prior to publishing his *Science of Logic* and include the *Phenomenology*) Hegel offers an imaginative and brilliant but obscure vision of political community that he retains in his later *Rechtsphilosophie* (which refers mainly to his lectures from 1817 to 1831 and his published *Philosophy of Right*) but translates there into concrete terms that allow this vision to serve as a practical theory, or a theory we can use to criticize and possibly reform existing practices.

The vision of which I speak is of an ethical community with shared values and customs. Hegel calls this community an "ethical substance" and characterizes its values and customs as *Recht-an-sich*.[4] Any encounter with this vision risks exposure to one of two charges, depending on which of two routes is taken to it: (1) We use Hegel's metaphors and images, but this may not lead us to a meaningful statement of what an ethical substance is; our account will be obscure. (2) We translate what we think Hegel means into language we understand, but this may not lead us to an explication of *Hegel*. Because I think the metaphors and obscure language Hegel uses in his early works when talking about ethical substances lack sense without translation into meaningful terms, I take the second route. My claim is that the vision loses its obscurity once we see its translation into the language of Hegel's *Rechtsphilosophie*—the language of right and freedom. By using Hegel's own language of right, I hope to avoid what many would regard as the danger inherent in this second route.

4.1   The Power That Punishes

We first want to understand what Hegel means in claiming that the power that punishes is not the state but justice. Hegel's point is that we can speak of right and wrong prior to the existence of criminal laws, and of a power or right to punish prior to the existence of a state prosecutor.

---

[4] On translating *Recht-an-sich*: Wallace translates *Recht-an-sich* as "right in the abstract" (Enz 531, 532), but this is very misleading, since *Recht-an-sich* does not refer to the abstract rights of which Hegel speaks in the *Rechtsphilosophie*. By *Recht-an-sich* I shall mean, and I think Hegel means, what is really right (*Recht*). Not all positive laws are *Recht-an-sich*, and certain actions may be *Recht-an-sich* even though no law or practice prescribes them. We might say that *Recht-an-sich* is that which is implicitly right; often when Hegel speaks of something as *an-sich* he means it is implicit. See for example HP 1:20–21. I shall use "right" and "just" interchangeably for *Recht*. On Hegel's use of *Recht* to refer to a conception of right going beyond a narrow legalistic notion of right, see ch. 3, note 1.

Unless we are die-hard Hobbesians this view should have some appeal,[5] and the following incident may help us see why. A gigantic young warrior of a village in the Upper Congo once violated a minor tabu and was unrepentant. The oldest woman of the tribe—"nearly 100 years old, grayhaired, toothless, shrunken and lean, so frail that a blow from the fist of the warrior would have crushed her skull"—found out and approached him indignantly. When she confronted him, he conceded and ran to the forest, apparently in shame. Comments the observer of this incident, "there was more power in her voice than in his muscle."[6] The power that punished here was not the physical strength of the state, but the power of right. Perhaps our muscular warrior shared in the old woman's conception of right, both being of the same tribe, and needed only her gaze to make explicit what he implicitly knew—that he had done wrong.

In explaining his view that the state is not the precondition for justice,[7] Hegel notes that many criminals give themselves up because they are not at peace with themselves until justice is served on them, his point being that crime brings its own call for justice; justice is demanded not merely by the state.[8] Hegel invokes the image of *Banquos-Geist* to make the point that the power of punishment has its source in the conscience of the criminal.[9] But what is the source of these pangs of guilt? The warrior doesn't seem to have felt guilt until another member of his tribe brought it out—the source of guilt seems to have been external to the warrior, although it seems also to have always been within him. Can we make sense of this?

There is an important (though very difficult) passage in Hegel's *Phenomenology* that helps us and lets us connect up the first of the points we are trying to understand, that the power that punishes is not the state but justice, with the second, that the modern state is an agent of justice. In the passage, paragraph 462, Hegel describes an ethical community—we may think of a small tribe that lacks the modern institutions that administer justice as we know it—in which one member commits a wrong against another, thereby bringing this community into "disequilibrium." (Actually, from the text it is not clear that the wrongdoer is of the same community as his victim. I am going to assume this for reasons that will become clear.) The community is "brought back to equilibrium by justice

---

[5] Thomas Hobbes claims that there is no such thing as right or justice prior to the existence of Leviathan and its laws and that justice is the keeping of these laws (*Leviathan*, ch. 15).

[6] Elsworth Faris, "The Origin of Punishment," p. 58.

[7] PR 100 Rem.

[8] Rph II, 1:276,16–18.

[9] On Hegel's use of the image of *Banquos-Geist*, see Igor Primoratz, *Banquos-Geist: Hegels Theorie der Strafe*.

[*Gerechtigkeit*]." Hegel says that this justice appears as human law, but equally as "the simple spirit [*Geist*] of the individual who has suffered wrong": "the individual himself is the power of the nether world, and it is his Erinys which wreaks vengeance." Hegel seems to mean that the avenger is the power that punishes, establishes right or justice, and brings back a "stable equilibrium." We know from passages in the *Philosophy of Right* that Hegel regards vengeance as the form punishment takes in the absence of the institutions of a modern state.[10] But we also know that Hegel thinks vengeance is subjective, and it would be inconsistent for him to claim that the angry victim is the measure of justice.[11] As we continue we see that he means something else. Hegel explains:

[a] His [the victim's] individuality, his blood, still lives on in the household, his substance has an enduring reality.

[b] The wrong which can be inflicted on the individual in the ethical realm is simply this, that something merely happens to him. The power which inflicts this wrong on the conscious individual of making him into a mere thing, is nature; it is the universality not of the community, but the abstract universality of mere being; and the individual, in avenging the wrong he has suffered, does not turn against the former [the community], for it is not at its hands that he has suffered, but against the latter [nature].

[c] As we saw, the consciousness of [those who share] the blood of the individual repairs this wrong in such a way that what has simply happened becomes rather a work deliberately done, in order that the mere being of the wrong, its ultimate form, may also be something willed.[12]

In this passage Hegel is opaque but also tantalizingly suggestive. What might he mean?

In (a) Hegel says that the wronged individual has a substance. By this Hegel means that the individual is part of an ethical substance, the community, and as we shall see in the following section, this means that the individual's conception of right conduct has as its source community standards of right. This idea helps make sense of the claim in (c) that "the consciousness of [those who share] the blood of the individual [victim] repairs this wrong": the individual victim shares the blood of the other members of his community; but more, he shares with the others who make up this substance a sense of right and justice. To wrong one is to wrong all, just as to attack a member of my family is to attack me. Referring to the Upper Congo example, we can infer from the old woman's

[10] PR 102. Hegel claims that the German word for justice, *Gerechtigkeit*, has its source in the German word for revenge, *Rache*. See Rph VI, 4:294.

[11] On Hegel's argument that revenge is subjective and contingent, see my discussion in sec. 3.3.1.2.

[12] PhdG 462, my insertions, division.

reaction that by violating the tabu the warrior had injured all the members of his tribe; and from his own reaction to her reproach we can infer that he had, in committing the wrong, injured himself as well.

Hegel says the wrong that put the ethical community into disequilibrium is an act of nature ([b]); it is something that merely happened ([c]). Again referring to the Upper Congo example, the punishment the old woman metes out to the warrior, in the form of reproach, transforms "what has simply happened" into "a work deliberately done" and "something willed." Only by this punishment is the existence of wrong established and is there the possibility of guilt, in both a legal sense (perhaps word of the incident gets around in the tribe and the warrior loses some of his privileges) and a moral sense (the warrior's feeling of shame). Our passage from the *Phenomenology* illustrates how radically anti-utilitarian is Hegel's retributive conception of punishment. In Hegel's view, we punish, not because this is the best way to respond to crime, but, rather, because punishing is the only way to express that certain actions are wrongs. Without the old woman's response there would have been no crime: not because if nobody discovers it happened it didn't happen, but because if nobody declares it's wrong it's not.

The community to which Hegel refers in our passage from the *Phenomenology* resembles more the Upper Congo tribe than the modern state he discusses in the *Rechtsphilosophie*: punishment is meted out not by an administration of justice, consisting in a determination of guilt and sentence by judge or jury, but by the fellow members of the community, who share in the wrongdoer's "substance." This ethical substance is ultimately the power that punishes. Hegel can say that justice appears as both human law and the spirit of the victim because both share in this ethical substance. But the wrongdoer too, as a member of this community, had "broken away from the balanced whole" and is brought back by justice to his own substance.[13]

The idea of ethical substance is central to both of the points we are trying to understand. The power that punishes is *Recht-an-sich*, which, as we shall see, is manifested in the ethical substance. But also, the ethical substance is (somehow) connected to the modern state, so that we may say that when the modern state punishes really what punishes is the ethical substance, and *Recht-an-sich*. Ethical substance is an idea that is central to the works of both the early Hegel and the Hegel of the *Rechtsphilosophie*. In the next section we shall examine what the early Hegel meant by this idea.

[13] In paragraph 462 of the *Phenomenology* Hegel does not say explicitly that what has "broken away" is the wrongdoer; Hegel does not indicate that the wrongdoer is a member of the same community to which his victim belongs. I have assumed this so that we could connect up this passage with the Upper Congo example, and I think it is a plausible reading.

THE POWER THAT PUNISHES

4.2   The Early Vision of Ethical Substance

With his images of the Eumenides and *Banquos-Geist*, and the passage
we have discussed from the *Phenomenology*, Hegel suggests that the
power that punishes is present *in potentia* in an ethical community, lying
in wait for any member who dares to violate the community's social morality. Some have criticized Hegel for this view, seeing in it a "phantas-
magoric ideology" at work legitimizing a practice, punishment, that is in
fact a political means of repression.[14] In Ossip Flechtheim's view, Hegel
believes there is a natural causality between crime and punishment.[15]
Flechtheim attributes Hegel's view to his coming under the influence of
antique tragedy: to the Greeks punishment seemed like fate, and so to
Hegel it appears as a "natural, godly, unconditional objectification of absolute *Geist*."[16]

From our reading of the *Phenomenology* we have reason to challenge
Flechtheim's claim that to Hegel punishment is a natural consequence of
crime: it is only the response of the accuser and of the ethical substance
that establishes actions as wrongs. Flechtheim is right to find significance
in Hegel's attraction to the ancient Greeks, but I think there is a better
account of this significance. That the Greeks viewed punishment as fate
need not imply that there exists some metaphysical causal mechanism to
mete out punishment; it might mean only that the Greeks attributed to
fate a power they held themselves, because they lacked self-awareness of
their own power. Hegel draws the latter implication. To Hegel, the ancient Greek city-state was an exemplar of an ethical substance. In his *Phenomenology* Hegel refers to the Greek polis as *das Glücke*, the happy
state, and his discussion there is an important source for understanding
what the early Hegel meant by ethical substance and helps us see that,
contrary to Flechtheim's view, Hegel regards it and not some divine force
as the power that punishes.

4.2.1   *Ethical Substance*

Hegel's *Phenomenology of Spirit* can be read as the story of the journey
of self-consciousnesses—us humans—toward a state of complete integ-

---

[14] Ossip Flechtheim, "Die Funktion der Strafe in der Rechtstheorie Hegels," pp. 9–11, 13.
For similar views see Flechtheim's earlier *Hegels Strafrechtstheorie*.

[15] Ossip, Flechtheim, "Die Funktion der Strafe in der Rechtstheorie Hegels," p. 12.

[16] Ibid.

rity, satisfaction, and comprehension of life in all its concrete richness.[17] The happy state—*das Glücke*—which Hegel describes in paragraphs 347–357 of the *Phenomenology*, exemplifies the unity and integrity, but not the self-knowledge, that we seek. Hegel tells us that this that we seek is implicitly in us, but that we do not know this explicitly: "It is Spirit which . . . has the certainty of its unity with itself. This certainty has now to be raised to the level of truth; what holds good for it in principle [*an sich*], and in its inner certainty, has to enter into the consciousness and become explicit for it [*für es*]."[18]

In the happy state individuals live in an ethical community, sharing a bond with their fellow members. Each acts according to the practices and laws, or *Sitte*, of his ethical community and in this way "is aware of the universal consciousness in its individuality as its [the individual's] own being."[19] In Hegel's view, the Greek who lived such a life acted unreflectively and on the basis of trust in the laws and customs given to him.[20] His life in the happy state may have been blissful, but it was also what Hegel calls immediate. The unreflective life in *das Glücke* consists of individuals working to fulfill their immediate or particular desires. It is because individuals are Spirit *an-sich*,[21] which is to say that they live in an ethical state such as the polis that is in fact a "universal sustaining medium,"[22] that through the satisfaction of his own needs the individual satisfies the needs of others, and that he is able to satisfy his own needs only through the labor of others.[23] The individuals themselves do not understand the true significance of individual labor and of life according to the *Sitte* of the polis—they do what they do because this is "what is done." They are not yet Spirit *für-sich* and do not know what Hegel knows, that by their individual activities they satisfy the needs of all and come to perceive their fellow citizens as themselves, all as of one substance.[24]

Hegel calls this happy state an ethical substance; and as we have seen,

---

[17] Any brief summary account of what the *Phenomenology* is about will no doubt be inadequate, but the following passages do support such a reading: on the quest for a state of satisfaction (*Befriedigung*), see, for example, PhdG 80, 163, 175. One criterion of *Befriedigung* is no longer to see death as limiting: see PhdG 80, 363–364, 452, 784; also, Charles Taylor, *Hegel*, p. 173. On the quest for absolute knowledge and self-comprehension, see, for example, PhdG 89, 438, 798, 808. Others have emphasized this point—see Robert Solomon, *In the Spirit of Hegel*, and Mark Taylor, *Journeys to Selfhood: Hegel and Kierkegaard*.

[18] PhdG 347.
[19] Ibid., 349.
[20] Ibid., 355.
[21] Ibid., 348.
[22] Ibid., 351.
[23] Ibid.
[24] Ibid., 351, 392.

in the *Phenomenology* he says this ethical substance is Spirit *an-sich*. In his happy state, or ethical substance, the individual is at home.[25]

Hegel speaks of the ethical substance as a ground to which Spirit returns after its journeys upon breaking away from this ground, this happy state.[26] Hegel writes, "Spirit, being the substance and the universal, self-identical, and abiding essence, is the unmoved solid ground and starting point [*Grund und Ausgangspunkt*] for the action of all, and it is their purpose and goal."[27] The happy state is the individual's origin and goal, his once and future home.

Hegel says that "Reason must [*muß*] withdraw from the happy state."[28] He gives two reasons. First, the law and custom, or "universal Spirit" with which the self-consciousness that is a part of the happy state identifies, is a "separate, individual" spirit—for example, it is the spirit of some particular Athens or Sparta—and this is too limited a spirit for human consciousness to identify with.[29] Later in the *Phenomenology* Hegel explains that limited ethical substances are self-destructive: they become shattered, leading to a multitude of separate atoms,[30] as a result of war.[31] The second reason Hegel gives why Reason must withdraw from the happy state is that an individual that is Spirit only immediately and implicitly, not explicitly, "is not aware of himself as being a pure individuality on his own account."[32] Such an individual, living unreflectively according to mere trust in the inherited laws and customs, lacks consciousness of what he really is: "[Spirit] must advance to the consciousness of what it is immediately, must leave behind it the beauty of ethical life, and by passing through a series of shapes attain to a knowledge of itself."[33] The Greeks identified with their happy state in an immediate way; they could not give an account of the grounds of their actions.[34] The final state of satisfaction, comprehension, freedom, and integrity sought by the subject of the *Phenomenology*, self-consciousness, is attained only by the subject acting not unreflectively according to trust in the inherited laws, but with comprehension of the grounds of these laws.[35]

[25] *Bei sich*; see PhdG 347, 533.
[26] Ibid., 348, 439–440, 680, 801.
[27] Ibid., 439.
[28] Ibid., 354.
[29] Ibid.
[30] Ibid., 476.
[31] Ibid., 475; cf. 455.
[32] Ibid., 355.
[33] Ibid., 441; cf. 347; 357, lines 25–27; 377.
[34] PR 147 Bem, p. 296.
[35] The necessity of reflection, or of what Hegel calls subjectivity, was discussed in sec. 3.3.2.

Hegel's view is that all of us become who we are by being born into an ethical community. At first, as children, we are "suckled at the breast of universal ethical life."[36] To a child, the norms it is taught appear "alien to it," but as the child grows it comprehends more and more, gaining insight into the rationality of the ethical life it had been taught. The Greeks, to Hegel, are in this respect like children: to the Greeks in the unreflective happy state, law "is not grounded in the will of a particular individual, but is eternal and valid in itself"; the ethical self-consciousness is "immediately one with the law." The law's origins are not questioned; law simply is. The ethical disposition of the Greeks, in Hegel's view, consists "just in sticking steadfastly to what is right, and abstaining from all attempts to move or shake it, or derive it."[37]

The subject who had left his ethical substance, withdrawn into a world where his actions are guided not by trust in the rightness of the customs and laws of his polis, but by his own standards of judgment, eventually returns to this substance. It had been his ground, a home in which he once blissfully and unreflectively dwelled; upon reflecting, he left this home in search of a commitment that would be his own, not merely given to him; and he eventually finds this commitment by returning to his old home, again to dwell in it, but with the newly earned comprehension that this is a commitment he has chosen for himself. Hegel thinks that Socrates plays a historically important role in the withdrawal from the original unreflective allegiance to the happy state. In his later lectures on the history of philosophy, Hegel says of Socrates that he marks a change in the spirit of the people.[38] According to Hegel, before Socrates morality was natural morality, people doing right unreflectively.[39] Socrates marks the stage of reflective, or subjective, morality, a morality where an individual subject determines what is right.

In the *Philosophy of Right*, Hegel characterizes the principle of subjectivity that Socrates embodied as necessary for freedom.[40] This necessity of reflective individuality appears in the *Phenomenology* as the necessity for self-consciousness to withdraw from and eventually return to its ethical substance; Hegel's argument there is couched in the language not of freedom, as in the later *Rechtsphilosophie*, but of Spirit: living in the happy state one is Spirit *an-sich*, and only by withdrawal and eventual return does one become Spirit *für-sich*. The plausibility of Hegel's early vision of an ethical substance that is our ground and goal depends, consequently, upon the plausibility of his conception of Spirit, or *Geist*.

[36] NL 115.
[37] PhdG 437.
[38] HP 1:407.
[39] PhdG 411.
[40] Cf. sec. 3.3.2.

That human beings are implicitly something called *Geist*, that they follow the dictates of and work for their community at first with an unreflective trust, but that they necessarily grow out of this condition of blind
trust and come to know themselves as sharers in or constituents of *Geist*,
is a central Hegelian idea.[41] Some, taking *Geist* as a metaphysical, cosmic
entity, consequently find Hegel's notion of ethical substance suspect.
Charles Taylor is obviously sympathetic with Hegel's conception of ethical community, but Taylor sees Hegel's conception ultimately as metaphysical. Taylor explains that for Hegel the public life of the state has a
crucial importance for men "because the norms and ideas it expresses are
not just human inventions. On the contrary, the state expresses the Idea,
the ontological structure of things. In the final analysis [the public life of
the state] is of vital importance because it is one of the indispensable ways
in which man recovers his essential relation to this ontological structure
. . . 'absolute Spirit.' "[42] Taylor has gone to great lengths to make clear
Hegel's view that the individual's ethical community is the individual's
very substance. He translates the idea of ethical substance into terms
someone who has no idea of what Hegel means by "Spirit" or "Idea"
could understand. For example, he explains that to say that the state or
community is the "substance" of the people is to say that "the individuals
only are what they are by their inherence in the community."[43] Taylor
then asks what it means to say this, and he answers:

> Our experience is what it is, is shaped in part, by the way we interpret it; and
> this has a lot to do with the terms which are available to us in our culture. But
> there is more; many of our most important experiences would be impossible
> outside of society. . . . So the culture which lives in our society shapes our pri-
> vate experience and constitutes our public experience, which in turn interacts
> profoundly with the private. So that it is no extravagant proposition to say that
> we are what we are in virtue of participating in the larger life of our society.[44]

Even if this is not entirely clear, resting on loose phrases such as "larger
life" and "interacts profoundly with," and metaphors such as "shapes,"
it is not a very foreign idea; in many respects it echoes Aristotle, who
maintains that we become virtuous only by acting in a virtuous way,
which we do by habituation, by acting in accord with the conventions of
our state, which is both natural and prior to the individual.[45] But Taylor

[41] Cf. sec. 1.3; and JR 253.
[42] Charles Taylor, *Hegel*, p. 386.
[43] Ibid., p. 379.
[44] Ibid., p. 381.
[45] See Aristotle, *Nichomachean Ethics* 2:1, 2:4; and Aristotle, *Politics* 1:2, 2:8. On the
Aristotelianism in Hegel's philosophy, see, for example, Joachim Ritter, *Hegel and the
French Revolution*, trans. Richard Dien Winfield, pp. 164–177; and Manfred Riedel, "Tra-

thinks that Hegel ultimately gives to his vision of ethical substance a metaphysical underpinning: "Where Hegel does make a substantial claim which is not easy to grant is in his basic ontological view, that man is the vehicle of cosmic spirit, and the corollary, that the state expresses the underlying formula of necessity by which this spirit posits the world."[46]

Others reject this reading of Hegel. For example, Robert Solomon writes in his commentary on the *Phenomenology*, "I could not be more in disagreement with Charles Taylor, otherwise a kindred spirit, who continually makes humanity into a 'vehicle' for Hegel's *Geist*, always a part of something 'greater than itself.' "[47] In Solomon's view, Hegel is a humanist; his *Geist* means not God, but humanity: "Hegel is a strictly secular, virulently anti-theological, and more or less anti-Christian philosopher."[48] Moreover, Hegel, in Solomon's view, is an anti-metaphysician: "It is Hegel who reduced all questions of being to questions about the structures and forms of human experience."[49] "The whole thrust of [the *Phenomenology*] is a demonstration of the strictly *human* context of human consciousness, in which Nature and all gods but human spirit are relegated to a small and unobtrusive place."[50] Even if we agree with Solomon that Hegel's metaphysics is secular, so that we think Taylor is wrong to claim that for Hegel man is the "vehicle of cosmic spirit," Taylor's point, what he calls a "corollary," that Hegel invokes his conception of *Geist* to establish the necessity, or absolute justification, of the state—its practices, institutions, and laws—remains a problem in Hegel's philosophy. Hegel claims to be a foundationalist, providing speculative insight into the necessity and absolute justifications of our practices, a necessity history reveals and of which Hegelian logic gives an account. My position as a nonfoundationalist is that we can make use of Hegel's interpretations of our social practices without privileging them as true on the basis of a metaphysics we cannot accept. As an elaboration and reworking of Aristotle's idea of a polis, Hegel's conception of ethical substance offers a potentially helpful way of thinking about political community and our shared social practices, including legal punishment. That Hegel links up his conception of ethical substance to his metaphysics of *Geist* in arguing for the necessity of the social practices of our ethical substance does not mean we must do the same. As we shall see, the later Hegel of the *Rechts-*

---

dition und Revolution in Hegels Philosophie des Rechts," in Riedel, *Studien zu Hegels Rechtsphilosophie*, pp. 100–134.

[46] Charles Taylor, *Hegel*, p. 387.

[47] Robert Solomon, *In the Spirit of Hegel*, p. 6.

[48] Ibid., p. 5.

[49] Ibid., p. 8.

[50] Ibid., pp. 198–199. In Solomon's reading, Hegel's God is "no more than self-conscious Spirit" (p. 256).

philosophie reformulates his vision of the ethical substance in a way that lets us make sense of it without recourse to the concept of *Geist*. The early Hegel also articulated the idea of ethical substance in ways that call to mind an Aristotelian political community rather than a vehicle of *Geist*. In the rest of this section we shall explore more thoroughly the Aristotelian interpretation of Hegel's idea of ethical substance.

4.2.2 Punishment and the Ethical Substance

In his *Jenaer Realphilosophie* (1805–1806) Hegel says that the law of the state acts against its member's particular self and upon his implicit (*ansich*) and universal self. The force of law is not that of "another against me" but of "myself against myself."[51] The force of law, or the power (*Macht*) that punishes those who violate this law, is the force not of pure power but of power I recognize. Through it I come to good.[52] Hegel adds that the power of the law is the common essence (*Gemeinwesen*) of the living people, the "substance" (*Substanz*); the substance is the power that punishes and is invoked by the criminal himself.[53] This passage, in its focus on law, is a somewhat more concrete account of the view Hegel expresses in paragraph 462 of the *Phenomenology*. The power that punishes is the ethical substance, the substance of the individuals sharing in an ethical life, and works through the law. In another early essay, his "System der Sittlichkeit," which is particularly obscure because Hegel was still using Friedrich Schelling's cryptic terminology, Hegel speaks of punishment as making the criminal whole again. The criminal sees himself as his own enemy and seeks external punishment as a quest for "totality."[54] If the criminal had committed a crime in another community, in whose ethical substance he did not share, punishment would not have this significance. In a passage from the later *Rechtsphilosophie* Hegel recounts how Napoleon was nearly killed by a German assassin in Vienna in 1809. The French, he says, could not reason with the assassin, who could not see that his action was a vile, low act. "The French treated him as a wild animal and shot him." Hegel's phrasing is significant—he does not say the assassin was punished, presumably because one does not punish wild animals. Hegel then makes his point: the assassin was shot because he could not be brought to see his error; no common ground ("*nichts Gemeinsames*") was shared between him and his victims.[55] Genuine punish-

---

[51] JR 235.
[52] Ibid.
[53] Ibid., 237, 240.
[54] Hegel, "System der Sittlichkeit," p. 467.
[55] Rph VI, 4:388,28–389,6.

ment, in this view, is a power presupposing an ethical substance that is shared among criminal, victim, and agent inflicting the actual punishment, so that we might see punishment as a sign of affection, the community's expression of concern for the criminal's own well-being.

Punishment is a measure to strengthen the community by vindicating and restoring right. Through it the ethical substance reinforces the sense of unity and community that make it a substance, and in this respect Hegel ascribes to punishment a function similar to that he ascribes to war.

4.2.3   War and the Ethical Substance

Hegel defends war by pointing to its ethical nature. Successful wars "actualize the Ideality of the state" by checking domestic unrest and consolidating state power at home.[56] War prevents a hardening of particularity by shifting our focus to the universal.[57] Through war we see that life and property are only finite and not absolute, and that the state exists not merely to protect life and property.[58] Classical liberals like Locke have trouble accounting for war and the sentiments of nationalism and patriotism it evokes, because they miss the point of why we live in a state: "The Understanding errs in saying citizens must defend the state in order to defend their property and life—they fall to contradiction because they miss the point."[59] The point they miss is that in war we are asked to risk life and property for something transcending the particular commitments to which life in civil society is dedicated.

War, like punishment, is what Hegel calls a determinate negation. Hegel says that man stagnates in peace, and he criticizes Kant's ideal of perpetual peace for ignoring the "necessity of determinate negation." "War is a negating negation and brings forth the infinite positive unity of the state."[60] The "negation" is the enemy, which war negates, and this negation of the negation leads to a strong sense of community identity and a "positive unity." War negates the enemy from without; punishment negates the enemy from within. Both are a struggle against opposition that helps define the ethical community. It is only through such struggle that the universal implicit within the ethical substance is reasserted and maintained.

Hegel is not saying that war is always good and that we must always

[56] PR 324 Rem.
[57] Rph II, 1:340,25–27.
[58] PR 324 Rem.
[59] Rph III, 276,11–17.
[60] Rph II, 1:338,26–30.

have lots of it.[61] In his lectures Hegel says that "war is the negativity of all finite things; war is necessary, but not too much war."[62] Hegel says that war is the less desirable means for the ethical community to prove its freedom and autonomy; the worthier means is to show itself as civilized, with the form of universal and legal relations.[63] Moreover, by giving an account of why at least some wars are valuable, Hegel in effect criticizes other wars that do not serve this purpose, for example wars waged in the interest of a faction of the society.

Hegel established his view of war already in the *Phenomenology*, where it plays a central role:

> The Spirit of universal assembly and association is the simple and negative essence of those systems which tend to isolate themselves. In order not to let them become rooted and set in this isolation, thereby breaking up the whole and letting the [communal] spirit evaporate, government has from time to time to shake them to their core by war. By this means the government upsets their established order, and violates their right to independence, while the individuals who, absorbed in their own way of life, break loose from the whole and strive after the inviolable independence and security of the person, are made to feel in the task laid on them their lord and master, death. Spirit, by thus throwing into the melting-pot the stable existence of these systems, checks their tendency to fall away from the ethical order, and to be submerged in a merely natural existence.[64]

Later in the *Phenomenology* Hegel repeats his argument that war preserves the whole of the community by making individuals caught up in lives driven by particular interests feel the power of death.[65] But he adds that war also tends to the destruction of the simple forms of ethical substances, the happy states such as the Greek poleis.[66]

This last point is very important, calling into question the Aristotelian conception of ethical substance we have been considering, drawing us into the debate about the metaphysical underpinnings of Hegel's vision, and, I shall argue, leading us to the later Hegel's clarification of the concept of ethical substance, which he achieves by using more persistently the language of right and freedom.

---

[61] For a brief reference to Hegel's reputation as warmonger, see Sissela Bok, *A Strategy for Peace*, p. 54, cited in *Owl of Minerva* 22, no. 1 (Fall 1990): p. 94.

[62] Rph V, 3:829,24–25; cf. Rph V, 3:829,28–830,6.

[63] Rph II, 1:339,14–29.

[64] PhdG 455.

[65] Ibid., 475.

[66] Ibid., 476.

4.2.4   Is the Ethical Substance Parochial or Universal?

The problem raised by this last point about war is this: how can the happy state be our ground *and goal* if one of the ways we withdraw from it is through its destruction in war? The happy states the Greeks knew destroyed each other and paved the way for the Roman Empire. Hegel says this process was necessary because it was necessary to withdraw from the happy state. But then Hegel must explain how this ethical substance of the Greeks can be both the ground and the goal of any self-consciousness, Greek or otherwise, for it seems there is nothing left to return to.

In the *Phenomenology* Hegel says of the happy state that it is Spirit *an-sich*. Hegel's answer to how self-consciousness can return to its former home is that it realizes that it is Spirit, which it was implicitly. The once and future home of self-consciousness is Spirit, which transcends particular ethical substances, which are "too limited."[67] It certainly sounds as if Taylor is right in arguing that in Hegel's view human beings share in the substance of some cosmic vehicle, *Geist*, which is something universal, transcending the boundaries of my community. But Hegel's discussion of the significance of punishment and war to ethical substances— that through these means the particular identity of a community is shaped and preserved—is coherent only if we view ethical substances as parochial, for example, the particular polis, tribe, or state in which I live. In this view the bonds of a community consist in a shared sense of identity, values, practices, laws, language, and in general a shared way of thinking that is distinct to this community and gives each member his or her identity. This account, though, contradicts the passages elsewhere in the *Phenomenology* where Hegel speaks of the ethical substance as Spirit *an-sich*, Spirit being universal, transcending the boundaries of any particular community.

Hegel's account is simply contradictory and confusing. Steven Smith argues that already in one of his earlier theological writings, which precedes the *Phenomenology* by several years, Hegel came upon the idea of Spirit; Hegel broke with the idea so central to Herder and Montesquieu of "individual national spirits" in favor of a universal, infinite Spirit. With this shift Hegel came to see people as part of a universal historical process, and this is a break from his earlier republicanism.[68] I am suggesting that Hegel never fully gave up this earlier republicanism. It is central still to his conception of ethical substance, and in particular to his views on punishment and war. It lurks in the later works and surfaces occasionally

---

[67] Ibid., 354.
[68] Steven Smith, *Hegel's Critique of Liberalism*, p. 50.

in ways that conflict with Hegel's grand teleological conception of history as Spirit unfolding.

The early Hegel's vision of community is exciting and profound: the Aristotelian idea of a shared political life, participation in which makes the partakers human beings rather than mere animals, is a promising antidote to what to some is the sickly liberal social-contract conception of the origins of political society. But, as I have been maintaining, the vision is obscure. Hegel is not clear about what it is precisely that we share in the happy state, and what it is we know, or are, when we return to it; nor what it is to which we return. His answers are that we had shared in Spirit *an-sich*, and we are Spirit *für-sich*. But as the disagreement by readers of the *Phenomenology* suggests, it is not obvious what this means. I believe that Hegel's vision of an ethical substance that is our ground and goal remains with him throughout his life, and that he succeeded, if only partially, in making it clearer in his later works.

4.3 *Recht-an-sich* in the *Rechtsphilosophie*

In the happy state, *das Glücke*, the ethical substance such as Athens or Sparta, the individual is "at home." Individuals withdraw from this state, which is their ground, only to return later, to go home again, this time with a newfound knowledge. But, we are left asking, knowledge of what? In his later work, in the *Rechtsphilosophie*, Hegel says that in the happy state the citizen obeys laws out of trust and is not really *free*. Hegel says that at first the laws appear as "given," but are not foreign, and the people come to know this.[69] He calls the original immediate unity of individual with happy state a "sickness" and "somnambulism."[70] When the citizen returns from his withdrawal, he has knowledge of why he should obey the laws; he obeys the laws, as he always had done, but for completely different reasons. The laws are justified to him, and he is genuinely free by obeying them, for he understands them to be his own, the product of his own will.[71] The early Hegel's vision remains but is translated consistently into the language of right and freedom, and I think this makes his vision more concrete and plausible.

[69] Rph III, 123,20–30.

[70] Ibid., 284,1–4; cf. Enz 320.

[71] Cf. Rph III, 123–124: Hegel speaks of laws as first given; then people develop a belief in the laws; then they develop a trust in the laws; and finally the people acquire knowledge of the grounds of the laws.

4.3.1 Early vs. Late Hegel

In the 1790s Hegel and his friends Hölderlin and Schelling, whose influence on Hegel is of great importance, shared in an aesthetic, romantic vision of a society of harmony, rational autonomy, and moral coherence. This vision is summed up in a fragment, the "Älteste Systemprogramm der deutschen Idealismus," generally regarded to have been the work of Hegel, written in perhaps 1796 or 1797:

> I am now convinced that the highest act of Reason, that in which it encompasses all ideas, is an aesthetic act and that truth and good are closely bound only in beauty. The philosopher must possess as much aesthetic power as the poet. Human beings without a sense of aesthetics are textbook philosophers [Buchstabenphilosophen]. The philosophy of spirit is an aesthetic philosophy. One can't be intellectually rich in anything, and especially in reasoning about history, without an aesthetic sense. . . .
>
> We must have a new mythology, but this mythology must stand in the service of the Idea, it must become a mythology of Reason.[72]

Dieter Henrich argues that the young Hegel shared Schiller's longing— "Beautiful world, where art thou? Return again"[73]—and that the circle of Hegel, Schelling, and Hölderlin were convinced that such a world could return: "This was the Rousseauism of the early Hegel. The beautiful polity of the Greek state was the promise that the revolutionary act held for him. . . . His work was to bring this polity before our eyes. . . . In the young Hegel hope for the future is theoretically grounded in an aesthetic of the political."[74] But, Henrich continues, as Hegel matured, the politics of aesthetics transformed into a politics of rationality:

> Now despite Hegel's assurance that the ideals of his youth had only been transformed into the system, this important element [the aesthetic] in his youthful ideal disappeared with the development of the system. . . .
>
> [For the later Hegel] the modern world owes its rationality to connections which essentially cannot be described as beautiful. If the concept of the rational

---

[72] In *Werke*, vol. 1, p. 234; and Johannes Hoffmeister, ed., *Dokumente zu Hegels Entwicklung*, pp. 219–221. For discussions of the authorship of this work, see H. S. Harris, *Hegel's Development: Toward the Sunlight, 1770–1801*, pp. 249–257; and Otto Pöggeler, "Hegel der Verfasser des ältesten Systemprogramms der deutschen Idealismus," pp. 17–32.

[73] Friedrich Schiller, "Die Götter Griechenlands" (1788), line 89, cited in Dieter Henrich, "The Contemporary Relevance of Hegel's Aesthetics," p. 204, note 16.

[74] Dieter Henrich, "The Contemporary Relevance of Hegel's Aesthetics," p. 204.

can no longer be defined in terms of aesthetic categories, then the possibility of a political aesthetic, a legacy of the Platonic tradition, disappears.[75]

Henrich's claim here is rather limited: not that Hegel's substantive philosophy or outlook changed with time, but only his mode of expression, from aesthetic and poetic to rationalistic. Others, though, argue that Hegel himself transformed, from a youthful idealist with utopian hopes into a conservative pessimist. In one view, the young Hegel, "brought up on the republican theorizing of Montesquieu and Rousseau," and who saw in the French Revolution "an attempt to recreate conditions of polis democracy," became disillusioned after the Revolution's failure to revive past political forms and "was led to a more sober appreciation of the opportunities afforded by modernity."[76] In another view, the older Hegel tames the longing for a new freedom that the younger Hegel expressed and seeks satisfaction not in a transformed and "fully human community" but in the realm of "speculative knowledge."[77] Still another commentator sees Hegel's philosophy beginning as a youthful zeal to change the world—"a philosophy of youth"—developing into a desire to work for the state—"a philosophy of manhood"—and eventually settling into a "philosophy of old age" that "detaches itself from opposition to particular objects or persons and withdraws into a harmonious relation to the universal precepts distilled from past experience of opposition."[78]

I think the argument that as Hegel matured he became passive and resigned, willing to accommodate himself to a less than ideal state, is mistaken. The vision of an ethical substance Hegel expressed in the *Phenomenology*, "System der Sittlichkeit," and other works is central, still, in the *Rechtsphilosophie*. So is Hegel's view, prominent in the *Phenomenology*, of the need for reflective individuality. Indeed, I am wary of claiming that there is any *difference* between the political philosophies of the early and late Hegel, apart from a new language: the ethical substance, in the *Rechtsphilosophie*, has become the modern state, and Hegel describes this ethical substance not, mainly, as Spirit *an-sich*, but as *Recht-an-sich*. The early Hegel does not typically use the latter phrase. It seems he had not yet become comfortable with the language of "right," and with a conception where "freedom is both the substance of right and its goal" and where "the system of right is the realm of freedom made actual" by will.[79]

---

[75] Ibid., pp. 204–205.

[76] Steven Smith, *Hegel's Critique of Liberalism*, p. 12.

[77] Bernard Yack, *The Longing for Total Revolution*. See my criticism of Yack's view in sec. 3.1.2.

[78] Clark Butler, "Introduction," in *Hegel: The Letters*, pp. 16–18.

[79] PR 4. This is not to say that Hegel gives up the language of Spirit.

4.3.2 Vision Translated

We have been concerned with two claims Hegel makes. First, the power that punishes is right; second, the modern state is the agent of right. We turned to Hegel's conception of ethical substance because Hegel suggests that the power that punishes is the power of justice (*Gerechtigkeit*), and that justice is meted out by the shared consciousness that is connected with the ethical substance in some way, though it is difficult to say precisely how, since the conception of ethical substance Hegel gives in his early work is opaque and contradictory. Our discussion so far gets us closer to an understanding of the first claim, but it does not help us much with the second. The early Hegel does not develop his concept of a modern state as an ethical substance, a "whole," certainly not with the persistence and specificity we find in the *Rechtsphilosophie*. In the *Philosophische Propädeutik*, which stands midway between the *Phenomenology* and the *Rechtsphilosophie*, Hegel speaks of the state as the society of people legally related in which each counts as a person; the immediate concern of the state is not to promote morality, religion, or welfare, but to guarantee and actualize formal or abstract rights to person and property.[80] Only later does Hegel develop the idea of the modern state as an ethical substance that is more than a mere collection of legally respected persons, and as the bearer of a right that is understood in a much broader sense than abstract Roman-law rights of personality.[81] By turning now to the *Rechtsphilosophie* we can see how for Hegel the modern state has become an ethical substance whose laws are *Recht-an-sich*, so that the punishment meted out by the modern state is a vindication and restoration of right.

In his *Lectures on the Philosophy of History*, given around the same time as the lectures on the *Rechtsphilosophie*, Hegel describes the state as an "individual totality." Its constitution is one with the "substance and

---

[80] Prop 246, 252.

[81] On Hegel's use of the word *state*, see Hans Maier, "Einige Historische Vorbemerkungen zu Hegels Politischer Philosophie," pp. 151–165. Maier argues that there was an ambiguity in the language of Hegel's day regarding the meaning of *Staat*: it was used often as a metaphor for a machine, or something external; but some used it as a moral concept of value ("der Staat soll sein"). Maier argues that the later Hegel elevates the "normative" meaning of the term, but the Hegel of the first decade of the 1800s uses *Staat* to mean the uniting of masses for collective defense of their property claims (pp. 157–159). In other words, the early Hegel follows German-law tradition by identifying the state with defense of property, while the later Hegel explicitly rejects this view. Cf. Shlomo Avineri, *Hegel's Theory of the Modern State*, ch. 3, in support of Maier's account of the early Hegel's definition of "state." Cf. also Hugh A. Reyburn, *The Ethical Theory of Hegel*, p. 236. Reyburn notes that in the *Phenomenology* there is no great appreciation of the state, and he suggests that political circumstances—Germany's weakness—account for this.

spirit" of the people, with the art, religion, philosophy, and in general the culture of the people.[82] "The history of a state, its acts, that which its forefathers brought forth, belongs to the state and lives in its memories—all of this is its possession, it makes up its substance, its being."[83] In his *Lectures on the Philosophy of Religion*, also of the Berlin period, Hegel says that the "national spirit constitutes the substantial foundation within the individual . . . it is the absolute ground of faith. By this standard it is determined what counts as truth . . . all individuals are thus born into the faith of their forefathers."[84]

The Hegel of the *Rechtsphilosophie* refers to the state repeatedly as substance.[85] To violate the demands of right established by the state is to contradict myself, or my "substantial foundations."[86] I do not limit myself by obeying the laws of the state, for it is my very nature to act in this way. To say that the state is an ethical substance in which I share is to say that it is natural for me to act in the way people of this state act. This way of acting obtains the form of right in a state,[87] so that by acting according to the laws and practices regarded as right I am acting in consonance with my nature. Law is not command, but rather it stipulates "what we already do by our own reason": we do not steal not because the law says not to steal; we have laws against theft only to formalize our practice of respecting the property of our fellow citizens.[88] The posited law of the state articulates what was already *Recht-an-sich*.[89] Hegel says there is little for the legislative power to do, since laws are already determined implicitly (*an-sich*).[90] But by whom? What is the source of *Recht-an-sich*?

In saying that laws are already determined implicitly, Hegel is *not* falling back on a theory of natural law that sees law as properly determined by either divinity or some faculty of deductive reason, so that the origin of law is external to human willing:

> Laws of right are given by the state, and hold together the life of human beings; laws of right differ from laws of nature, which simply are, are valid, suffer no atrophy (although in particular cases they are violated). Here, in order to know what is law, we must pay attention to the normal patterns of nature. These laws (of nature) are correct; only our representation of them can be false. The standards of these laws are outside of us, and our cognition of them adds nothing

---

[82] PH 64–65(46).
[83] Ibid., 72(52).
[84] PRel 195.
[85] PH 72–73(52–53); Enz 514–517; PR 258.
[86] PR 126 and Rem.
[87] Ibid., 152.
[88] Rph VI, 4:603,25–26.
[89] PR 217 Z.
[90] Rph V, 3:749,22–27.

to them . . . only our cognition of them can be furthered. . . . But with laws of right, spirit raises itself . . . these laws are not so absolute as the laws of nature; they originate from men; man does not stop with existing laws, but rather claims to have within himself the standard of what is right.[91]

There can be no crimes against laws of nature as there are against laws of right, because "[i]n nature the highest test is, that a law above all is; in laws of right mere existence does not imply validity . . . opposition is possible here between what is and what should be."[92] Laws of right are made by human beings. But they are not arbitrary; they inhere in the ethical substance, which no single person makes, just as no one makes the constitution of a state.[93] For Hegel, a constitution does not arise at a determinate point in time, but rather it builds itself up in many stages, reflecting the "substance of the spirit of the people [*Volksgeist*]."[94] Laws reflect the values of the society in which we are educated. They change as the substance itself changes.[95] The laws are rooted in the spirit of the people and develop as the *Volksgeist* develops.

At one time laws *were* made, and Hegel speaks of the maker as the founder of the state, a figure often drawn larger than life:

> Laws are the ground or scaffold of a people, they belong to the oldest memories—they are ascribed to gods and heroes. . . . Lawgivers have a lasting influence. [One thinks of] Confucius, Manus, Moses, Solon, Numa. . . . The lawgivers are eternally honoured, and they are present in our daily life. But the groundings of these laws are often said to be older than these men, they are eternal, divine—[one thinks of] Antigone. In this way they *appear* as natural laws, something unchanging.[96]

Even though laws are made by individuals who seem to be gods, these laws are still the product of the *Volksgeist*; tyrannical laws are due not to the tyrant, but to the spirit of a people that accepts such laws: "It is false to say that through the power of a prince a nation could be deceived; deception occurs over particular things; but as to the laws, these belong to the people. The source of unfree laws lies not in the arbitrary will of an individual, but with the nature of the will of the people."[97] Invoking

---

[91] Rph V, Preface.

[92] Ibid. The point that there can be no crimes against laws of nature is an implication I have drawn from Hegel's passage; Hegel does note that in particular cases laws of nature are violated, but these cases are anomalies and don't earn the moral approbation crimes merit.

[93] PR 273 Rem, p. 178.

[94] Rph VI, 4:659,25–30.

[95] Rph I, 220,565–566; cf. PR 298.

[96] Rph VII, Preface, 4:918.

[97] Rph VII, 4:921–922; cf. JR 246.

the thought of Machiavelli, Hegel adds that the founder becomes superfluous once education (*Bildung*) instills obedience and eventually a rule
of law.[98] Hegel argues that law based *merely* on the arbitrary will of one
individual will not survive; he says that Charlemagne's constitution was
just, but it dissolved after his death because it was based not on the spirit
of the people but on one man.[99]

For Hegel, *Recht-an-sich* is implicit, it is already there, lying in wait. It
inheres in the *Volksgeist*. Its origin is the founder of the practices, laws,
and institutions that constitute the ethical life of the people. Some Hegel
scholars, I think unduly influenced by the *Phenomenology*, understand
Hegel to claim that the origin of right lies elsewhere, namely, in the mutual recognition of humans as free beings or persons. For example, Steven
Smith argues that for Hegel rights (as opposed to right—Smith is not careful to distinguish the two) "have their ground in the individual subject, or
Wille."[100] Hegel gives a "crypto-state-of-nature" theory of rights that is
based on the "struggle for recognition."[101] Smith writes that for Hegel
"the desire for recognition is the standard by which to judge the adequacy
of our political institutions and the quality of our civic life."[102] The "right
to recognition" is the modern state's "soul and purpose."[103] To Kurt Seelmann, too, in Hegel's view we are free when we are recognized by others
as a free person, and a crime is a wrong because it violates not *Recht-an-
sich* but the victim's whole person, thereby destroying the relation of recognition and respect.[104] Punishment, in this view, restores not *Recht-an-
sich* but the relation of mutual recognition and respect.[105] With this view
it is difficult to account for Hegel's claim that injuring one self-consciousness injures all. We might say that the criminal sets an example and therefore disturbs the tendency of all mutually to respect each other as persons,[106] but this is unconvincing and misses the point of Hegel's account
of *Recht-an-sich*. Hegel argues that the universal character of a crime is
not that it will be an example to others; its universality is already con-

---

[98] JR 247.

[99] PH 440(365); 444(368–369).

[100] Steven Smith, *Hegel's Critique of Liberalism*, p. 107.

[101] Ibid., p. 115.

[102] Ibid., p. 117. One wonders how a "desire" can be a "standard."

[103] Ibid., p. 123; cf. pp. x–xi, 114. Smith does write that ethical relations "precede the
will and provide it with a determinate content and focus" (p. 130), but he doesn't expand
adequately on the implications of this point for his claim elsewhere that in Hegel's view the
basis of right lies in mutual recognition.

[104] Kurt Seelmann, "Hegels Straftheorie in seinen *Grundlinien der Philosophie des
Rechts*." Both Seelmann and Smith rely heavily on the "master and slave" passage in the
Phenomenology in supporting their view that the origin of right is in mutual recognition.

[105] Ibid., p. 690.

[106] Ibid.

tained in the act, just as his punishment is already in the will of the criminal. To break the law is to violate our own nature, because *Recht-an-sich* is already in us. Hegel rejected already in 1811 the view that the origin of right is in mutual recognition: "Recognition of property is not based on reciprocity [*Gegenseitigkeit*]; *I acknowledge another's property not because he acknowledges my property . . . but because the will is to be acknowledged in and for itself [an und für sich].*"[107]

Hegel does think that human willing is an important path to right; only that is right to me which I will. But individual wills do not create right, they approach it. Right already exists implicitly. "Government is the conscious power of unconscious custom," and historically "it is *not* the case that each citizen recommends a law and all agree to it."[108]

In Hegel's view a twofold movement is involved in the determination of right: one movement is that of will, but the other is of the ethical substance, in which we exist at first immediately, but which we eventually come to will for ourselves. Hegel's well-known criticism of classical liberal contract theory is based largely on his insistence that right is determined not solely by subjective willing, but that it exists already as *Recht-an-sich* in the *Sitte* (customs) of the ethical substance: "the subjective will also has a substantial life . . . the ethical whole, the state."[109] For Hegel, there is no necessary conflict between willing one's own particular interest and satisfaction and willing according to the dictates of a rational state: "Just as little is it the case that when I do the good, this is necessarily opposed to my satisfaction. The distinction does not resolve into incompatibility of the both sides; rather, I do the universal as subject, for in that lies my satisfaction."[110]

In the previous chapter on Hegel's conception of freedom, we saw that for Hegel laws are right if human beings can be understood to be free living in accord with them. We are free under laws we know we have the possibility of renouncing; this possibility is essential to our being free under law. We appropriate as our own content the laws of our ethical community by an act of *begreifen*, or comprehension; we choose the laws—originally given to us—because they are justified to us. The laws of the state are right because we are free in them. Now we can connect up this conception of freedom with the conception of ethical substance. Hegel claims that human beings are born into a community in which they live unreflectively. This community shapes who they are; it is their substance.

---

[107] Prop 237, my emphasis. While the passage cited speaks of the origin not of right but of property, I think we can infer from it that Hegel thinks the origin of right is not in mutual recognition, since in Hegel's view property is an essential embodiment of right.

[108] Ibid., 247.

[109] PH 55(38).

[110] Rph V, 3:388,1–18.

But they are truly free only by fulfilling the demands of this community when they choose their commitment to it upon reflection and with an insight into the rationality of the demands this commitment entails. These laws, practices, and institutions, having always guided the individual, as child and adult, were always right, or *Recht-an-sich*; but an individual is free in acting in accord with the demands of these laws and practices only when he wills them on the basis of insight into the rationality of the demands.

The vision of ethical substance we find in the early Hegel is couched in the language of Spirit rather than of right and freedom. In the *Phenomenology* Hegel speaks of the consciousness of the Greek citizen as limited and immediate—the citizen of the polis does not identify himself with Spirit. His defect is a failure to know that he is really a part of a cosmic vehicle that survives his polis. To agree that this is a defect requires we assent to a teleological conception of history and a metaphysics that sees ethical substances as essentially transparochial. Besides being implausible, the account contradicts passages elsewhere in the *Phenomenology* on war and punishment that are coherent only by assuming that ethical substances are essentially parochial. In the *Rechtsphilosophie* the defect of the Greek citizen is not (merely) his lack of prophetic knowledge, but his blind, unreflective attitude toward the practices and laws of his community. The Greek is unfree because he lacks knowledge of the rationality of these practices and laws, of their right. Whereas in the *Phenomenology* Hegel says of the Greeks that they were only Spirit *an-sich*, the later Hegel says that the Greeks were not truly free, because they obeyed laws out of mere trust. His account of ethical substances can be understood, without assent to a metaphysical postulate that there is a cosmic vehicle called *Geist*, as part of an account of freedom. This is not to say that the later vision is unambivalently on the "parochial" side, or is unproblematic. As we shall see in the next section and in chapter 6, to be free does not mean to reconcile oneself to whatever parochial laws and practices exist in one's society: Hegel thinks there are standards of rationality that let us criticize some laws and practices, though he is elusive about what these standards are.

4.3.3   Is the Vision Plausible?

For Hegel, the objective reason for punishing a criminal is that justice demands this: *Recht-an-sich* lies in wait for the criminal who injures the community of which he is a part. The community is the criminal's own substance, and in injuring it the criminal injures himself. Punishment vindicates and restores right. In the *Rechtsphilosophie* Hegel characterizes the modern state as the community that is the ethical substance of its members, so that the criminal laws of this state are *Recht-an-sich*. These laws are objectively justified, are right, and when we understand this, we are free in obeying them.

Hegel's view presupposes a great deal. Hegel is a "communitarian" insofar as he rejects the classical liberal assumption that the authority a state has over its citizens derives from the consent each citizen gives to be constrained by the state, a consent expressed by a social contract.[111] Hegel thinks that if we are to be free in a state we must consent in some sense to its laws. But, for Hegel, we are born into our community and it shapes us through *Bildung* (education, cultivation, formation) into who we are, so that when we arrive at the age classical liberals regard as the age of consent, our choice of the standards by which we think we should be guided has already been determined for us.

Inasmuch as Hegel's project is to show the importance of community and the inadequacy of classical liberal accounts of the origin of our laws and practices, it is a project we might want to support (though few classical liberals claim to be giving an historical account of laws' origin). But Hegel's project is far more ambitious. Hegel also means to show that modern states are rational, their laws expressive of a shared conception of right; and this project will seem troubling, if not utterly preposterous and irresponsible, given our experience with religious, ethnic, tribal, racial, gender, and class conflicts dividing not only modern states, but even our own cities and local communities. Is Hegel's vision of a modern state as an ethical substance whose laws are *Recht-an-sich* at all plausible?

In considering this question here, I shall focus on the following issues: How does Hegel justify his claim that the modern state is an ethical substance, and that we are free by living in accordance with its laws, practices, and institutions, which are right? Does Hegel leave room to say that some modern states are not ethical substances whose laws are *Recht-an-sich*, or does he rather leave us unable to criticize a state such as Nazi Germany, whose laws strike us as terribly *wrong* and *irrational*? And finally, does Hegel's vision of the modern state as an ethical substance assume that there are homogeneous community standards, an assumption that would seem patently false given the great deal of disagreement there typically is among members of communities, and over so many issues of importance?

We have already seen that sometimes Hegel suggests that right is something parochial, not universal;[112] if this is so, how could Hegel lend criti-

---

[111] On the communitarian/liberal debate, see, for example, Nancy Rosenblum, ed., *Liberalism and the Moral Life*; Michael Sandel, *Liberalism and the Limits of Justice*; and Amy Gutmann, "Communitarian Critics of Liberalism," pp. 308–322.

[112] See sec. 4.2.

cal support to the citizen of a particular ethical substance that has its own parochial standards of right that we want to say are terribly wrong? Was Nazi Germany an ethical substance whose laws are *Recht-an-sich*? Is *any* modern state?

Sometimes Hegel seems to suggest that *by definition* any set of customs or way of doing things is right. Socrates' death was just because to his ethical substance Socrates was destructive.[113] Yet Hegel says also that Socrates' death was tragic, because it resulted from a confrontation between two legitimate claims of right: the absolute right Socrates could claim inasmuch as his insistence on subjecting the law to his own judgment of its rightness is in Hegel's view historically necessary; and the relative right of the ethical substance as manifested in Athenian laws and practices.[114] So Hegel *does* have some conception of right that transcends particular community conceptions of right, for he thinks Socrates was right to criticize his Athens; and Hegel also thinks that an ethical substance whose practices and laws include, say, slavery is not *Recht-an-sich*. But Hegel says also that *Recht-an-sich* is a feature of states. In his discussion of international law he notes that there is no power to decide *Recht-an-sich* when states dispute. Hegel concludes not that in theory there is no *Recht-an-sich* apart from what a state declares, but that *Recht-an-sich* must be realizable, and where there is no judge it is not; it remains an "ought."[115] Hegel has a philosophy of history that he calls an account of the development of world spirit, and he says the right of this universal spirit is highest; world history is the judge among states: "Weltgeschichte ist Weltgericht."[116] This philosophy of history is premised on the metaphysical view that ultimately history is the realization of freedom. Freedom is the standard by which world history judges among states, and by which we can criticize particular ethical substances.

Hegel thinks we can criticize existing practices by using parochial standards, standards immanent in these practices; but Hegel also claims to have the justifications of practices—he not only uses the principles he finds immanent in the practices of marriage or punishment, or in the institutions of private property or hereditary monarchy, to criticize the actual practices or institutions when they diverge from these principles, but he claims to justify these as opposed to alternative practices or institutions. Hegel takes the universalistic position that there are certain practices and laws any rational modern state *must* have. The force of this must is metaphysical.[117] Hegel ultimately justifies his claim that the modern

---

[113] HP 1:439, 443–444, 446.
[114] Rph V, 3:309,14–16.
[115] PR 330 Z; cf. PR 333 Rem.
[116] Ibid., 340.
[117] I shall say more about how Hegel avoids cultural or historical relativism in sec. 6.2.

state is an ethical substance, that its practices, laws, and institutions are
right, and that through them we realize our freedom, by a metaphysics
that sees history as the development of *Geist*, which is instantiated in
world-historical peoples, with the modern state as its final instantiation.
Freedom, to Hegel, is not *just* reconciling oneself to whatever community
in which one lives; nor are these laws, practices, and institutions of our
community right merely because we come to feel at home in them—this
would be a "procedural" conception of right and freedom. Hegel, rather,
adopts a substantive conception; he believes there are specific institutions
a rational modern state must have. This lets him criticize certain parochial
ethical substances such as Nazi Germany or apartheid South Africa. Hegel's claim that we are free by obeying the laws of the modern state rests
on a metaphysical conception that sees history as progressing toward its
telos, the characteristic feature of which is a modern state with those rational institutions Hegel describes in the *Philosophy of Right*. Hegel implies that all modern states will of necessity come to have these rational
institutions; and as Steven Smith has noted, this concept of rational necessity in history rests on "an apparently benign faith in historical prog-
ress which the experiences of the 20th century have done much to undermine."[118]

The necessity or rationality of the institutions Hegel describes in the
Philosophy of Right—private property, contract, marriage, hereditary
monarchy and others—is a teleological necessity. If we reject the idea of
teleological necessity, as I think we should, what is left to justify these
institutions? Steven Smith, acknowledging that Hegel is not clear about
what standard there is for saying something is rational, suggests that in
Hegel's view an institution is rational if it adapts and survives over time:
"rationality is a fully functional concept."[119] This is an attractive alternative account that I might endorse but for one defect: merely to show a
thing has a function need not be to show it is rational or justified. Some
critics of legal punishment acknowledge that the practice has a function,
but they do not thereby conclude punishment is rational.[120] For Hegel, to
say a practice is rational is to say it is necessary, and Smith's account of
what Hegel means by rationality, that a practice is rational if it serves a
function, does not capture the sense of necessity I think Hegel means. The
functionalist argument Smith imputes to Hegel seems to me to be a modified version of the view that a practice is justified merely because it exists;
Smith seems only to add the requirement that the practice must exist for
some time and therefore prove to be functional. We know that Hegel ex-

---

[118] Steven Smith, *Hegel's Critique of Liberalism*, p. 212.
[119] Ibid., p. 225.
[120] For example, Karl Menninger sees punishment as functioning to release our primitive
urges for vengeance, urges he thinks we should be above (*The Crime of Punishment*).

plicitly rejects the view that its mere existence justifies a practice. There is something right about what Smith says—that a practice exists and maintains itself, and serves a function, is a point in its favor. But Hegel demands more of an institution or practice he regards as rational. By virtue of its persistent, functional existence, the practice becomes a part of our ethical life, our culture, our *Bildung*; it shapes us, becomes a part of ourselves. *This* makes it justified.[121]

This suggests a third way we might understand Hegel to justify his view that the modern state is our ethical substance and that its practices, laws, and institutions are right. This interpretation is suggested by several passages in Hegel's texts, but in ignoring Hegel's metaphysics it is more a revision than an accurate account of his views, although the revisionist account *is* based on points Hegel did make. I think such a revision is warranted, for it lets us take advantage of Hegel's insights without compromising what I take to be a modern commitment to nonfoundational justifications. According to this view, Hegel thinks commitment to the practices and institutions of our ethical community is justified because only by participating in them do we give meaning to our lives. Hegel holds that individuals "only have worth as an appearance of the ethical substance,"[122] that man "can't be simply a private person,"[123] that "in ethical life the individual is on an eternal plane" and has his essence and meaning "solely in the whole,"[124] that in the ethical substance each individual has his place, "is something," finds himself and his meaning:[125] "The state, its laws, its arrangements, constitute the rights of its members . . . what their ancestors have produced, belongs to them and lives in their memory. All is their possession, just as they are possessed by it; for it constitutes their substance [*Substanz*], their being."[126] By virtue of their existence, the practices of our ethical life are already a part of us, and we have expectations that hinge on their being there.[127] We will not have a

---

[121] Cf. sec. 2.2, on Hegel's substantive conception of rationality: a practice is rational that embodies the values of the community in which one has grown up and partakes. Cf. sec. 3.2.2, on how we are free in commitments that make us who we are, that constitute our identity. And cf. sec. 6.2, on how for Hegel something is rational if it constitutes our identity.

[122] Rph V, 3:503,11–13.

[123] Rph III, 206,23.

[124] Hegel, "System der Sittlichkeit," p. 480.

[125] PH 99(74).

[126] Ibid., 72(52).

[127] Something like the argument that what is is good in part because it is has been defended by Robert Nozick. Nozick, in defending the right of "domestic protective associations" to have a monopoly on the power to punish, argues that they do not deserve to have this power, but the power is still legitimate because people expect them to have this power; people count on it. Similarly, teenagers may happen to meet regularly at a certain shop; everyone knows they all meet there and all count on convening there. If you try a different

meaningful life identifying with just *any* set of shared practices. Hegel's point goes beyond Edmund Burke's, that without commitment to *a* state "no one generation could link with the other" and "men would become little better than the flies of a summer."[128] The reason our life has meaning only by participating in the shared ethical life of our community is that *this* ethical life is special; it has shaped who we are and in it we are at home.

It is essential to see that this argument, which we might call Hegel's "existential" justification of commitment to the laws of a state, does not pretend to be a justification of particular laws. When Hegel speaks of individuals having their place in the world as obedient members of their states, he is stepping back from the details about our practices, trying to reconcile individuals to practices as a whole.[129] Later we shall see that Hegel *does* criticize particular laws of modern states; indeed, I shall argue that the critical power of his political theory is one of its most distinctive features.

Hegel's "existential" argument, that we are part of a greater whole, part of a tradition that outlives us, which by identifying with gives us meaning, is convincing only if we can understand ourselves to be at home in our state. I think this is not a weakness but an advantage of the "existential" over the metaphysical account of Hegel's argument: it does not pretend to command compulsory or logical assent, which, given the nature of the activity about which we are speaking, justifying practices as a whole, makes appropriate its emphasis on persuasion rather than logical compulsion. Hegel points to our connectedness, to the ways in which we share in a common identity, with the hope of persuading us that the power that punishes is "we," and not "them" against "me." To be sure, Hegel uses language suggesting he thinks his account is not merely persuasive but correct. From his rhetoric it seems clear enough that Hegel assumes the role not of persuader but of teacher. But I can see no reason why this prevents us from regarding his account as not an exposition of metaphysical truths but an interpretation aiming to persuade.

But can Hegel hope to persuade us? To a citizen who does not feel at home in or a part of the state, this "existential" justification does not really justify obedience to the state. The persuasiveness of Hegel's argument depends on the possibility of our reconciling ourselves to this state and its laws and practices in general (as opposed to agreeing with every particular law). As theorist, Hegel tries to persuade the citizen of the mod-

---

place, you won't be successful. The shop does not deserve, is not entitled, to be the meeting place. It just is (*Anarchy, State, and Utopia*, p. 140).

[128] Edmund Burke, *Reflections on the Revolution in France* (Harmondsworth, Eng.: Penguin, 1968), p. 193.

[129] See sec. 6.3.

ern state that its laws and practices are essentially rational, when they are. Hegel argues that our state is our substance and gives us our identity, makes us who we are through our having been brought up in this state. But is it plausible to assume, as Hegel does, that there is a single community with which we all identify? And even if there were such a community, is it the state? Some of us think of the state as a bureaucratic machine that *undermines* community values.[130]

The latter objection is perhaps the easier for Hegel to meet. Hegel *defines* "state" to mean an ethical substance, a community with shared ethical practices and values; and while this is counter to ordinary usage, including the usage of *Staat* in his own Germany,[131] it is perfectly legitimate for him to stipulate a definition for special purposes. Which community should a San Franciscan think of as her version of Hegel's *Rechtstaat*, or ethical substance? The United States? California? San Francisco? Each make laws she is obligated to obey. Hegel seems to have in mind the nation-state when he speaks of the *Staat*; but insofar as we identify with more local communities and share in the ethical life distinct to them, they are *part* of our ethical substance.[132] The former objection, that there is no ethical substance with which any of us identify, is more serious. The governments to which we are subject rule over peoples of different cultures, heritages, religions, and ethnicities. Many individuals identify themselves more closely with their street gang than with their state. If Hegel is telling those who by any objective measure are not a part of the state, are actively excluded from it, that this state is their substance, then there is something very wrong with his project. But, as we shall see in chapter 6, Hegel does not insist that those who are not at home in the state nevertheless feel at home there. Rather, he uses his conception of the modern state as ethical substance as a standard by which he criticizes states in which the free will of its members "does not come into existence."[133]

For Hegel, laws or practices are right to us if we can understand them to be integral parts of an ethical life in which we are at home; but to those who are not at home in this ethical life, who live in a community divided

---

[130] See, for example, John Leo's editorial in *U.S. News and World Report*, July 24, 1989, p. 56: Leo, complaining of liberal efforts to protect the right of the homeless "to sleep wherever one collapses," argues that "as always, the Achilles' heel of liberalism is its reflexive tendency to convert every social or moral or political problem into a dramatic confrontation between a beleaguered individual and the all-powerful, menacing state. The community is nowhere to be found." Leo thinks such liberal efforts, aimed at the state, destroy community values. What I find interesting is his explicit separation of "state" and "community," a separation Hegel would not have made.

[131] Cf. note 81, above.

[132] In the following pages I shall use *state* to refer not only to a nation-state, but also to more local communities that make laws and are granted police powers.

[133] See ch. 5, note 35, and corresponding text.

and lacking a shared sense of right, the laws and practices of the community will not be right—this is the position Hegel takes in criticizing Roman law.[134]

We might think that in claiming that the modern state is an ethical substance, and that its laws and practices reflect a shared sense of right, Hegel assumes there must be a homogeneity or unity, at least in moral judgment, among members of a modern state, in which case our own political experience would compel us to reject Hegel's claims. We are of different social classes with conflicting interests, of different genders with unequal opportunities, of different racial, ethnic, and religious groups. What to one person is law and justice, to another is repression and injustice. What to one is a moral and religious tradition, to another is intolerant fanaticism and superstition.

But I think it is a mistake to think that Hegel assumes that modern societies are the coherent happy unities he thinks existed in ancient Greece. Hegel is quite aware that his Germany is no classical Athens. He acknowledges that its members go off "in every direction" to satisfy their particular needs, "accidental caprices," and "subjective desires,"[135] and that it is easy to lose sight of the ethical order and assume that the state is

---

[134] In the *Philosophy of History*, Hegel contrasts the origins of Greek ethical life with those of Roman law; he suggests that the unattractiveness and ultimate failure of the Roman Empire are due to Rome's lack of an ethical substance that Roman law could reflect. Prior to the Trojan War Hegel says the Greeks lacked an ethical bond. But through his personal strength (as opposed to force) Agamemnon assembled the Greeks and led them to victory, and the collectivity he created, while not resulting in a lasting political union, provided the foundation upon which the Greek poets created an eternal picture of the youth and spirit of Greece; the poets created a *Bild* that became the basis of the *Bildung* that shaped Greek ethical life and created the ethical substance. In Hegel's view the Greek ethical substance was a collective shaping, an origin very different from the classical liberal social contract (PH 277–294[225–239]). Rome, in contrast to Greece, was made by force (*Gewalt*) as an asylum for criminals and rabble (PH 344–346[283–285]; 360[296]—Sibree translates "Räubern" as "freebooters"). There was no ethical bond keeping Rome together, only the force of formal law (PH 345–347[284–285]). Rome lacked a natural morality or family ties; wives were seized by conquest (PH 348[286]). To Hegel, Rome was a spiritless unity (*geistlose Einheit*) (PH 373[308]). The lack of Roman spirit is reflected even in Roman games—the Romans, unlike the Greeks, were mainly spectators; "their own spirit was not in the games" (PH 357[293–294]; cf. PH 297–298[242–243] on Greek games). Lacking ethical bonds, Romans took flight into Stoicism, Epicureanism, and Skepticism, "all of which sought to make one indifferent to what reality presented" (PH 385[317–318]). Hegel says that this lack of an ethical bond is reflected in the harsh Roman law. Rather than custom determining law, as is the case in Greece, in Rome formal law is the basis of Roman custom (PH 351[289]). Hegel's judgment of Rome—it is harsh, cold, indifferent (cf. HP 2:234–235)—and his suggestion that Rome fell because of its "particularization," its lack of an ethical basis for unity (PH 374[307–308]), reflect his view that an already existing custom and shared spirit must be the basis of just law.

[135] PR 185.

nothing but an association of different individuals satisfying their particularity. The central task of Hegel's political philosophy is to get us to look behind this appearance, what Hegel calls "civil society," and see the underlying unity and connectedness of its members, to view this collection of people sharing certain practices and traditions not merely as civil society, but as a "state," with all the ethical connotations that word has for Hegel. Hegel believes that civil society, a realm of difference and alienation, can become coherent in thought. The early aesthetic vision of Hegel, which calls for "a new mythology," transforms into a philosophy of right that understands an essential unity and rationality to be implicit in civil society. To say that there is an essential unity or rationality is not to say that we all agree about every moral judgment. It is to say that despite the differences among us—gender, race, class, national origin, occupation, religion—we all share in a common identity.

Hegel must leave open the possibility that the modern state is not our home. We shall consider whether he does. But his project is aimed essentially at getting us to see the positive connections that exist between us, so that we will come to think as a community. Hegel argues we will be justified in thinking in this way: his task is not, like Burke's, to get us to be happy in pleasing illusions.

Five

Hegel's Immanent Criticism of the Practice of Legal Punishment

5.1 Ideals in Practice

Political theorists are not often taken seriously. Their ideas are expressed mainly in academic journals unread by those who practice politics. The theorist typically is relegated to the far corner of a university social science department, tolerated, perhaps, out of a sense of duty to our intellectual traditions. One reason for this is that most theorists seem to have nothing to say of relevance to practitioners, to those working within our institutions and practices and coping with the problems of everyday life. Theorists are often perceived as outsiders, occupied with the profound and timeless, not the mundane and ordinary. I am convinced that political theory must speak to practitioners. The best theorists, while necessarily distanced from existing practices in order to get a more perspicuous view of them, return from their journey to step back inside the practice, in order to engage with practitioners.

Hegel confronts the philosophical issue "why punish?" by developing an elaborate theory that sees the laws of a modern rational state as the articulation of right; that understands practices, institutions, and laws to be right if we are free by living in accord with them; and that claims that the criminal, who violates right, violates his own implicit will, his own ethical substance, and that punishment by the state expresses his true will, and makes him free. But Hegel does more than give this justification of the practice as a whole. In the *Philosophy of Right*, and in his lectures on the *Rechtsphilosophie*, Hegel steps "inside" the practice; he uses his philosophical conception of why we punish at all to resolve problems commonly faced by those working within the criminal justice system. It is this turn to the practical, this stepping back inside the practice, that is distinct about Hegel's political philosophy. It is a turn that previous commentators have not seen Hegel take. In this chapter we shall see how Hegel is an immanent critic of legal punishment. He uses his theory of why we punish at all, of the principle immanent in the practice, to criticize features of the actual practice that do not accord with that principle.

Legal punishment is a complex practice, itself consisting of several "subpractices," including, among others, codification of crimes, choke hold, citizen's arrest, stakeout, pretrial detention, parole, plea bargaining, bail, habeas corpus, execution, fines, imprisonment, arraignments. All of these can be grouped into one of five subpractices: lawmaking, clutching (arrest and pretrial detention), the determination of guilt, sentencing, and the infliction of punishment.[1] Distinct problems arise within each of these subpractices. Consider the case of a murderer we convict, sentence to death, and execute. If one asks "why punish?" in this context, one might mean any of the following distinct questions: Why punish *for murder?*— which takes the general form, for what actions should we punish? Why may *the state* punish this person? Why punish *this* murderer? Is punishment appropriate if this person did not intend to commit a crime, perhaps because she was unaware of or unable to prevent what she did? Why punish *by execution*? Other problems are also typically raised from within the practice: Should we punish a person whose guilt was established only by inclusion of evidence illegally obtained? Should we use expedients such as plea bargaining?

One promising strategy for resolving such problems is to apply the principle(s) we think immanent in the practice as a whole. To decide whether to punish someone who is "insane" or who cops a plea, or to inflict capital punishment, we ask whether doing so is consistent with our conception of why we punish at all.[2] This strategy, of immanent criticism, is the one Hegel adopts. For Hegel, the reason we legally punish is to vindicate right. Hegel understands the practice to be justified on not utilitarian but retributive grounds: we punish for the sake of justice. Hegel's interpretation of legal punishment rests on his account of the free will and of right, and on his interpretation of social practices as a whole. In this chapter we shall see how Hegel counsels us about the practical problems that arise within the criminal justice system by applying to the subpractices of legal punishment in which the problems emerge the retributive principle that legal punishment vindicates right and makes the criminal free. We shall see how Hegel is a practical theorist of legal punishment; but we shall also see how the power of his theory is circumscribed. I do not argue that Hegel the theorist provides the solutions to all the problems vexing judges, lawyers and legislators—about some problems Hegel is ambivalent; other times he refrains from taking a position on a partic-

---

[1] "Clutching" is a term used by Joel Feinberg in his essay "Crime, Clutchability, and Individuated Treatment," in *Doing and Deserving*, pp. 252–271. My use of the term is broader; Feinberg does not regard someone held in pretrial detention as being clutched (p. 265). I discuss clutching, and develop the idea of "subpractices" of legal punishment, to a much greater extent in my *Punishment: Theory and Practice*. For my purposes here, the division of legal punishment into five subpractices serves only to order the discussion in this chapter.

[2] See Mark Tunick, *Punishment: Theory and Practice*, ch. 1, sec. 1.

ular controversy, on the grounds that there are limits to what philosophy can say about the details of a practice. At these times Hegel offers little guidance. The power of his theory is limited; but Hegel *does* offer guidance, and guidance is much needed in steering through a practice as contested as legal punishment.

5.2   Lawmaking: What Should Be Made Criminal?

At the lawmaking stage of legal punishment, we want to know what actions merit the imposition of the penal process. According to some utilitarians, for whom the purpose of punishment is to augment social utility, we should punish only those actions that tend to decrease social utility.[3] For example, to Richard Posner, who gives a modified utilitarian account, the criminal law exists to promote economic efficiency and maximize wealth: "The major function of criminal law in a capitalist society is to prevent people from bypassing the system of voluntary, compensated exchange—the 'market', explicit or implicit—in situations where, because transaction costs are low, the market is a more efficient method of allocating resources than forced exchange."[4] Given this account of why we punish at all, Posner argues that we should punish only those actions that bypass markets and therefore create inefficiencies in the economy. To some retributivists, for whom punishment serves not to augment social utility however understood, but to express society's condemnation of morally blameworthy acts, we should punish only those actions that society regards as morally wrong.[5]

In Hegel's view, we legally punish to vindicate right, and so we should punish only those actions that violate right. But what counts as violating right? Utilitarians such as Jeremy Bentham might also agree that we should punish only actions violating right, but they would mean by right whatever augments social utility or promotes economic efficiency. Some classical liberals would mean by right the rights individuals have to their person and property, what Hegel calls abstract rights. Hegel means by right the contents of the free will: practices, institutions, and laws are right if we are free in them. For Hegel, right includes the abstract right to

---

[3] Jeremy Bentham, *An Introduction to the Principles of Morals and Legislation.*

[4] Richard Posner, "An Economic Theory of the Criminal Law," p. 1195. For technical reasons Posner distinguishes his view from a utilitarian theory; see ibid. p. 1196, note 9.

[5] Henry M. Hart, Jr., "The Aims of the Criminal Law"; cf. Joel Feinberg, *Doing and Deserving.* Feinberg himself opposes the view that we should use the criminal law to punish inherently immoral acts that otherwise do not harm or cause offense to others; see Joel Feinberg, *The Moral Limits of the Criminal Law,* vol. 1, Introduction; and vol. 3, chs. 17 and 18.

property, but also the moral right of conscience, and the rights connected with the commitments of ethical life in which we come to our freedom.[6] Consequently, Hegel thinks that we should make criminal not merely actions that violate the abstract right to property.

It is easy to miss this point. Because Hegel places his account of crime in the section "Abstract Right,"[7] some Hegel scholars infer that he thinks only violations of the abstract right to one's person and property should be made criminal.[8] But, for Hegel, crime is an attack on an embodiment of the free will, and though property is such an embodiment it is not the only, nor the highest one.[9] In his discussion in "Abstract Right" Hegel remarks that crime, "so far" and "to begin with," is specified as the violation of rights to property, indicating that as his account develops, so too will his conception of what counts as a crime.[10] As we proceed in the *Philosophy of Right* Hegel tells us that wrong is an injury to abstract rights *and* to welfare.[11] Once we get to the account of the state, the highest content of the free will, we are told that a civil servant commits a crime in failing to perform his duty,[12] and that an injury to the state or to the person of the prince is the highest crime.[13] Hegel would oppose classical liberals like John Stuart Mill who insist that there can be no victimless crimes;[14] for Hegel, treason is one of the highest crimes, even though such an act may have no assignable victim. Crimes include not merely individual but social harms, including the violation of the customs and values of

[6] On the connection Hegel sees between right and freedom, see the introduction to chapter 3.

[7] Hegel divides the *Philosophy of Right* into three sections: "Abstract Right," "Moralität," and "Sittlichkeit" (Ethical Life). In the first section he gives an "abstract," or incomplete, account of social reality that recognizes only persons with legal rights. The account in "Abstract Right" brackets all particular features or ethical commitments individuals have and is therefore inadequate. In the second section, a richer (what Hegel calls more "concrete") account of this same social reality is given: persons now are viewed as individuals with intentions, purposes, and moral responsibilities—but we still bracket their social commitments, such as to family, civil society, state. In the final section, what Hegel claims is the richest or most concrete account of social reality, the individual is viewed as entirely situated in the various commitments of ethical life. For discussion, see "The Structure of Hegel's *Philosophy of Right*," chapter 8 in Mark Tunick, "The Justification of Legal Punishment: Hegel's *Rechtsphilosophie* as Practical Theory."

[8] For example, Peter Stillman, "Hegel's Idea of Punishment," pp. 169–171, 180.

[9] Rph V, 3:300–301.

[10] PR 95 Rem.

[11] Rph VI, 4:585,32–33; cf. PR 229.

[12] PR 294 Rem.

[13] Ibid., 282 Rem.

[14] John Stuart Mill argues in *On Liberty* that "over himself, over his own body and mind, the individual is sovereign" and that coercion of the criminal is justified only for the "protection of his fellow creatures, individually or collectively" (pp. 69, 146). Where there is no individual or collective "victim," there is no crime, and no justified punishment.

our ethical community. In Hegel's view, there are standards of right implicit in the spirit of a people who share in an ethical substance; there is a social morality, violations of which count as crimes. Hegel thinks the criminal law should proscribe not only acts that violate individual rights, but also acts that are immoral though they do not violate the abstract rights of any assignable victim.[15]

In holding that a society's criminal law reflects its shared sense of right, Hegel clearly opposes those who would restrict the scope of the criminal law to morally neutral acts; but also, as a consequence, he commits himself to what seems to be a relativist position that sees as futile any effort to determine by abstract, universal principles the proper content of the criminal law, futile for the reason that this content depends essentially on the spirit of the particular people.[16] Hegel gives the example of how the Egyptians did not punish for theft if the thief informed against himself, and they would even allow such thieves to keep a fourth of what they had stolen. Hegel says this made sense in Egypt because the Egyptians valued cunning, and such a practice would encourage this "virtue."[17]

For a society deeply divided about what is right and wrong, as ours is regarding many acts—abortion, flag burning, consensual homosexual sodomy, distribution of pornography—Hegel's principle that the law reflects the people's ethical substance is not helpful. Hegel does say that positive laws should be limited to the external character of actions and should not concern "inner" feelings.[18] He says that the Ten Commandments are true and rational but are not suitable as a criminal code, precisely because they concern our "inner" thoughts.[19] But the commandment against adultery, or a law prohibiting abortion or homosexual sodomy, proscribes not thoughts but actions. Are such laws right? By in-

[15] Peter Nicholson argues that for Hegel wrong means not merely illegal but immoral, and therefore to break the law is to act immorally; wrongs are immoral *because* it is immoral to violate law. By arguing that wrongs are immoral only because it is immoral to disobey the law in general, Nicholson suggests that for Hegel all particular laws are established independently of moral standards. But for Hegel some particular laws *are* determined by moral standards. See Peter Nicholson, "Hegel on Crime," pp. 116–117.

[16] Hegel says also that contemporary conditions, the danger of the moment, and other contingent factors determine the content of a particular criminal code (PR 234).

[17] PH 254(205): "Theft, we are told, was forbidden; but the law commanded that thieves should inform against themselves. If they did so, they were not punished, but, on the contrary, were allowed to keep a fourth part of what they had stolen. This perhaps was designed to excite and keep in exercise that cunning for which the Egyptians were so celebrated." Hegel is not advocating this practice; Egyptian customs were in his view not rational. Hegel distinguishes between practices that are relatively justified and practices that are absolutely justified. See my discussion in chapter 6, where I take up the problem of whether Hegel is an ethical relativist.

[18] PR 213, 270 Z; Rph V, 3:649–650; Rph VI, 4:540,24–28.

[19] Rph III, 219,13–17.

voking his conception of why we punish at all, Hegel offers an important alternative to the classical liberal account of the proper scope of the criminal law. But when we want to know whether to make criminal actions that are not violations of abstract rights, threats to the institutions of the state, or affronts to what is indisputably society's shared sense of right, Hegel offers us little guidance.

5.3   Clutching: Hegel on Political Crime

At the stage of clutching, or arrest and pretrial detention, the modern state confronts the suspect, and the suspect might ask, who are *you* to take hold of me? By identifying clutching as a distinct aspect of the practice of legal punishment, we are able more clearly to articulate concerns about the practice that are closely connected to fundamental questions regarding the nature and extent of legitimate state authority: Why may the *state* punish? Is disobedience of its laws ever justified? What limits are there to state interference in our private lives? While these issues are seldom directly raised in our criminal justice system, they are relevant to two sorts of issues that *are* occasionally raised in practice. The first sort, concerning the extent of legitimate state interference, is more common. To what extent may the police search and seize those suspected of committing a wrong or regulate our lives to prevent us from committing wrongs in the future? The second sort of issue concerns the nature of state authority: Is it just to punish someone who acts in protest against the state? Is it just to punish what we might call political crimes?[20]

In this section we shall focus on Hegel's views on the latter issue. But Hegel says a few things about the former issue as well, and it is worth considering these. Hegel does not treat systematically the issue of the limits to state interference and the extent to which the state may clutch, but there is a suggestive passage in his first series of lectures. Hegel criticizes Johann Gottlieb Fichte's conception of a police state, where "one can't go out without his pass," as a "gallery, where everyone always watches everyone." Evidently Hegel thinks this is too intrusive. In a later series of lectures Hegel finds it "difficult to say" what counts as a justified ground of suspicion, noting that we must balance the right of the police to clutch on suspicion with the interest we have in personal freedom.[21] And in the earlier lectures Hegel says that "we can accept that the police may not enter a house without special orders, for the inner goings on of the family

---

[20] On the concept of political crime, see Gustav Radbruch, "Die Überzeugungsverbrecher"; Stephen Schafer, *The Political Criminal*; and Austin Turk, *Political Criminality*.
[21] Rph VI, 4:593,9–16.

must not be observed." Something is wrong if one sees police officers everywhere. Hegel says a secret police would be better, so long as its aim is to secure a free public life,[22] but he describes the practice in London of rewarding police spies for their "catches," thereby giving them a subjective interest in imputing crimes to others, as "the greatest abyss of corruption."[23]

To Hegel the point of clutching is to further the welfare of all and preserve the abstract rights of each. Hegel thinks the point of having police is to secure the safety of person and property in general and to secure our subsistence and welfare as our right, as necessary to our freedom.[24] The police do not just annul wrong, they hinder it.[25] On the basis of his interpretation of the purpose of the police, Hegel argues that the clutching of possibly innocent suspects is justified on the grounds that to further the public welfare we need not merely respond to wrongs that occur, but prevent them from occurring. This means that measures are needed that limit otherwise just (*rechtlich*) actions.[26] The police can require us to be careful so we do not injure others accidentally.[27]

Hegel maintains that civil society has a duty to secure the subsistence and welfare of its members, a duty that corresponds to the "right" of civil society to wrench these members away from their families and make them dependent on civil society,[28] and this shapes his position on the other issue raised by the subpractice of clutching, the issue concerning the very nature of legitimate state authority: is it just to punish political criminals?

Given his reputation as philosopher of the Prussian state and archconservative, we might expect Hegel to have little tolerance for political criminals—those who do not recognize the legitimacy of the state's power to punish, who do not regard the state's laws as an articulation of right. Some passages support this expectation. Political crime is an act of nonconformity, and Hegel sometimes suggests that nonconformity is a crime: "You must do something that counts universally, you can't be just a private person. . . . To want to do something unheard of would be a crime."[29]

Some might defend the illegal actions of political criminals because these actions are done for a greater good. In his lengthy discussion at the

[22] Rph I, 163,665–678; Hegel is not advocating a secret police here, certainly not the sort with which we are familiar in recent history.

[23] Ibid., 163,678–688.

[24] PR 230.

[25] Rph V, 3:691–62.

[26] Rph III, 189,25–28.

[27] Ibid., 190,4–5; cf. PR 232.

[28] PR 238 Z.

[29] Rph V, 3:637–638.

end of the section "Moralität," Hegel sharply criticizes those who commit crimes with good intentions—we might think of Robin Hood, who robs the rich to help the poor, or Raskolnikov, who murders for a greater good:

> Theft in order to do good for the poor, theft or flight from battle for the sake of fulfilling one's duty to care for one's life or one's family, murder out of hate or revenge (i.e. in order to satisfy one's sense of one's own rights or of right in general . . .)—all these actions are made well intentioned and therefore good. . . . [But] in this abstract good the distinction between good and evil has vanished together with all concrete duties; for this reason, simply to will the good and to have a good intention in acting is more like evil than good.[30]

Hegel's point is not that those subject to the law must obey it whether they agree with it or not; on the contrary, he thinks that subjects have a right to know the good of the law.[31] His point is that not just any standards will do in criticizing the law. We must appeal not to subjective standards such as hate, the desire for revenge, or what we feel is right, but to the objective standards already implicit in our law and practices. Hegel sometimes discounts the revolutionary implications of the right of the subjective will to know the good of the law: he says there is this right of the subject to agree or be convinced that the law is right, but "on the other side . . . the state can't wait for the understanding of others."[32] So long as right is embodied in the laws and practices of the modern state, there is no excuse or justification for the citizen to oppose them.[33] Here Hegel's position is, in effect, that the right to (dis)agree with the laws is meaningless *if* the laws *are* right.

Hegel gives the authority of the state and of custom tremendous weight against my subjective authority because it is the universal against my particularity: I must therefore have great doubt in my authority to challenge such a power.[34] But Hegel does not leave the individual confronted with injustice impotent. To Hegel, legal punishment is justified *if* the state that punishes is our ethical substance, *if* its practices, institutions, and laws are the contents in which the free will comes into existence. But if my free will does not come into existence in the state, I have no corresponding duty to the state.[35]

---

[30] PR 140 Rem, p. 97.

[31] Rph V, 3:414–415.

[32] Rph VI, 4:352,25–29.

[33] Cf. ibid., 4:352,30–353,2.

[34] Ibid.

[35] Ibid., 4:154,12–21: "Der Mensch hat das Recht dazu, denn was realisirt werden soll ist der freie Wille, dieser ist sein eigener und wenn dieser nicht zum Dasein kommt so ist er nicht gebunden . . . insofern [der freie Wille] als solcher nicht zum Dasein kommt, hat er

If for Hegel legal punishment is justified only when it fulfills the purpose of vindicating right and making the criminal free, then we might expect Hegel, were he consistent, to condemn as unjust punishment in a society whose laws do not reflect a universal will, a shared sense of right. Hegel does just that. In a fragment from his early Frankfurt period Hegel characterizes punishment intended to reform but meted out by an unjust state as tyrannical: "To regard man with cold understanding as essentially a worker and producer, to be improved and commanded, becomes the greatest tyranny, because the goal of the whole, to attain the best, is a foreign goal to man if the whole is not just."[36]

This criticism of some legal punishment is not an aberration in Hegel's thought, nor the exclamation of a young and still radical intellectual who later accepts injustice with passivity, but it is consistent with Hegel's later *Rechtsphilosophie*: only when our state is the object of our implicit will, the universal within us, is state punishment just. In the set of lectures recently discovered by Dieter Henrich we find other passages where Hegel criticizes punishment in an unjust society: "Where one class [*Stand*] controls the administration of justice [it is in their hands], they exercise a right of domination [*Herrenrecht*] over the citizens, more or less like serfdom."[37] For Hegel, serfdom is contrary to freedom,[38] and therefore to right.[39]

Hegel goes on to suggest, in a lengthy passage from the newfound lectures, that rebellion of the sort the political criminal undertakes is sometimes justified. The passage, so intriguing that its discovery was reported in the magazine *Der Spiegel*,[40] is translated in the appendix to this chapter. In it, Hegel describes how, in a society sharply divided between rich and poor, the poor person feels himself excluded and ridiculed by virtue of his status; he confronts the arbitrary will of others, his freedom is entirely contingent on their will. "Envy and hate emerge on the part of the poor against those who have something." And from this inevitably arises an "inner anger"—Hegel plays on the double meaning of the word *Em-*

---

kein Recht, insofern auch keine Pflicht" ("Man also has the right that his free will should be realized, it is his own, and if it does not come into existence, then he is not bound . . . insofar as the free will as such does not come into existence, there is neither right nor duty").

[36] "Fragmente historischer und politischer Studien aus der Berner und Frankfurter Zeit" (ca. 1795, 1798), in *Frühe Schriften* (Hegel, *Werke*, vol. 1), p. 443 (fragment 16). The original reads: "Mit kaltem Verstande die Menschen bald als arbeitende und produzierende Wesen, bald als zu bessernde Wesen zu betrachten und zu befehligen, wird die ärgste Tyrannei, weil das Beste des Ganzen als Zweck ihnen fremd ist, wenn es nicht gerecht ist."

[37] Rph III, 186,29–33.

[38] PH 529–530(448); PR 274 Z.

[39] See the introduction to chapter 3 on the connection Hegel sees between freedom and right.

[40] *Der Spiegel*, no. 52 (1983): pp. 130–132.

pörung, which can mean revolt. After describing the plight of the "rabble," Hegel then makes a remark in which Henrich finds great significance: "Earlier we had seen the right of distress as relating to a momentary necessity. Here necessity no longer has this purely momentary character."

Henrich writes: "Nowhere else in all of Hegel's work do we find the conclusion Hegel unambiguously arrives at here, albeit in a hesitant statement concealed in a reference to a previous passage: the poor have in civil society a right to rebel [*Recht zum Aufstand*] against the order which prevents the realisation of their freedom."[41]

Henrich explains how Hegel compares this right to rebel with the right of distress, which declares the right to take another's property when in extreme danger of losing one's life.[42] Henrich says, "The necessity of poverty is not this. . . . This necessity rather arises out of the form of organisation of society as such. And so Hegel says, 'here necessity no longer has this purely momentary character.' This can only be understood as a declaration of the right against the society itself that denies to the wills of the poor their existence, and the carrying out of the realisation of these wills."[43] Henrich adds, "There is no other passage in Hegel's works where he explains revolution not merely as an historical fact and necessity, but as a right based on the systematic analysis of institutions that are present even for Hegel. No wonder that this account is arrived at in an indirect form."[44]

Perhaps Henrich exaggerates the radical character of Hegel's *Rechtsphilosophie* by reading too much into this single passage. Henrich implies that the Hegel of the *Rechtsphilosophie* advocates revolution, but Hegel could well think the poor have a right to outrage, even a right to resist unjust social conditions, yet advocate not revolution but reform as a strategy for action. In his late essay on the English Reform Bill, Hegel is also critical of laws that favor one class of society at the expense of another. He writes with disgust and sarcasm of the disproportionately harsh punishment prescribed by, and actually inflicted under, England's game laws. He notes that these laws serve only the aristocrats who made the laws and who then sit in judgment in their capacity as magistrates and jurymen.[45] Yet in this essay Hegel argues not for revolution but for suitable reform, the last hope for *preventing* revolution. Hegel is critical of the proposed

[41] Dieter Henrich, "Vernunft in Verwirklichung," p. 20. "Recht zum Aufstand" is Henrich's term; it does not appear in the lecture notes.
[42] See PR 127–128.
[43] Dieter Henrich, "Vernunft in Verwirklichung," p. 20.
[44] Ibid.
[45] "The English Reform Bill," in *Hegel's Political Writings*, trans. T. M. Knox, pp. 300, 309ff.

English Reform Bill about which he writes, because the bill's premise is that the unequal representation resulting from England's positive law violates abstract principles of equality, and these abstract principles, while rational in general, could, if applied to England in particular, with its common-law tradition, lead to revolution. Yet Hegel is ambivalent about the Reform Bill—it *does* attack real injustices. Hegel sees the need for altering institutions but suggests the Reform Bill is not the right blueprint for change, because it is *too* revolutionary.

The passage Henrich believes unique for its explicit advocacy of revolution is not inconsistent with the *Rechtsphilosophie* as a whole—a point on which Henrich, rightly concerned with establishing the importance of his find, does not elaborate in his brief introduction to his edition of the lecture notes. While Hegel's strategy as political theorist is to try to make us feel at home in our world, he does not obtain the bliss of reconciliation by blinding himself, or us, to manifest injustices. Hegel was certainly aware that his society was polarized and that many people lived on the margin who "can't and don't want to be politically active."[46] In an earlier work Hegel wrote that, in the happy state of the Greeks,[47] the will of the individual and the will of the universal are one and the same; each is the universal "immediately," and "no protestation occurred here."[48] But in the modern state individuals satisfy their particular interests, and the possibility therefore arises of opposition to the universal. Particularity, while essential to our freedom, can lead to "corruption and misery."[49] Hegel also sees structural reasons why opposition occurs within a modern state. Capitalism causes class polarization: "The man with capital can live off of his profits and always seek more at the expense of the poor"; "where there is wealth there is poverty."[50]

Still, it is important to see that the sort of revolution Hegel would advocate under such divisive circumstances is different from the sort Marx and Marxists advocate. For the latter, revolution implies an uprooting of the bourgeois system of private property and the capitalist mode of production. Hegel, rather, would call us back to the ideals of that very system. In Hegel's view, the problem with a society polarized along class lines in which a "rabble" are marginalized is not with the ideals of that society's practices, laws, and institutions, but with the failure of society to live up to those ideals. Hegel would insist that each had the right to private property, to work, and to obtain his or her welfare. Hegel would

[46] Rph III, 268,1–3.
[47] See sec. 4.3.1.
[48] "Es findet kein Protestieren hier statt" (JR 250). Of course, Hegel ignores women and slaves; and in any case his vision of Greek society is certainly contestable.
[49] Rph V, 3:574–575.
[50] Rph VI, 4:494,20–495,10.

be a revolutionary, then, in the original sense of that word, by calling us back to the ideals from which we have departed.[51] The difference between Marx and Hegel here is analogous to the difference between on the one hand the person of the far left who, outraged by the widespread poverty in the inner cities, calls for an overthrow of the economic system, social welfare programs included, which she believes engenders the impoverishment of an entire class, and on the other hand the reformist who sees the problem of poverty rather as a failure properly to administer the social welfare programs in place.

There are deep-seated reasons why modern societies must be polarized. Rather than shut his eyes to facts that go against his conception of a rational modern state, Hegel acknowledges that "where there is misery, the concept dissolves."[52] Hegel criticizes the punishment of political criminals on the basis of his interpretation of the point of our social practices, and of the state as our ethical substance. The poor, like all individuals, have a "right to demand that civil society care for [their] particularity." Hegel says they have the right to work.[53] A society where some do not have the opportunity to work, or obtain a subsistence living, is unjust. For Hegel, the significance of crime is that by committing it the criminal violates his own rational will and injures "all others."[54] Crime no longer has this significance in a divided society: "Where the classes of society are estranged from each other, there the members of one class are least troubled by the injury to a member of another class."[55] The illegal actions of those excluded from such a society are comparable to the resistance a conquered people puts up against a master. Hegel says such rebellion is not a crime against the state, since it is no violation of the idea of the state.[56] He implies that a society of such class divisions is not really a state, even if it has a government, makes war, and collects taxes, and that the "punishment" meted out by this "state" is not really punishment.

Earlier I suggested that the issue of political crime *is* occasionally relevant to our actual practice of legal punishment. In practice, when the question of political crime arises the issue gets transformed from what it is originally—a question of the legitimacy of state punishment—to the question of whether to allow a justification defense of "necessity." In

[51] On this original sense of "revolution," see Hannah Arendt, *On Revolution*, pp. 34ff. Cf. my discussion, sec. 6.1.

[52] Rph V, 3:573,27–33.

[53] Rph III, 191–192; cf. PR 240 Z, where Hegel says that "every man has the right to demand subsistence from [civil society]" but also that civil society "has the right to press [its members] to provide for their own livelihood."

[54] PR 218.

[55] Rph III, 177,11–14.

[56] PR 281 Z, p. 289.

criminal law doctrine, justification is distinguished from excuse. The difference is the same as between being forgivably wrong (excuse) and being right (justification). If someone can show he committed an otherwise criminal act out of "necessity," his act is justified and not considered a wrong.[57] In our practice the necessity defense is almost never successfully invoked. Hegel provides a strong argument for why we might want to change that and take more seriously those who argue for the defense as a justification. I think an interpretation more consistent with Hegel's political philosophy as a whole, of the newly discovered passage where Hegel applies the right of distress to the economically and socially marginal of a society, is that it suggests the legitimacy not of revolution, but of the legal defense of necessity in certain criminal cases involving political crimes.

5.4   Determination of Guilt

The suspect who is clutched for violating a criminal law becomes a defendant in the next subpractice, the determination of guilt. In this section we shall see how Hegel uses his interpretation of legal punishment as a whole to answer the question of what counts as being guilty and to defend the practice by which we often determine guilt: trial by jury.

5.4.1   Justifying Due Process

The process of legal punishment concerns criminal actions, and actions either were or were not done. Before we can mete out justice, we must make a legal determination of guilt: "*Recht-an-sich* has to prove itself to the court—a process in which there may be a difference between what is right implicitly (*an sich*) and what is provably right."[58] Part of doing justice is convicting only the guilty; another is making sure we do not unduly burden innocent persons in our search for the guilty.[59] Both objectives require rules of procedure and evidence: "In court the specific character

---

[57] See Edward Arnolds and Norman Garland, "The Defense of Necessity in Criminal Law."

[58] Enz 531. Wallace translates *Recht-an-sich* here as "abstract right" and *an-sich* as "abstractly," which I think is a mistake. Abstract right refers to the formal conception of right (right to one's person and property) and does not encompass all that is *Recht-an-sich*.

[59] Sometimes unduly burdening innocent persons obstructs our search for the guilty. Hegel criticizes the use of torture to extract confessions, not because of its cruelty, but because it is unreliable and may lead the innocent to confess. Rph VI, 4:579,33–580,7; cf. 4:583,2–13.

which rightness acquires is that it must be demonstrable. When parties go to law, they are put in the position of having to make good their evidence and their claims and to make the judge acquainted with the facts. *These steps in a legal process are themselves rights*, and their course must therefore be fixed by law."[60] Following rules may prevent us from determining the truth about whether right was violated. Hegel's point is that commitment to due process, though entailing this risk of doing injustice, is part of right: "If I can not prove it in court, it is no right."[61]

Submitting ourselves to the demands of due process—for example, excluding evidence illegally obtained that otherwise could rightly lead to conviction—is part of what we must do to determine right. But, Hegel insists, we must not lose sight of the point of having a legal system: to stipulate what is right and wrong and punish those who commit wrongs. Legal formalities are a necessity, but they should help rather than hinder the legal system in carrying out its fundamental purpose. Recall how Hegel criticizes the "empty formalism" that allowed a Bartholomew Thompson to escape justice because his name was not accurately recorded on the complaint.[62] We find among Hegel's transcripts of articles he had read in the *Morning Chronicle* other anecdotes of injustice caused by strict adherence to rules of procedure, and Hegel's response. Hegel finds it "intolerable" that a Catholic priest may not prevent a murder the intention of which he hears about in confession; referring to what seems to be the same case, Hegel writes that a "wretch escapes punishment" because a girl could not describe him according to the technical standards required. Hegel also was sufficiently struck to record a case where a conviction for theft could not be enforced because one of the jurors was later found to be underage.[63]

While these passages suggest Hegel might be sympathetic to those who criticize our submitting to the demands of due process at the expense of finding out the truth, other passages suggest he might simply waver. Hegel says that principles of justice do not decisively argue for either England's practice of granting the right to refuse to testify against oneself or the continental practice of demanding testimony: "While the interest of justice is to bring truth to light, also it is not to be expected that someone incriminate or accuse himself."[64] We might criticize Hegel for not taking a clear stand, but on the other hand we might think he is just being consistent and honest: on some issues our principles leave us wavering. Procedures may prevent us from punishing the right person, hampering jus-

---

[60] PR 222, emphasis in original.
[61] Ibid., 222 Z.
[62] Rph III, 175,21–27.
[63] Michael J. Petry, "Hegel and 'The Morning Chronicle,' " fragments 12, 63–65.
[64] Rph VI, 4:583,15–584,28.

tice; but they also may prevent us from punishing the wrong person, hampering injustice. The defender of justice must be ambivalent about such procedures.

Ideally a defendant's guilt would be determined by a free confession: "it is the greatest honor to aim for a confession and the agreement of the perpetrator."[65] With such a confession not only do we have the greatest certainty of punishing the right person,[66] but also we respect the freedom of the criminal.[67] But often the criminal will not confess, and we must rely instead on what Hegel calls "extraordinary punishment." Extraordinary punishment is meted out to those determined to be guilty on the basis not of a confession but of a jury's verdict.[68] Hegel uses his interpretation of the practice as a whole, of legal punishment as making free the criminal, who shares in the ethical substance of his community, in justifying jury trials. In Hegel's view, with the jury's verdict the "soul of the criminal speaks: I have done it."[69]

The most prevalent argument justifying juries is that they provide "an inestimable safeguard against the corrupt or overzealous prosecutor and against the compliant, biased, or eccentric judge."[70] Current debate about juries focuses on whether the advantages of jury trial outweigh its costs; opponents contend that legal issues are too complicated for laypeople, while proponents argue that twelve heads are better than one, and that the jury system provides an important civic experience.[71] Hegel would think that this current debate misses the whole point of why we have juries. In Hegel's view, the jury system is justified not on the grounds of utility, but by the "concept of the matter."[72] The jury, whose members are part of the criminal's community and share in the same ethical substance, represents the criminal's soul and expresses his implicit will. Its verdict is a quasi confession. Juries satisfy the "right of subjectivity and self-consciousness,"[73] that is, the demand that the judgment of condemnation "is not alien to the criminal."[74]

Hegel uses his interpretation of the point of juries to criticize the actual practice: when the jury does not represent the criminal's soul because the

---

[65] Ibid., 4:579,1–7; cf. PR 227.

[66] Rph VI, 4:578,21–27.

[67] Ibid., 4:579,16–20.

[68] Enz 531 Rem.

[69] Rph VI, 4:580,28–32.

[70] *Duncan v. Louisiana*, 391 U.S. 145 (1968), majority opinion of Justice Byron White.

[71] These and other arguments are recounted in Harry Kalven and Hans Zeisel, *The American Jury*, pp. 7–9.

[72] Rph V, 3:687,18–21. Hegel adds that "utility is never capable of giving the last decision on a matter" (ibid.)

[73] PR 228 Rem.

[74] Rph V, 3:683.

society is divided along class or religious lines, the jury's judgment *would* be alien to the criminal. Hegel transcribed a commentary he read in the *Morning Chronicle* that argued that in such divided societies a jury system is impossible:

> The institution of juries is unsuitable in all countries in which the population is divided into castes, whether political or civil. It would for example be a mockery to try a negro by a jury of white planters.—Every cause of dispute between a Protestant and a Catholic becomes a trial of strength between the two castes, and as the Protestants have the law in their hand they naturally exclude the Catholics from juries in party causes, and use the law merely as an engine for upholding their influence and punishing their opponents.[75]

Hegel not only was exposed to this idea, but he was interested enough to copy it down, perhaps to be used in future lectures. Since for Hegel the jury represents the "soul" or "conscience" of the defendant, by virtue of their all sharing in the same ethical substance, it is no wonder that he was struck by a passage arguing that in a society so divided that we could not speak of its members sharing in one substance, a jury could deliver only sham justice in cross-class cases.

Hegel's justification for open and public jury trials is similarly based on his general conception of the practice of punishment as a whole. Open trials fulfill the "absolute right of subjective consciousness to know the laws."[76] Still, Hegel acknowledges that there are reasons to support both open and closed trials.[77] Sometimes there is a public need that a trial be closed, as when a crime is "unclean."[78]

In our own criminal justice system, a vast majority of cases never go to trial. Perhaps as many as 90 percent of all cases are "plea bargained."[79] Plea bargaining refers to the exchange, between prosecutor and defendant, of reductions in charge for a plea of guilty. Plea bargaining allows tremendous savings in resources. The prosecutor (the state) avoids the cost of trial, and the defendant gets off with a lighter, though certain, sentence. There are persuasive utilitarian reasons for plea bargaining. But when we punish someone who cops a plea, we are punishing them for

---

[75] Michael J. Petry, "Hegel and 'The Morning Chronicle,'" fragment 27. The fragment was written in 1827, so Hegel never had the opportunity to use it in his *Rechtsphilosophie* lectures (he stopped lecturing on this subject in 1826, and resumed in 1831, but he died after giving only two lectures).

[76] Rph VI, 4:561,20–21; cf. PR 224.

[77] Rph III, 181–182.

[78] Rph VI, 4:564,16–22.

[79] *New York Times*, Feb. 12, 1975, p. 1; Malcolm Feeley, *The Process Is the Punishment*, p. 186.

something they did not do.[80] If we think the point of punishing at all is to express our condemnation of an act we regard as wrong and to vindicate right, we might think plea bargaining misses the point of why we punish.[81] We might expect Hegel to make such an objection. Hegel says nothing about plea bargaining.[82] The closest he comes is in a passage in the lectures critical of a jury that fudged the facts of a case by finding a theft that was in fact greater than forty shillings, and therefore punishable by death according to English law, to have been a theft of less than forty shillings, and therefore not subject to capital punishment. Hegel does not condone the law that imposes death for a relatively trivial crime, but neither does he condone the mixing of legal consequences with a determination of facts; the investigation of facts should be "pure."[83] If Hegel is willing to condemn a jury for punishing a defendant for a lesser offense not actually committed, albeit for benevolent purposes, perhaps he would condemn a prosecutor whose plea bargain, offered not even out of benevolence but merely to clear court dockets, results in the punishment of a person for a lesser offense not actually committed. Hegel insists that we punish for the sake of justice, and he would strictly scrutinize a penal system that sacrificed justice for some other purpose.

5.4.2   Hegel on Accountability

Once settled on the process and procedures for determining guilt, we need to know by what standards we should determine whether a defendant is guilty. In most cases in our own practice we punish only those persons who *intended* to do the wrong of which they are accused. We require the presence of *mens rea*, or vicious will. The offender had to have had a choice whether to commit the wrong. Many statutes make such a mental state a requirement for criminal liability; one cannot commit larceny without intent, by definition. Intent is also a requirement in a broader sense: the law typically absolves those unable to comply with the law, for example infants or the insane. The law allows certain defenses that excuse persons from criminal liability. For example, the law excuses those whose "act" of wrongdoing was involuntary.[84] Some utilitarians, who reject the

---

[80] This is not a trivial objection. See Mark Tunick, *Punishment: Theory and Practice*, ch. 4, sec. 3.3.1.

[81] See ibid.

[82] His Prussia no doubt had no such practice. Present-day Germany does not even have the practice—see John Langbein, "Land Without Plea Bargaining: How the Germans Do It," *Michigan Law Review* 78 (1979): pp. 204ff.

[83] Rph VI, 4:577,7–23.

[84] For discussion, see Sanford Kadish, *Blame and Punishment*, pp. 82–87.

retributive principle that we punish for the sake of justice or to condemn blameworthy actions, suggest that criminal intent should be irrelevant to guilt and hold to the principle of strict liability.[85] Some retributivists, however, insist that there is no crime without *mens rea*, or intent, for we cannot rightly blame people for something they did not intend to do.[86]

It is difficult to get clear Hegel's view on accountability, as disagreement among commentators indicates. Some criticize Hegel for placing too much importance on the criminal's subjective reasons for acting—on intent—when in fact human behavior is largely socially determined.[87] Others take Hegel to be a theorist of strict liability who claims that we are responsible for our jeopardizing behavior apart from whether we intended any wrong.[88] Andrej Piontkowski takes both sides. In his view, one of the most important theses in the *Rechtsphilosophie* is that a person is to be judged criminally responsible on the basis not of intent or disposition, but of action—by objective criteria independent of subjective intention.[89] But elsewhere in the same work Piontkowski declares that Hegel does not advocate strict liability and, rather, sees the need for subjective accountability.[90] What *is* this view of Hegel's that causes such confusion?

One thing is clear: Hegel insists that human beings must be held accountable only for what they have willed. This view has underlying it Hegel's entire conception of right and freedom:

> The state of innocence consists in the fact that nothing is good and nothing is evil for human beings; it is the state of the animal. Paradise is in fact initially a zoological garden [*Tiergarten*], it is the state where there is no accountability. An ethical state of humanity begins only with a state of accountability or of capacity for guilt, and this is now the human state . . . to have guilt means to

[85] See Lady Barbara Wootton, *Social Science and Social Pathology*, and "Diminished Responsibility: A Layman's View." On strict liability offenses, see Richard Wasserstrom, "Strict Liability in the Criminal Law," pp. 731–745. Wasserstrom notes that there is still a notion of fault in strict liability. Even according to a strict liability standard the state would not punish randomly chosen people in response to a wrong I unintentionally commit—the state would punish me (p. 742). Wasserstrom emphasizes the similarities between strict liability and negligence (p. 745).

[86] See Henry M. Hart, Jr., "The Aims of the Criminal Law."

[87] S. W. Dyde, "Hegel's Conception of Freedom," pp. 668–669; A. A. Piontkowski, *Hegels Lehre über Staat und Recht und Seine Strafrechtstheorie*, pp. 270, 276.

[88] Gustav Radbruch, *Der Handlungsbegriff in seiner Bedeutung für das Strafrecht*; Karl Larenz, *Hegels Zurechnungslehre*; and Peter Böning, *Die Lehre vom Unrechtsbewußtsein in der Rechtsphilosophie Hegels*.

[89] A. A. Piontkowski, *Hegels Lehre über Staat und Recht und Seine Strafrechtstheorie*, pp. 274–275.

[90] Ibid., pp. 238–242.

be accountable, that this is one's knowledge and one's will, that one does it as what is right.[91]

In Hegel's view, guilt is for an act. The necessity that there be an act makes wrong the *labeling* of people as criminals. In the *Phenomenology* Hegel criticizes physiognomists for taking as signs of one's intention external features such as one's handwriting, voice, or facial lines, as if such features could reveal "the criminal" or "the poet" regardless of the acts of the individual being investigated.[92] For Hegel, "the true being of a man is rather his deed."[93] Phrenologists, too, are culprits, in trying to link physiology with behavior. Phrenologists focus not on outer signs, as do the physiognomists, but on the "thing"—the skull. Phrenologists claim that the actuality and existence of man are his skull bone.[94] But, says Hegel, this view is wrong. It takes what may be a fluke, a bump on the skull, as an indication of future criminal activity,[95] whereas a crime consists in not an inner possibility but an actual deed.

Hegel specifies his theory of accountability in the section "Moralität" in the *Philosophy of Right*. There he says that I am accountable for what belongs to my purpose (*Vorsatz*).[96] Hegel distinguishes purpose from intention (*Absicht*). The arsonist's *purpose* in striking a match is to light it; his *intention* is to burn down the house. Purpose is immediate; intention concerns the worth of the act, how it is to be evaluated or assessed.[97] The intention of an act is the universality the act has in the eyes of the subject.[98] Intention is "relatively universal,"[99] in that what the subject takes to be the worth of the act may differ from its objective worth. The distinction between purpose and intention corresponds to another distinction Hegel makes, between deed (*Tat*) and action (*Handlung*). When I carry out my purpose I do my *deed* (burn down a house), but my deed is in fact an *action* with consequences I might or might not have intended (I burn down the house next door, as well). Hegel says I have blame (*Schuld*) for my deed. I might do x, and x leads to y, though I did not intend that y occur. I am accountable only for x, even though I have also at least indirectly caused y.[100]

One reason, no doubt, why Hegel's account has been mistaken for that

[91] PRel 214.
[92] PhdG 319–320.
[93] Ibid., 322.
[94] Ibid., 331.
[95] Ibid., 335–336.
[96] PR 115.
[97] PR 114.
[98] Ibid., 114 Bem, pp. 213–214.
[99] Rph VI, 4:312,9–19.
[100] PR 115 Z.

to which it so far bears no resemblance whatsoever—an account of strict liability—is that immediately after declaring that I am responsible only "insofar as the abstract predicate 'mine' belongs to the alteration in the state of affairs resulting from my deed,"[101] Hegel says in paragraph 116 that we may be held accountable if a thing of ours (our hammer, our car, our dog) causes damage, even though this occurs not as our deed or with our having purposed it, since the thing is ours and contingency is inherent in the concept of will.[102] In other words, just after declaring the requirement of intent, Hegel proposes what sounds like a standard of strict liability. But to see the sense in which Hegel actually advocates this standard, and whether Hegel has fallen into a blundering contradiction, we must read on.

In paragraph 117 Hegel restates the intent theory of paragraph 115, saying that the subjective will has the right to be held to blame only for what it purposed or knew, and that an action is the deed of the subject only if the subject knew the presuppositions of the action. In his lectures Hegel illustrated this point with the example of Oedipus. The action of Oedipus was parricide, but Oedipus's purpose, not knowing his victim was his father, was to commit only murder; he should be blamed only for murder. The action was parricide, his deed was murder. Similarly, a hunter who mistakes a man for an animal and shoots him can be blamed for his death but not for murder.[103] "[T]he deed [sic] can be entirely different than imagined, but the will is accountable only for what it presupposed and aimed for."[104]

Here Hegel seems to oppose strict liability; how, then, shall we make sense of paragraph 116? One way is to see that two principles are at work: accountability for the embodiments of my will, such as my pets, my children, my possessions;[105] and accountability for what my subjective will purposed.[106] But why make this distinction, and why hold that I should be accountable only for what I purpose, or immediately intend, yet also hold that I am accountable for actions of others, and of things, that I do not directly will, that I have not purposed at all?

In paragraph 118 Hegel voices opposition to strict liability once again: the subjective will has the right to be held accountable for the first consequence, the purposed consequence, of its deed. He notes that the Greeks, who in Hegel's view failed to recognize the right of subjectivity, held a person accountable for the whole scope of his deed, that is, they

---

[101] Ibid., 115.
[102] Ibid., 116; cf. 41, 42.
[103] Rph V, 3:358–359; cf. PR 116 Bem, p. 217.
[104] Rph II, 1:283.
[105] PR 116.
[106] Ibid., 115, 117.

imputed to the person the whole action—Oedipus was held accountable for parricide.[107] But Hegel introduces an important qualification that helps resolve our questions: we can be negligent. "Negligence can occur and this can be more or less punishable; one must know what one does and has before him."[108] Though we can be held accountable only for what we purpose, we have the responsibility of knowing the universal character of our act, of knowing its inevitable consequences.[109] The arsonist, as a thinking being, cannot justly claim that she meant only to light a match; she had the responsibility to know that doing this on a windy day a flame's leap from a grass hut could burn down the hut. Hegel's introduction of the concept of negligence is consistent with and a consequence of his dialectical account of will that is the foundation of his interpretation of social practices. The concept of negligence implies that the will does not act exclusively by its own standards but has objective responsibilities. Its actions are part of an objective world it shares with others. By being held to a standard of negligence, we are held to objective standards, connected up to the values implicit in our ethical life.

Hegel completes the move from a subjective to an objective theory of accountability in paragraph 120, which announces the "right of intention": "The right of intention is that the universal quality of the action shall not merely be implicit but shall be known by the agent, and so shall have lain from the start in his subjective will. Vice versa, what may be called the right of the objectivity of action is the right of the action to evince itself as known and willed by the subject as a thinker." Hegel has us impute to the criminal the intention that it would have taken for a rational human being to have undertaken the misdeed, which no truly rational human being would undertake upon reflection. In his marginal notes Hegel explains that the subjective purpose of a thief may be to steal a thing to enjoy it, but the universal consequence is to threaten society and property.[110] Any rational human being would know that to steal is to make society unsafe. We respect the criminal as a rational human being by imputing to him the capacity to know what any rational human being should know, by explaining his crime as the product of a split will.[111] By holding the criminal responsible in this way, we respect him as a *free* human being.[112] We treat him as an agent who wills the nature of his action.[113] In Hegel's view, we have a responsibility to know not only what

---

[107] Ibid., 118 Rem; cf. Rph III, 92–93.

[108] Rph VI, 4:315,22–25.

[109] PR 118 Z; PR 118 Bem, p. 222.

[110] Ibid., 120 Bem, pp. 227–228.

[111] See sec. 2.2.2.

[112] Rph V, 3:370,11–24.

[113] Rph VI, 4:325,23–30.

we do—that doing this could lead to a wrong—but also that certain actions are wrong. Human beings have the responsibility to know the universal worth of their act. This duty corresponds to the right not to be held responsible for what could not be known.[114]

Hegel offers a philosophical justification for the requirement of intent and the negligence standard of liability that is based on his interpretation of the purpose of punishing at all. He also applies his account to a particular, pressing problem: whether we should allow the insanity defense. Again we find in Hegel not an irrelevant metaphysician and detached idealist, but a political theorist taking up practical concerns. Peter Steinberger has already pointed to Hegel's discussion of criminal accountability and the insanity defense as an example of how "Hegel's theory [of punishment] is by no means merely abstract or irrelevantly metaphysical."[115] But there is, I think, a problem with Steinberger's discussion of Hegel's views. Steinberger, rightly attentive to how Hegel takes up practical questions, in this case at least loses sight of the principles underlying the *Rechtsphilosophie* as a whole that Hegel uses to address these questions. Steinberger ends up imputing to Hegel an *anti*-retributive position by suggesting that Hegel would deny the guilt of a person who committed a crime twenty years previously but who had reformed in the interim, prior to his late capture.[116] With respect to the insanity defense, Steinberger

---

[114] Peter Böning, in his book-length interpretation of Hegel's theory of accountability, emphasizes Hegel's insistence that the state take into consideration whether the defendant was aware that her action was wrong (*Unrechtsbewußtsein*). Böning suggests that this "liberal" position has been missed because everybody assumes Hegel's theory of the state is antiliberal (*Die Lehre vom Unrechtsbewußtsein in der Rechtsphilosophie Hegels*, pp. 17–18). Böning argues that for Hegel there is an essential difference between violations of abstract rights, what Böning calls *Straftaten*, and police offenses (*Polizeivergehen*), or violations of regulations of the police power. *Straftaten* are fixed and determined apart from the whim of legislators, but police offenses represent a selection of many possible means of suppression; their scope has no limit beyond custom (pp. 74–75). *Straftaten*, argues Böning, "have a universal quality in and for themselves and don't first receive this via the contingent (*zufällig*) positing of a law" (p. 77). Böning then argues that, in Hegel's view, proof that the criminal was conscious of doing wrong is required only for police offenses, not for *Straftaten*, because we already assume the subjects of the state know *Straftaten* are wrong, having acquired this knowledge not by nature but through being brought up and formed (*bilden*) in society (pp. 88, 96–97). Böning is right to point out that the consciousness of wrongdoing, which Hegel imputes to criminals, who have the "right" to know the universal worth of their actions, is cultivated through *Bildung*. But we learn about all wrongs through *Bildung*. Böning is mistaken, I believe, to assume that Hegel sharply distinguishes between acts (*Straftaten*) that are wrong prior to their being codified in the criminal law and acts that are wrong only because they are so codified (*Polizeivergehen*). *Straftaten* are not prior to the establishment of penal laws, though Hegel's placing of "Abstract Right" prior to the section in the *Philosophy of Right* on the police and the state might give that impression.

[115] Peter J. Steinberger, *Logic and Politics: Hegel's Philosophy of Right*, p. 145.

[116] Ibid., pp. 142–143.

then finds that Hegel "would view insanity as a perfectly adequate defense," but concedes that he "gives us little help in" distinguishing a rational agent from a lunatic in "actual cases,"[117] and so Steinberger turns to
his own speculation that Hegel would share Derek Parfit's idea of a complex self that changes.[118] Steinberger concludes that Hegel would hold
simultaneously that we are so complex that we are not responsible for
what an "earlier self" did, and that we are simple, continuous selves, still
responsible for our earlier deeds. From this he concludes that for Hegel
the person reformed twenty years after his crime and finally caught would
be "completely guiltless."[119] From imputing to Hegel this notion of a
complex self Steinberger concludes also that Hegel would have us decide
cases of drunkenness by, on the whole, holding "the sober self somehow
responsible for the drunken self."[120] He suggests Hegel would punish the
drunken killer, "perhaps" not for murder, but "for some lesser but still
serious offense."

We should be skeptical of Steinberger's speculations not only because
there is no textual evidence that Hegel held a view of a "complex self" as
Parfit and others understand this term (a point Steinberger acknowledges), but also because the conclusions Steinberger draws tend to contradict what we should expect Hegel to say on the basis of his understanding of why we legally punish. The recently discovered set of lectures Hegel
first gave on the *Rechtsphilosophie* includes an extensive remark on the
issue of insanity and criminal responsibility. Hegel notes that to hold me
accountable for a crime requires I must have: (1) consciousness of the
situation, and (2) a capacity to make the purpose of the act a maxim, to
universalize the act. Hegel says children lack (2) because they are not yet
rational creatures.[121] Anger, drunkenness, and insanity weaken a person's
consciousness, but, says Hegel, we must always honor (adult) human beings by imputing to them knowledge of the universal aspect of their act.
Of course such persons may not know the true value of their act when
they commit the crime; therefore we allow for mitigating circumstances,[122] which, for Hegel, are a matter of mercy, not right.[123] Hegel's
account here is not an aberration hidden away only in the lecture notes,

[117] Ibid., p. 139.
[118] Steinberger draws on Derek Parfit's conception of changing selves in Parfit's "Later
Selves and Moral Principles," in A. Montefiori, ed., *Philosophy and Personal Relations*
(London: Routledge and Kegan Paul, 1973), and on the notion of a "complex view" of the
self as changing, in Amelie Oksenberg Rorty, ed., *The Identities of Persons* (Berkeley: University of California Press, 1976).
[119] Peter J. Steinberger, *Logic and Politics: Hegel's Philosophy of Right*, pp. 141–143.
[120] Ibid., p. 143.
[121] Rph I, 65,173–176.
[122] Ibid., 65–66.
[123] PR 132 Rem.

but it is consistent with his conception of legal punishment and is made clear in the *Philosophy of Right*: "The claim is made that the criminal in the moment of his action must have had a 'clear idea' of the wrong and its culpability before it can be imputed to him as a crime. At first sight, this claim seems to preserve the right of his subjectivity, but the truth is that it deprives him of his indwelling nature as intelligent."[124]

5.5   Sentencing

Among the issues connected to the subpractice of sentencing is whether we should allow discretion to the judge in determining how much punishment the convicted criminal receives. On this issue of judicial discretion Hegel offers us only a few morsels. From the principle that the people should know the law Hegel concludes that there should be little discretion, for nobody can anticipate law if it is judge-made. "Law must be contained in the lawbooks and when done rationally, little will be left to the judge."[125] Yet Hegel is aware that statute law by its nature is rigid, and he argues that sometimes we must go by the spirit and not the letter of the law.[126] The judge, Hegel says, stands up for the "substance of right" against distortions that arise by a rigid application of the law's letter. Ideally the spirit of the law would be put in writing, but in practice we need some discretion.[127]

Discretion in practice often means individualizing sentences, tailoring them to the criminal. Some retributivists might oppose this practice on the grounds that justice demands treating all equally, while other retributivists might favor individualized sentencing on the grounds that true justice can be meted out only by taking into account the particular features of each case. Hegel says very little on the topic,[128] but there is one passage suggesting his support of individualized sentencing: "Other considerations for making punishment more severe are if [the crime] was premeditated, or if this was the criminal's first crime; in the former case the action is the result of a more intensive will; in the latter case we [consider whether] crime has come to be customary for this person."[129] Hegel's rea-

---

[124] Ibid., 132 Rem, p. 89.

[125] Rph VI, 4:535,26–28; cf. PR 211 Z.

[126] Rph III, 174–175.

[127] Ibid.

[128] In his much earlier *Jenaer Realphilosophie* (1805–1806) Hegel writes that the penalty should take into account one's class, so as to preserve the social standing of the punished (JR 258–259). Igor Primoratz argues that this view is later dropped (*Banquos-Geist: Hegels Theorie der Strafe*, p. 26). But see Rph III, 89,9–14.

[129] Rph I, 150,266–151,278.

soning here is drawn in part from his account of the will—the more intensive the will to do wrong, the more deserved is severer punishment. Again Hegel applies to particular problems the principles he adduces from the practice as a whole.

Another issue regarding sentencing has been a recent focus of attention: whether it is permissible for victim-impact evidence to be used in the sentencing phase of a criminal trial. In a 1991 decision, *Payne v. Tennessee*, the majority of the Supreme Court, overturning decisions by the Court of just two and four years previously, held that the Constitution permits evidence about the victim and the impact of the victim's death to be introduced in a capital murder trial. In this case, Pervis Payne was convicted by a jury on two counts of first-degree murder and one count of assault with intent to commit murder in the first degree. The victims of his offenses were twenty-eight-year-old Charisse Christopher; her two-year-old daughter, Lacie; and a surviving three-year-old son, Nicholas. Chief Justice William Rehnquist, in his majority opinion, quoted from the disputed closing arguments of the prosecutor concerning the impact of Payne's crimes on Nicholas:

> But we do know that Nicholas was alive. And Nicholas was in the same room. Nicholas was still conscious. His eyes were open . . . he knew what happened to his mother and baby sister. . . . There is obviously nothing you can do for Charisse and Lacie Jo. But there is something that you can do for Nicholas. . . . Somewhere down the road Nicholas is going to grow up, hopefully. He's going to want to know what happened. And he is going to know what happened to his baby sister and his mother. He is going to want to know what type of justice was done. He is going to want to know what happened. With your verdict, you will provide the answer.

The majority argued that victim-impact evidence such as this "serves entirely legitimate purposes." "For the jury to assess meaningfully the defendant's moral culpability and blameworthiness, it should have before it at the sentencing phase evidence of the specific harm caused by the defendant." Against the charge that such victim-impact evidence encourages arbitrary sentencing based on the sympathies and emotions rather than on reason, Justice David Souter, in his concurring opinion, responded,

> Any failure to take account of a victim's individuality and the effects of his death upon close survivors would thus more appropriately be called an act of lenity than their consideration an invitation to arbitrary sentencing. Indeed, given a defendant's option to introduce relevant evidence in mitigation, sentencing without such evidence of victim impact may be seen as a significantly imbalanced process.[130]

[130] See 111 S. Ct. 2597 at 2601–2603, 2614–2619.

In *Payne v. Tennessee* the Court considered the strictly constitutional issue of whether the introduction of victim-impact evidence violates the Eighth Amendment, and therefore the distinct issue of to what extent the Constitution places limits on the authority of states to devise criminal procedures and remedies.[131] While Hegel of course has nothing to say about this issue of U.S. constitutional law, his theory of legal punishment does provide a powerful rebuttal to the substantive position taken by the Court's majority. Hegel, as we have seen, distinguishes justice in a modern state from revenge justice. The measure of revenge justice is the will of the particular victim; the measure of justice in a modern state is the will of the community, as articulated in law. A defendant's guilt or moral culpability is determined by the nature of the act, the extent to which it violates our shared conception of right. To base justice on the felt hurt of the victim is to impose a subjective and arbitrary standard and to degrade the moral character that punishment has. Hegel would have the majority of the Court rethink the meaning and purpose of punishing at all.

5.6   Infliction of Punishment

Retributivists are often criticized for insisting we punish wrongs for the sake of justice, yet being unable to show how punishment can be commensurable with the wrong committed, other than by resorting to the crude and barbaric and surely unacceptable measure of the *lex talionis,* "an eye for an eye." Granted crimes are things we want to prevent, either because we think they are wrong or because they decrease social utility, but why inflict punishment on those who commit crimes? And if we must, how can we decide how much?

A few commentators have asked why Hegel thinks we should punish and not merely publicly denounce the criminal. David Cooper and Igor Primoratz both defend Hegel, arguing that, empirically, only punishment possesses the required strength and the necessary seriousness and weight of negation.[132] This is partly right but obscures Hegel's actual argument that the physical, nonverbal punishment both Cooper and Primoratz understand by "punishment," in contrasting it with mere public denunciation or "verbal reaction,"[133] may be necessary in societies that are internally weak, where crime poses a great danger to public safety, but

---

[131] This case will be most remembered, I suspect, not for its resolution of the substantive issue, but for its bearing on the principle of *stare decisis*. See the dissents by Justice Thurgood Marshall and Justice John Paul Stevens.

[132] David Cooper, "Hegel's Theory of Punishment," in *Hegel's Political Philosophy,* ed. Z. A. Pelczynski, p. 167; Igor Primoratz, *Banquos-Geist,* pp. 77–78.

[133] Igor Primoratz, *Banquos-Geist,* pp. 77–78.

unnecessary in other societies. In principle punishment need not consist in the infliction of physical pain. The very question raised by Cooper and Primoratz, why punish as opposed merely to denounce publicly, itself is based on the confusion that punishment must be something more than public denunciation, a confusion shared also by Peter Steinberger, who insists that for Hegel public denunciation, reform, and deterrence are all inadequate responses to crime—we must "punish"[134]—and Ossip Flechtheim, who claims that Hegel never shows why the negation of the negation must have the form of punishment, where any other legal sanction would do: "Hegel never unambiguously derives punishment."[135]

In Hegel's view, unless we punish, right is not vindicated, and this explains why we cannot sit back and do nothing when a crime is committed. The principle that right must be restored also dictates to an extent what counts as punishment. Hegel says that punishment must be perceptible or felt (*empfindlich*), but he does not mean it must hurt physically: shame is felt.[136] Cooper and Primoratz would surely consider the death penalty as punishment, yet Hegel says the death penalty sometimes is *not* felt.[137] The fear of execution is felt and felt painfully by many people, but in a case where a murderer is not "receptive" to death, as when he thinks he will receive eternal salvation, Hegel says the judge should commute the sentence to imprisonment to make punishment felt. Hegel argues also that a fine is not punishment because it is not felt by the rich.[138] Hegel adds that a fine, and restitution in general, is acceptable for civil but not criminal cases, since with crime the universal will and not just that of the victim has been injured. Compensation responds only to the damage to one's property, not to the damage to right and the "*an-sich* existing will."[139]

Hegel argues that punishment should condemn and stigmatize the criminal,[140] and therefore that the criminal trial should be public: open trials are already part of the punishment of the criminal.[141] But he says little about how much punishment is needed. The reason for his silence is that Hegel thinks there are limits to what philosophy can determine:

But the determinate character given by the Concept to punishment is just that necessary connexion between crime and punishment already mentioned; crime,

[134] Steinberger takes "punish" to mean "inflict pain," in his "Hegel on Crime and Punishment," p. 863.
[135] Ossip Flechtheim, *Hegels Strafrechtstheorie*, pp. 105–106.
[136] Rph VI, 4:285,23–32.
[137] PR 99 Bem.
[138] Rph VI, 4:285.
[139] Rph V, 3:308,21–30. Cf. PR 98: compensation is for damage to external possessions in a civil suit; and Igor Primoratz, *Banquos-Geist*, pp. 78–80.
[140] Rph I, 148,176–180; 148,195–196.
[141] Rph VI, 4:563,27–28.

as the will which is implicitly null, *eo ipso* contains its negation in itself and this negation is manifested as punishment. . . . The qualitative and quantitative characteristics of crime and its annulment fall, then, into the sphere of externality. In any case, no absolute determinacy is possible in this sphere.[142]

Reason cannot determine whether justice requires forty or thirty-nine lashes.[143] It is with some irony that Hegel says "too much or too little in these cases is an injustice."[144] "A criminal code cannot hold good for all times."[145] Hegel argues that the customs of a people determine what is commensurable. The nature of society shapes its penal code; "a penal code belongs to its time and the condition of its civil society."[146] "How retribution is fixed depends essentially on the custom [*Sitte*] of the people and also in part on the differences in class."[147] Hegel notes, for example, how "the Jews gave thirty-nine strokes since forty seemed a holy number and to give one less was seen as moderation."[148] In China, where in Hegel's view there is no self-reflection, penal measures are based on fear and are in effect a means of discipline; they are consequently severe and corporal.[149] This lack of subjectivity in China is reflected in their practice as a whole: Hegel notes that Chinese penal law disregards intent, and so one is hanged even for accidentally causing someone's death.[150] In India the caste system is reflected in the manner of punishing: Brahmans do not answer for crimes, and the codebook of Manu bases punishment largely on caste.[151] The spirit of the early Teutonic race also shaped its practice of meting out punishment. Murder was only fined, because it was seen not as an injury to the honor of the family but as a particular act lacking universality.[152]

Culture matters in determining what punishment fits what crime, but so do factors intrinsic to certain crimes: "Highway robbery is more serious than robbery in a village because its effect is to endanger universal communication, [and this] makes [highway robbery] seem dangerous."[153] Contingent factors also enter into the consideration of how much punishment is commensurate to the crime. The danger the crime poses to society

---

[142] PR 101 Rem, p. 72.
[143] Ibid., 214 Rem.
[144] Ibid.
[145] Ibid., 218 Z.
[146] Ibid., 218 Rem.
[147] Rph III, 89,9–14.
[148] Rph VI, 4:542,7–9.
[149] PH 161–165(127–131).
[150] Ibid., 163–164(129–130).
[151] Ibid., 190(152); 193(153–154).
[152] Ibid., 424–425(352–353).
[153] Rph VI, 4:279,17–28.

depends on circumstances, just as there is a great difference between a
spark thrown on gunpowder and one thrown on plain earth.[154] How
much to punish depends on the stability of society: "Above all the injury
is not so serious if the society is secure, if the universal is so fixed that it
cannot be injured."[155] If the society is wavering, punishment must serve
as an example. Thus in times just following war it is suitable to increase
the severity of punishment.[156]

By arguing that what counts as just punishment is a function of a society's values and stability, Hegel appears to commit himself to a relativist
position. Yet he is an ambivalent relativist. We can see this from his considerations of one of our most pressing problems: whether we should inflict capital punishment. Commentators disagree about whether Hegel
thinks the death penalty is just in some instances or whether he rejects it
in principle. Primoratz and Flechtheim think Hegel is for the death penalty on the principle of the *lex talionis*: they point to the remark to paragraph 100, where Hegel criticizes Cesare Beccaria, the famous opponent
of capital punishment. But a careful reading of the remark shows that in
it Hegel does not endorse capital punishment but merely criticizes Beccaria's *reason* for opposing capital punishment, that the state is a contract
and no one would have originally entered that contract were the state to
have the power of execution. They point also to a passage from the additions: "Now although requital cannot simply be made specifically equal
to the crime, the case is otherwise with murder, which is of necessity liable
to the death penalty; the reason is that since life is the full compass of a
man's existence, the punishment here cannot simply consist in a 'value,'
for none is great enough, but can consist only in taking away a second
life."[157] This is the sole passage where Hegel advocates the death penalty
for murder, and some commentators have either ignored it or refused to
give it determinative weight. For example, Hugh Reyburn writes "Although Hegel does not say so, there seems to be no reason why the extreme penalty must be regarded as the death sentence: penal servitude for
life, outlawry, or any other form of the total loss of rights, is an equivalent
of the death penalty; it is death so far as the rights of the person are concerned."[158] David Lamb argues that Hegel was opposed to the death penalty. In Lamb's view, Hegel does not think a rational modern state should
execute criminals, since the point of punishment is to reconcile the wrong-

[154] Ibid., 4:729,11–18.
[155] PR 96 Bem, p. 184.
[156] Rph III, 178,1–5. This need not imply that Hegel thinks that in a deeply divided society
where standards of right are in dispute severe punishment is justified. We have seen that
Hegel would say that punishment in such a society is unjust.
[157] PR 101 Z; cf. Rph V, 3:318–319.
[158] Hugh A. Reyburn, *The Ethical Theory of Hegel*, p. 154.

doer with his ethical community or to deter potential wrongdoers.[159] Hegel does say in his lectures that by commuting the death penalty to imprisonment we can make reform a goal, and that doing this does not violate his retributive principles,[160] but Lamb goes too far in suggesting that reform or deterrence is for Hegel "the point of punishment." David Pare is closer to the truth in saying that "although Hegel's retributivist philosophy of punishment is both logical and humane, it does permit capital punishment."[161]

Hegel's acknowledgment of the limits of philosophy in determining appropriate amounts of punishment forces him to make a "relativist" concession and accept the use of the death penalty, but it does not prevent him from criticizing a society forced to resort to this extreme form of punishment: the moral fabric of such a society is weak. In a fragment from his Frankfurt period he wrote that the Greeks did not resort to public executions to deter, because they were ethically strong: "the claimed necessity of cruel public punishment shows nothing more than the little trust that the lawgiver and judge can have in the ethical feeling of their people."[162]

5.7 Hegel as Practical Theorist

We have seen how Hegel applies to practical problems concerning legal punishment his political philosophy—his conception of right as the content of the free will, embodied in the practices, institutions, and laws of a modern state that we can understand to be our ethical substance. Hegel's criticism takes the form of immanent criticism, in that the principles he uses as standards by which to criticize or justify aspects of our practice are adduced from his interpretation of existing practice.

But we have also seen Hegel's ambivalence. Hegel's principle that we punish to mete out justice does not help him to decide whether we should force testimony against oneself for the sake of bringing truth to light; he uses his principles to defend public trials but admits an exception when a crime is "unclean." He fails to guide us if we want to know whether to make criminal actions about whose morality our society is divided.

When Hegel does become practical, he begins to compromise principles, turn consequentialist, waver. Applying theory is hard. The temptation is great to make exceptions to the principles to which we hold in

---

[159] David Lamb, *Hegel and Modern Philosophy*, p. 165.
[160] Rph VI, 4:553,28–31.
[161] David Pare, "Hegel's Concept of Punishment," p. 73.
[162] "Öffentliche Todesstrafe" ("Public Execution"), in *Frühe Schriften* (Hegel, *Werke*, vol. 1), p. 442 (fragment 15).

theory when we face tough, practical choices. Some will see in Hegel's vacillations and concessions the weakness of an idealist who hypocritically sells out when confronted with the contradictions of the real world to which he blinded himself; others, the compromises of a dialectician who insists that our ideals adapt to the exigencies of our practices. I share in the latter judgment. While Hegel's wavering and waffling show how circumscribed the power of his theory is, they are the necessary cost of his willing to be practical, political. Hegel tries systematically to order in terms of their right the numerous commitments that make up our ethical life. Perhaps he set for himself an impossible task. Hegel's uncertainty is greatest when he confronts conflicting values, for example, when he tries to balance the demands of due process with the demand of getting at the truth. The problem on which Hegel wavered is analogous to a problem with which we grapple—whether we should invoke the exclusionary rule, which prohibits the admission of evidence seized in violation of the Fourth Amendment's proscription against unreasonable searches and seizures. Application of the exclusionary rule means that sometimes a guilty criminal goes free. Yet refusal to apply it means that the courts have almost no power to enforce the Fourth Amendment.[163] We value both protection of society and the principle that wrongdoers should be brought to justice, on the one hand, and judicial integrity and the rights of individuals that the Fourth Amendment was constructed to protect, on the other. Sometimes values conflict, and it is difficult to say which are more important. Values within a practice may conflict with each other or with values external to the practice. Hegel rarely acknowledges explicitly that our practices sometimes contain conflicting, perhaps incommensurable values.[164] The closest he comes is when he admits there are limits to what philosophical speculation can recommend. His wavering and vacillations are an implicit acknowledgment.

As immanent critic, Hegel adduces the principle(s) underlying a practice in order to criticize the actual practice when it diverges from the princi-

---

[163] For discussion, see the exchanges between Yale Kamisar, who defends the exclusionary rule on the grounds of both principle and consequences, and Malcolm Richard Wilkey, who opposes the rule for its frustrating crime control (*Judicature* 62, no. 2 [August 1978]; 62, no. 5 [November 1978]; and 62, no. 7 [February 1979].) For empirical evidence that the exclusionary rule leads to the release of otherwise guilty persons and is ineffective as a deterrent to police misconduct, see Steven R. Schlesinger, in *Judicature* 62, no. 8 (March 1979). But for compelling counter evidence, see Peter F. Nardulli, "The Societal Cost of the Exclusionary Rule: An Empirical Assessment"; and Thomas Davies, "A Hard Look at What We Know About the Costs of the Exclusionary Rule: The NIJ Study and Other Studies of Lost Arrests."

[164] He does acknowledge the clash between the abstract right to property and the right to life in his discussion of the right of distress, PR 127–128.

ple(s). The immanent critic presupposes the essential justice of existing practices, for it is from these practices that the immanent critic gets the standards with which he criticizes actual practices. Hegel, we saw, presupposes that our state is essentially rational. Hegel thinks that we can feel at home, and be free, in the state. This does not mean he thinks every aspect of our practices, laws, and institutions is right or ideal. But, as we shall see, Hegel thinks we can reconcile ourselves to a less than ideal actuality by an act of theory. Hegel believes that historically an ethical life emerges that is on the whole or essentially rational, so that the standards Hegel uses as immanent critic will be rational. But, we must ask, what is the immanent critic to do if our practices are bad root and branch? Does Hegel's commitment to immanent criticism, to the materials at hand, and to the metaphysics that to him ultimately justifies the materials at hand, leave him unable ever to be a radical critic? It is to these crucial questions that we shall turn in the final chapter, in which we shall step back and reflect on Hegel's political philosophy as a whole.

Appendix to Chapter Five _____

Translation of Passage from Rph III on Political Crime

From Hegel, *Philosophie des Rechts: Die Vorlesung von 1819/20 in einer Nachschrift*, ed. Dieter Henrich (Frankfurt am Main: Suhrkamp Verlag, 1983), pp. 195–196.

The poor person feels excluded from everything and ridiculed, and from this inevitably arises an inner anger [*Empörung*]. He has the consciousness of himself as infinite, free, and he comes to demand that external existence accord with this consciousness. In civil society it is not merely a natural need with which the poor man has to struggle; the nature opposing the poor man is not simply a being, but a will. The poor man feels himself as relating himself to arbitrary will [*Willkür*], to human contingency, and from this comes the outrage [*Empörende*] that in the last analysis he is put in this conflict by the arbitrary will of other human beings. Self-consciousness appears driven to this point where there is no more right, where freedom has no existence. At this point, where the existence [*Dasein*] of freedom has become something entirely contingent, inner anger [*Empörung*] is inevitable. Because the freedom of the individual has no existence, the recognition of universal freedom vanishes. From this condition arises the shamelessness we find in the rabble [*Pöbel*]. The rabble arise mainly out of a developed civil society. When the individuals aren't yet self-conscious of their rights, they remain in natural poverty. This natural poverty leads at least to unemployment and usually to idleness. When this happens, any hope of modifying one's self-confidence is lost.[165] Envy and hate emerge on the part of the poor against those who have something.

Earlier we had seen the right of distress as relating to a momentary necessity. Here necessity no longer has this purely momentary character. In the emergence of poverty the power of particularity comes to existence against the reality of the free. Herein is the basis leading to the infinite judgment of the criminal. The crime can well be punished, but this punishment is contingent. In the uniting of substance in its entire scope lies a uniting of objective right in general.[166] Just as on the one side poverty is

[165] My reading of "Damit gehen die Modifikationen des Selbstgefühls überhaupt verloren."

[166] This last passage is obscure also in the German, as Henrich notes. Hegel seems to mean that the ethical substance dissolves when the rich and the poor are so divided that the laws

HEGEL'S IMMANENT CRITICISM

the root cause of the rabble's plight, and of the lack of recognition of right [*Nichtanerkennung des Rechts*], so on the other side the wealthy acquire the same way of thinking as the rabble. The rich man regards all as for purchase for himself, because he knows himself as the power of particularity of self-consciousness. Wealth can thus lead to the same ridicule and shamelessness that is characteristic of the poor rabble. The disposition of the master over the slave is the same as that of the slave. The master knows himself as the power, just as the slave knows himself as the realization of freedom and the idea. Insofar as the master knows himself as master over the freedom of the other, so vanishes the substance of spirit. Here we find the bad conscience not only as inward, but as an actuality that is recognized.

---

of the society are seen by the poor as serving only the capricious interests of the wealthy. A crime, or an infinite judgment, expresses the poor man's total rejection of the rich man's conception of legal justice; and punishment, to the poor man, is arbitrary, not the criminal's real will, not *Recht-an-sich*.

Six

Theory and Practice

6.1 The Power of Theory: Kierkegaard vs. Marx

A single man, no home, no meaningful job, sits in an East Oakland jail, convicted of buying crack, which he takes to escape his miserable life. A Berkeley Hegelian speaks to him on behalf of the state: "As you sit in your cell, you feel unfree. But you aren't. We are punishing you because you have broken our laws. But these laws are your laws as well, and really you are punishing yourself. It is your implicit, rational will to act in accordance with the law, and in doing so you are really free. When you take crack, your natural will overcomes your true will. By punishing you we are respecting you as a rational being who lost control (it happens to all of us sometimes). When you reflect you should realize that really the will that punishes you is your own. It is only your unreflective side that makes you feel unfree. As you sit in your cell, reflect, and then rejoice in your freedom."

Not very convincing. Our Hegelian assumes that this man is at home in the laws, practices, and institutions of the state, and that he sees or can come to see as right what they declare to be right. But maybe this man is homeless in more than one sense. Maybe he does not share in the values of the state. Given the facts of his life, maybe it would not even be rational for him to will its laws. He might think of himself as a member not of the state that punishes him, which he regards as a "They," but, say, of his street gang. His gang might provide him with an identity and meaning the state denies him. In his gang he counts as somebody, he has prestige and purpose, he feels at home; in relation to the state he is a nobody who has nothing. The rules as practiced are rigged against him and his like. Couldn't we even say that, in light of such facts, if this man did feel at home in the state he would have things all wrong?

Does Hegel want the convict to feel he is at home in his state, and free in his punishment, even when he is not? Is Hegel's objective as political theorist to fool us into believing we are at home when in fact we are not?

Before we answer these questions, let us take a very different example. A married woman meets an attractive man and wants to have sex with him. She knows she should not, but she really wants to.[1] Our Hegelian

---

[1] Perhaps it is quaint to say that "she knows she should not," given the prevalence of

speaks: "Your commitment to your husband seems like a chain right now. But pause and reflect. Think of the importance of your commitment, what it means to you. Weigh the momentary pleasure you might get from satisfying your natural will against the potential loss breaking this commitment would mean to your life. Think! Which is the real chain: your commitment, or this desire?"

If Hegel's theory is right that marriage is essentially a strong ethical commitment in which the partners are free, even though they each may at times feel unfree when required as part of the commitment to renounce certain desires, and if Hegel's interpretation of marriage fits the facts of this woman's marriage, then our woman may well decide to remain faithful, in which case theory has its day. But suppose the marriage has problems; for example, the husband had already been unfaithful, or for some other reason the facts of this marriage do not fit Hegel's account of marriage as a strong mutual ethical commitment. Theory might be silenced, or might even encourage the tempted woman to satisfy her desires.

Facts matter. If by all accounts of the East Oakland man's actual life it makes no sense to say he is at home in his state, or that it is his highest commitment, then the theorist's most honest advice to him might well be, "Make a break for it!"[2]

Hegel is torn. He would feel the pull of facts silencing the theorist: the single, unemployed man is not at home in his state, and the wife with the unfaithful husband is not at home in her marriage. Yet Hegel feels also the power of theory, not to *change* facts, but to devalue, or have us persevere even in the face of, some facts. Hegel would not claim that theory can change facts: he would not insist to a woman married to a promiscuous husband that really her husband is faithful; nor would he insist to the marginalized and homeless man that really he has a house and a meaningful job. But with a sufficiently persuasive theory of marriage or

---

extramarital sex in our society. Later, in discussing the dialectical relation between actual and ideal, I shall take this up.

[2] The two cases, of the single East Oakland man and of the wife, seem different. The woman chose to marry her husband, and she might have done otherwise. But did the single man ever choose his state? Clearly not in the same way. Some commitments, it seems, we explicitly choose, like those we make to a spouse or to our friends. Other commitments are less clearly the product of an explicit choice: has a lawyer chosen her career, given that she couldn't get an appointment as professor of philosophy and rather than be a waitress decided to go to law school? Some commitments we seem to be born into—our natal family, state, perhaps religion—but we can speak of these as choices insofar as we choose to remain committed to them after the fact. While we have no say about our natal family, our commitment to it, and our fulfillment of the obligations entailed by our commitment, *are* a matter of choice. While the case of the East Oakland man born into a state is different from that of a wife choosing her husband (and also from that of an immigrant who makes an explicit choice of citizenship), in both cases we can speak of a choice.

the modern state as commitments in which we are free, the theorist might get our convict, or our wife, to feel at home and free in these commitments despite the facts. But here facts tug at Hegel: as we shall see in this chapter, Hegel does not want us to feel at home when in fact we are not. His goal is not to invent a happy pill to ease the pain of our chains by making us feel free. Hegel wants us to *be* free, to *be* at home, and recognize that we are *when* we are.

But for Hegel there is no sharp distinction between "being at home" and "feeling at home." For Hegel, thought itself changes being. Interpretation has ontological status. By our theoretical act of comprehension, an act of interpretation, we shape the world, it becomes what it is (for us); yet interpretations can be inadequate to the world. Things, after all, rarely are as theory has them. The line between thinking and being, between what the world is in itself and what it is for us, sometimes seems to vanish for Hegel; other times it reappears but remains elusive. Similarly, the line between real and merely felt unfreedom is thin and hard to draw. Is the fact that the East Oakland man can get only demeaning work, or none, or must turn to an underground economy to obtain a decent income and some dignity,[3] enough to show he is not at home in the state? The facts of this man's life are a pity, but do they prove he is unfree in the state? Perhaps these facts reflect mere contingencies, or bad luck, so that they prove nothing about the "essential" relation this man has with his state. Which facts tug so hard that Hegel gives up on the power of theory to have us persevere in the face of them?

Hegel gives accounts of various commitments—to property, to spouse, to state—call them "ideal" accounts, or accounts of "ideal commitments." When we do what ideal commitments require we are free in them. A life of ideal commitments might be called *ideality*. Ideality might

[3] Consider this account by Philippe Bourgeois, "Just Another Night on Crack Street," in the *New York Times Magazine*, Nov. 12, 1989, p. 62: "Most of the people I have met are proud that they are not being exploited by 'the White Man.' All of them have, at one time or another, held the jobs . . . that are objectively recognized as among the least desirable in American society. They see the illegal, underground economy as not only offering superior wages, but also a more dignified workplace." Bourgeois explains what this dignity is like: "The feeling of self-worth that the street level dealer's lifestyle offers cannot be underestimated. A former manager of a coke-shooting gallery who had employed a network of a half-dozen sellers, lookouts and security guards before he was jailed, explained to me that the best memories of his drug-dealing days were of the respect he received from people on the street—as a dealer, when he drove up in one of his cars to pick up the day's receipts, a bevy of attentive men and women would run to open the door for him and engage him in polite small talk. Others would offer to clean his car. He would invite a half-dozen friends and acquaintances out to dinner in expensive restaurants almost every night" (p. 94).

not correspond with *actuality*, or life as it actually is. Hegel claims that his ideal accounts are interpretations of actuality. Of course actual life is messy; things rarely are as theory has them. But what if actuality is almost never like ideality? How bad does actuality have to be before we declare that commitment to its ideals entails giving up our actual commitments, as when the homeless man resists the law because "this is not justice" ("I don't get anything from the system; it isn't just, so why play by its rules!"), or the woman pursues love outside of her marriage because "this is no marriage!"[4] How bad does actuality have to be before we give up our commitment to its ideals? At what point are we so much not at home that Hegel would stop trying to make us feel at home and instead get us to reassess our actual commitments, perhaps to break them and form new ones? In the rest of this chapter we shall work for an answer to these questions.

To some, the world is so chaotic that they not only are not at home in it, but they cannot make sense enough of it even to secure the comfort of at least feeling at home. In their view, we cannot extract from the tangle of conflicting values and commitments any conception of ideality. To systematize, to order, to find principles by which we can make sense of the world and happily live our lives in it, is a mistake, is to be untrue to a random and essentially contested universe. We are deceived by prophets who claim to find order, to make sense of the world. According to this understanding we are not at home and cannot feel at home. In this world there is no need for theory, just as there would perhaps be no need for theory in a world in which we were perfectly at home and felt at home.

The need to theorize arises from a sense of crisis: we think we can feel at home, but we don't. Some theory is content with getting us *just* to feel at home, to live in an ideality oblivious to actuality. Other theory insists we must be at home and suggests that we change actuality. Hegel's theory belongs to the latter sort. In the following section, I shall take the work of Soren Kierkegaard as theory of the former sort, so that by contrasting it with Hegel's we can better understand what Hegel is up to.

---

[4] Some argue that the true revolutionary does precisely this: rather than setting up new ideals, she appeals to the old ideals in challenging the existing order. Hannah Arendt writes, "Nothing could be farther removed from the original meaning of the word 'revolution' than the idea of which all revolutionary actors have been possessed and obsessed, namely, that they are agents in a process which spells the definite end of an old order and brings about the birth of a new world. . . . In the seventeenth century, where we find the word for the first time as a political term, the metaphoric content was even closer to the original meaning of the word, for it was used for a movement of revolving back to some pre-established point and, by implication, of swinging back into a preordained order" (*On Revolution*, pp. 36–37).

6.1.1   Feeling at Home Though We Are Not: Kierkegaard's
Knight of Faith

Kierkegaard raises the possibility, if we are strong enough to be "knights of faith," of holding to ideality regardless of actuality. In *Fear and Trembling* Kierkegaard asks us to imagine that

> [a] young lad falls in love with a princess, and this love is the entire substance of his life, and yet the relation is such that it cannot possibly be realized, cannot possibly be translated from ideality into reality. Of course, the slaves of the finite, the frogs in the swamp of life, scream: That kind of love is foolishness; the rich brewer's widow is just as good and solid a match. Let them go croaking in the swamp. The knight of infinite resignation does not do any such thing; he does not give up the love, not for all the glories of the world.[5]

The frogs of whom Kierkegaard speaks are the pragmatists who insist that an ideal is of no value if it cannot be made actual. Whether the ideal can be made actual is of no matter to the knight of infinite resignation—the ideal is of no less value for being unattainable.

In this passage Kierkegaard refers to a knight of infinite resignation. The difference between this knight and the knight of faith is the difference between Socrates and Abraham. The former renounces actuality for the ideal and suffers as a tragic hero. The latter, the knight of faith, also renounces actuality, but he has faith in what is impossible and absurd, that his ideal will become actual. Were the young lad in Kierkegaard's story a knight of faith, "[h]is love for that princess would become for him the expression of an eternal love, would assume a religious character, would be transfigured into a love of the eternal being, which true enough denied the fulfillment but nevertheless did reconcile him once more in the eternal consciousness of its validity in an eternal form that no actuality can take away from him."[6] With faith we can feel at home in an idealized love, impervious to the contingency the finite world brings to actual love. No one can take away one's ideal love.

For Kierkegaard, the renunciation of an actuality that threatens ideality is a spiritual move, a move resembling Stoic withdrawal from the world: "Spiritually speaking, everything is possible, but in the finite world there is much that is not possible. The knight, however, makes this impossibility possible by expressing it spiritually, but he expresses it spiritually by

---

[5] Søren Kierkegaard, *Fear and Trembling*, trans. Howard V. Hong and Edna H. Hong, pp. 41–42. I shall refer to passages from this work as expressing Kierkegaard's views, even though this "dialectical lyric" is said to be authored by Johannes De Silentio.

[6] Ibid., pp. 43–44. The passages I cite refer to the former knight, but his moves are made also by the knight of faith.

renouncing it. The desire that would lead him out into actuality but has been stranded on impossibility is now turned inward, but it is not therefore lost, nor is it forgotten."[7] This renunciation of an actuality that contradicts the ideal is, for Kierkegaard, an act of faith, an apolitical act in the extreme: "From the moment [the knight of faith] has made the movement, the princess is lost. . . . He is no longer finitely concerned about what the princess does, and precisely this proves that he has made the movement infinitely."[8]

Politics is about acts in the finite world, the world of actuality. We can bring ideals to our politics, but unless our ideals bear on actuality, unless we can use them to effect change practically, they are not political. For Kierkegaard, the world in which politics makes a difference is unimportant. The only world that counts is a world of spirituality, a world unconstrained by the demands of the possible. For Kierkegaard, we can feel at home, though not in the actual world, by transfiguring actuality into an ideal, by an act of faith. Commitment to an ideal world does not require one to feel at home in, be committed to, or be reconciled to the actual world. If anything, it replaces actual commitments. Kierkegaard's knight is at home somewhere, but not here. In this world he is a pilgrim and a stranger.

6.1.2   Changing House to Feel at Home: What Counts as Change?

It is precisely this turn away from reality that Hegel criticizes so vehemently as a "Hindu fanaticism of pure contemplation,"[9] and in the *Phenomenology* associates with Stoicism, Scepticism, and the unhappy consciousness.[10] The Stoic's aim, he says, is to be free in thought, "to maintain that lifeless indifference which steadfastly withdraws from the bustle of existence, alike from being active as passive, into the simple essentiality of thought. . . . Stoicism is the freedom which always comes directly out of bondage and returns into the pure universality of thought."[11] The problem Hegel sees in Stoic freedom is that it "has only pure thought as its truth, a truth lacking the fullness of life." For Hegel, "freedom in thought . . . [is] not the living reality of freedom itself."[12] The knight of faith's love is enduring and fixed, not subject to the vagaries of human

[7] Ibid., p. 44.
[8] Ibid.
[9] PR 5 Rem.
[10] PhdG 197ff.
[11] Ibid., 199.
[12] Ibid., 200.

caprice and contingency. But it is not real love. Real love objectifies itself. An ideal love cannot conceive.[13]

To be fully free we must return to actuality. We must be practical, political. It is not enough just to think. To be practical is not to be unthinking or to have no ideals. It is to actualize thought, to put ideals into practice. But how?

6.1.2.1 MARX: MUST CHANGE THE BUILDING

In his introduction to the *Contribution to the Critique of Hegel's Philosophy of Right* Marx reflects on the relation between theory and practice, between ideality and actuality: "It is clear that the arm of criticism cannot replace the criticism of arms. Material force can only be overthrown by material force; but theory itself becomes a material force when it has seized the masses. Theory is capable of seizing the masses when it demonstrates *ad hominem*, and it demonstrates *ad hominem* as soon as it becomes radical. To be radical is to grasp things by the root."[14]

Theory grasps things. The German word Marx uses for grasp, *fassen*, is ambiguous, as is its synonym, *begreifen* (and as are the English "to grasp" and "to comprehend"). We have already seen how Hegel plays with this ambiguity: Does grasping mean an act of understanding, merely, or does it mean a physical taking hold of? Is the task of theory to change our consciousness or to change the world? Marx is famous for declaring that philosophers "have only interpreted the world, in various ways; the point, however, is to change it."[15] Is the theoretical act of grasping merely an interpretation of the world, or does it count as changing the world? If we come to a new interpretation, have we not changed the world?

In his *Critique* Marx distinguishes interpreting from changing by distinguishing theory from practice. He sees the two as connected: "theoretical emancipation has a specific practical importance."[16] But, for Marx, theory by itself is not enough to make actual an ideal. Marx thinks Germany lags behind other European countries because its intellectuals only philosophize; they don't get their hands dirty in political struggles. Germany has "accompanied the development of the modern nations only

---

[13] So the line between "being" and "feeling" is crucial. But sometimes it is easy to draw; other times it is not so easy.

[14] Marx, *Critique*, in Robert C. Tucker, ed., *The Marx-Engels Reader*, 2nd ed., p. 60. Karl Marx and Friedrich Engels, *Marx-Engels Gesamtausgabe* (MEGA), vol. 2, p. 177. In citing from this work henceforth, the first number refers to the Tucker edition, the second to the German edition.

[15] *Theses on Feuerbach*, in Tucker, p. 145.

[16] Marx, *Critique*, p. 60 (177).

through the abstract activity of thought, without taking an active part in the real struggles of this development."[17]

Theory must penetrate practice; the two must unite to conceive a new, theoretically informed actuality: "Just as philosophy finds its material weapons in the proletariat, so the proletariat finds its intellectual weapons in philosophy. And once the lightning of thought has penetrated deeply into this virgin soil of the people, the Germans will emancipate themselves and become men [*Menschen*]."[18] For Marx, philosophy must use "material weapons." Philosophy must be realized by action; action must be informed by philosophy. Marx is disgusted with his Germany because "practical life is as little intellectual as intellectual life is practical."[19] The intellectual must acquire the tools with which to demolish existing institutions and practices.

For Marx, theory's grasping is a mental act that leads to a physical taking hold of. To be at home requires we tear down social institutions. The failure of Germany's political revolution was precisely that it left "the pillars of the building standing."[20] The Russian Marxist Evgeny Pashukanis clearly emphasizes this view, that for being at home in the world, mere theory or grasping in the sense of understanding is not enough:

> The forms of bourgeois consciousness cannot be eliminated by a critique in terms of ideas alone, for they form a united whole with the material relations of which they are the expression. The only way to dissipate these appearances which have become reality is by overcoming the corresponding relations in practice, that is by realising socialism through the revolutionary struggle of the proletariat.[21]

6.1.2.2   HEGEL: INTERPRETATIONS CHANGE

Where Marx and his epigones emphasize the sense of *fassen* or *begreifen* as "physically to take hold of," Hegel, while acknowledging this sense of the word, emphasizes the other sense. In his *Lectures on the History of Philosophy*, in discussing Cicero's account of Zeno, Hegel explains the double meaning of *begreifen*:

> Zeno illustrated the moments of [the appropriation of truth] by a movement of the hand. When he showed the open palm he said that this was a sensuous perception; when he bent the fingers somewhat, this was a mental assent through which the conception is declared to be mine; when he pressed them

[17] Ibid., p. 61 (178). We shall see that Hegel agrees. See sec. 6.2.
[18] Ibid., p. 65 (182).
[19] Ibid., p. 64 (181).
[20] Ibid., p. 62 (179).
[21] Evgeny B. Pashukanis, *Law and Marxism*, trans. Barbara Einhorn, p. 194.

quite together and formed a fist, this was comprehension, just as in German we speak of *begreifen* when by means of our senses we lay hold of anything in a similar way.[22]

Begreifen is both a mental appropriation and a physical movement, a taking hold of. For Hegel, grasping in thought leads to a physical taking hold of the world through an act of will. We understand actuality as ideality by a mental act, commit ourselves to this actuality, and will accordingly. Practical activity, for Hegel, results from willing guided by thought.

We can see what this process of thinking and willing, of making actual the ideal, is like by returning to the example that engaged Kierkegaard, of being in love. We have a picture of our ideal love. Hegel insists our ideal derives from actuality, so we can think of our picture as being of our actual beloved. Our beloved is not always like our ideal picture, perhaps not as caring or intelligent or energetic or beautiful as our ideal. This is why commitment is so important. Actuality does not always live up to ideality. We commit ourselves to our love with the ideal in mind. We are committed to an ideal with which we do not always, or even often actually, live. Yet we remain committed, not because the ideal blinds us to the facts, to what the actual is really like, but because we think that what really counts in the actual is the ideal. Commitment to an ideal entails acceptance of an actuality that cannot always live up to the ideal. Hegel's conception of theory is based on the assumption that so long as we can see the ideal in the actual, abstract it out, we can be free in our commitment to a less than ideal actuality.

Marx suggests that Hegel's brand of theory by itself merely interprets and reconciles, makes us feel at home, but that to be at home we must get up out of the philosopher's armchair and seize material tools with which we change the world through action. But for Hegel practical theory, the act of grasping, both interprets and changes. In thinking, we might reconcile ourselves with the present, choosing to keep our commitments; or we might be critical of the present, in one of two ways: we might see a discrepancy between aspects of actuality and ideality and try to bring actuality closer to the ideal, while at the same time modifying our ideal more closely to fit actuality—it is in this dialectical activity that the immanent critic engages; or we might see an irreconcilable discrepancy between actuality and ideality and declare either that commitment to ideality entails giving up our actual commitments or that we need to formulate a new conception of the ideal. This is radical criticism. The immanent critic remains committed to existing understandings of both the actual and the ideal (we can revise and be committed), while the radical critic gives up on one or both. In all three cases, of reconciliation,

---

[22] HP 2:250–251.

immanent criticism, and radical criticism, we are thinking and then acting.

Marx and Hegel part ways on whether interpretation itself constitutes action and change, but also on whether practical theory *must* be radical. For Marx, the task of theory, at least in capitalist society, is to criticize at the roots, not to reconcile. Where Marx and Pashukanis argue that to translate their sort of theory into practice we must tear down and build anew, for Hegel this translation does not necessarily require radical change.[23] Few will disagree that, unlike Marx, Hegel opposes radical criticism. We shall consider later in this chapter the extent of Hegel's opposition. What is more controversial, and central to the interpretation of Hegel I am putting forth, is that Hegel sets against radical criticism, such as we find in Marx, not a conservatism, but a different form of criticism, immanent criticism. By an act of interpretation, Hegel develops from existing laws, practices, and institutions an account of their purpose(s) and the principles to which we must adhere if we are to realize their purpose(s). With this ideal account, Hegel criticizes actuality when it diverges from the ideal immanent in actuality. For Hegel, the theorist's foremost objective is to make actual the ideal by a process of thinking and willing that reconciles us to our existing commitments, or at most offers immanent criticism. Often Hegel sounds as if he rejects the very possibility of radical criticism, insisting that if we come to feel at home we *will* be at home. But Hegel is ambivalent. Sometimes actuality comes to look nothing like ideality. Our existing commitments feel like chains, and we want

---

[23] We have already seen how for Marx Germany's failure was in leaving "the pillars of the building standing" (Marx, *Critique*, p. 62 [179]). In the *Eighteenth Brumaire* Marx again says that the first French Revolution failed because it perfected the state machine "instead of smashing it" (cited by V. I. Lenin in *The State and Revolution*, p. 34). Marx calls for "entirely revolutionising the mode of production," a process that will upend not only the institution of private property, but also the whole of bourgeois jurisprudence, which, Marx tells the capitalists, "is but the will of your class made into a law for all" (*Communist Manifesto*, in Tucker, pp. 490, 487). Lenin seized on the passages in Marx that seem to equate criticism with castigation or the complete uprooting of the old: the working class must "break up, smash" the state machinery; the task is to "smash the old bureaucratic machine at once and to begin immediately to construct a new one" (Lenin, pp. 46, 59).

In another reading, Marx insists not on pulling everything up by the roots, but on building a new society from within the old. But I think it is a mistake to read Marx as an immanent critic. Marx does not try to rescue practices within capitalist society, such as legal punishment or marriage, by bringing us back to their true purpose—he rejects their purpose, rejects these practices root and branch. The standards for justice by which Marx criticizes the old and calls for a new society no doubt are immanent within the old society, and of course the means of change, the proletariat, organize and work from within the old society; but with respect to practices and institutions (not all, to be sure—Marx says nothing about practices such as playing chess, producing plays, grading exams, etc.), Marx insists on not reform but revolution—and by revolution he does not mean keeping our commitments.

to break them. Hegel calls us back to actuality when we feel like with-drawing. Yet he recognizes that sometimes we have good reasons for wanting to escape actuality. Hegel calls us back also to ideality.

Kierkegaard's knight of faith avoids the conflict between ideal and ac-tual. Hegel insists we live it. For Hegel, theory and practice are in dialec-tical tension; in the next section, we shall look at this tension by unpack-ing the enigmatic and famous sentence "What is rational is actual and what is actual is rational."[24] While in this sentence Hegel seems to claim that the ideal is actual, and the actual is the ideal, so that there is no room for criticism, he is really trying to express this complicated tension.

6.2   "The Actual Is the Rational"

What is rational is actual and what is actual is rational. On this conviction the plain man like the philosopher takes his stand, and from it philosophy starts in its study of the universe of mind as well as the universe of nature. If reflection, feeling, or whatever form subjective consciousness may take, looks upon the present as something vacuous and looks beyond it with the eyes of superior wisdom, it finds itself in a vacuum. . . . [T]he great thing is to apprehend in the show of the temporal and transient the substance which is immanent and the eternal which is present.

The first line of this famous passage from the preface to the *Philosophy of Right* has come to be used as a one-sentence summary of Hegel's polit-ical philosophy, and, as we would expect of a brief summary, it oversim-plifies and trivializes this complicated philosophy.

In claiming that "the actual is the rational" Hegel has often been un-derstood to justify all existing status quos, to give up criticism. Rudolf Haym writes, "All that Hobbes or Filmer, Haller or Stahl have taught, is relatively open minded in comparison with the famous phrase regarding the rationality of the real in the sense of Hegel's preface. The theory of divine free grace and the theory of absolute obedience are blameless and innocuous in comparison with the frightful doctrine which canonizes the subsisting as such."[25] To Sean Sayers, Hegel's philosophy "gives not crit-icism but consolation; it teaches us to give up the restless desire to con-demn and repudiate the existing order." In this view, to say "the actual is the rational" is to say "there is no place here for criticism—no need for it";[26] Hegel's dictum is not "loose exaggeration and rhetoric on Hegel's part," but "an essential ingredient of his philosophy and of his ideal-

[24] PR Preface, p. 10.
[25] Rudolf Haym, *Hegel und seine Zeit*, p. 367. Cited in Hugh Reyburn, *The Ethical The-ory of Hegel*, p. 63 note.
[26] Sean Sayers, "The Actual Is the Rational," pp. 147–148.

ism."[27] Another commentator, Andrew Arato, understands Hegel to be claiming that "after reflection the existing ethos will turn out to be rational," a claim Arato finds "astonishing." "But what if after the most thorough reflection, the opposite turned out to be the case?" Arato understands Hegel's dictum to exclude the possibility that there can be a clash between right and duty, between the rational will of the subject and the laws and institutions of the state.[28] Sidney Hook similarly concludes that Hegel, rather than being critical, accommodates himself to whatever power is in place at the time: "But [Hegel] nowhere tells us when the 'existent' becomes irrational. His judgment is always *ex post facto*. Like those who invoke God's will and wisdom in history, the exact equivalent of *die List der Vernunft* [the cunning of reason], he is always wise after the event. Until then he is on the side of the 'Powers that Be.' "[29] Ossip Flechtheim calls Hegel's philosophy "passive" and writes, "unable to realize his ideal, Hegel idealized reality." To Flechtheim, Hegel's world "was the best of all possible worlds, not needing any fundamental innovations and revolutions, at most small corrections and narrow reforms."[30] Theodor Adorno, too, echoes the view with which we are by now all too familiar:

> Hegel stills criticism: whoever relies on the limited activity of his own Understanding is called by Hegel with the political pejorative "Raisonneur"; he accuses him of vanity, because he doesn't think of his own finitude, is incapable of comprehending and submitting to a higher totality. This higher order is according to Hegel the existing. . . . The individual citizen should capitulate before society.[31]

These commentators take Hegel to be justifying whatever laws, practices, and institutions exist, some imputing this position to Hegel's idealism. Yet none makes clear exactly how Hegel's idealism works: Is Hegel claiming that ideality actually exists? Or that we should merely regard actuality as ideal, as rational? The former position is patently absurd and is not Hegel's. But is the latter? We must unpack Hegel's dictum to see precisely what he is claiming.

The first step in seeing what Hegel means is to see that perhaps Hegel does not really mean what he has published. We already know that Hegel published his *Philosophy of Right* following censorship decrees in Prus-

[27] Ibid., p. 148.

[28] Andrew Arato, "A Reconstruction of Hegel's Theory of Civil Society," p. 1365.

[29] Sidney Hook, "Hegel Rehabilitated?" p. 56.

[30] Ossip Flechtheim, *Hegels Strafrechtstheorie*, pp. 16, 26, 119.

[31] "Kritik," in *Die Zeit*, no. 26, June 27, 1969. Cited in Ernst Topitsch, *Die Sozialphilosophie Hegels als Heilslehre und Herrschaftsideologie*, pp. 72–73.

sia, and that he had practical reasons to accommodate himself to the Prussian government, to appear to legitimate the powers that be.[32]

There is some evidence that the version of the dictum Hegel published is an exoteric variation of an esoteric dictum with a very different message. In his lectures on the *Rechtsphilosophie* immediately preceding the publication of the *Philosophy of Right*, notes of which were recently discovered and published in the German by Dieter Henrich, Hegel is reported to have said, "what is rational becomes actual; and actuality becomes rational."[33] With this version Hegel clearly distances himself from the indefensible claim that actuality is by definition rational. Still, Hegel might be understood to claim that there is a metaphysical guarantee that our institutions are bound to become rational, or that our standards of rationality are bound to adjust to fit those institutions, and so this version is insufficient to dispel the charge that Hegel passively accommodates himself to what is, waiting until it *becomes* rational.[34]

In another version, recorded during the last series of *Rechtsphilosophie* lectures he gave, Hegel repeats that "what is actual is rational" but adds,

> But not everything that exists is actual. The bad self-destructs and is a non-entity. Freedom is to comprehend [*fassen*]; this is just how theoretical spirit frees itself. What spirit does not comprehend [*begreifen*] stands opposed to it, is something other for it. If spirit comprehends it, then it has the substance of the thing and it is in spirit, it is at home in it [*bei sich selbst*]. If I have the concept of the sun, I am of course not in possession of its external existence, but I am in possession of its substance.[35]

In this passage Hegel makes use of a distinction, between actuality and existence, that he explains in his *Lesser Logic*. There he refers to his famous and often misunderstood dictum: "In the Preface to my *Philosophy of Right* are found the propositions: 'What is rational is actual', and 'what is actual is rational'. These simple statements have given rise to expressions of surprise and hostility, even in quarters where it would be reckoned an insult to presume absence of philosophy."[36] Hegel says he had assumed the readers of his *Philosophy of Right* would have "enough intelligence to know" that "existence is in part mere appearance, and only in part actuality." For Hegel, existence includes "any freak of fancy, any

---

[32] See my discussion in sec. 1.2.

[33] "Was vernünftig ist, wird wirklich; und das Wirkliche wird vernünftig" (Rph III, 50–51).

[34] Another passage from the lectures is just as ambiguous: "The state *must*, in its institutions, be a temple of reason" (Rph I, 246, 448–449). Perhaps the "must" reflects a yearning, which means there is no metaphysical guarantee that the state will be a temple of reason. But the "must" is ambiguous.

[35] Rph VII, 4:923,14–25.

[36] Enz 6.

error, evil and everything of the nature of evil, as well as every degenerate and transitory existence whatever," and it is a mistake to include such contingencies as part of actuality: "As for the term actuality, [my] critics would have done well to consider the sense in which I employ it. In a detailed *Logic* I had treated among other things of actuality, and accurately distinguished it . . . from the contingent, which, after all, has existence."[37]

The version of Hegel's dictum that we find in the lecture notes Henrich discovered deflects the criticisms of the published dictum: Hegel does not identify the actual with the rational, for the actual must *become* rational. But with this distinction between actuality and existence we need not assume there is an exoteric and esoteric, true Hegel. With his elaboration in the *Encyclopaedia* we can find the true Hegel in the published *Philosophy of Right*, though we might wonder why Hegel published a formulation he surely knew would bring confusion.[38]

With the distinction between actuality and existence in hand, we can understand "the actual is the rational" to mean, not that every aspect of existing society is rational, but, rather, that society consists of essentially rational institutions, practices, and laws that nevertheless might occasionally make irrational demands on us.[39] Such bursts of irrationality we are to regard not as actual, but as merely existing.[40] With his distinction Hegel postulates a three-level ontology consisting of the ideal, the actual, and the existing, and he claims that the ideal, or the theoretical account of rational laws, practices, and institutions, is, or becomes, actual.

Hegel's dictum expresses his judgment that existing irrationalities do

[37] Ibid. On the distinction between existence and actuality, see also PH 53 (36) ("Only that which is divinely executed is, has actuality; what does not measure up to God's plan is merely foul existence"); and PR 1 Bem ("Actuality is the realization of the Concept; existence lacks the Concept [*begriffslos*], is contingent and untrue").

[38] We have just seen that Hegel expected his readers to know the difference between actuality and existence, but nevertheless he must have known that the formulation in his preface would be construed by some of his readers (perhaps nonphilosophically minded government officials?) to justify whatever exists. Might Hegel even have been counting on the ambiguity of his dictum?

[39] There are further complexities to Hegel's view. Hegel does not think that all societies are "essentially rational"; for example, classical Athens, India, and Africa are not, according to Hegel. Hegel gives content to "rationality." There is, in his view, a standard of "truth" by which we can judge whether institutions and practices are rational. This standard of truth is connected to Hegel's conception of freedom. We could never be truly free living in a caste system, or in democracy as practiced in classical Athens, and therefore such institutions and practices are not rational. Hegel says they are not "true," though they are "correct" (or appropriate) for those societies. See note 88, below, and corresponding text.

[40] Hegel goes on to declare that they are not truly real. (See Rph V, 3:727,19–35: "a bad state merely exists, like a sick body; it has no true reality [*wahrhafte Realität*].") This is a much stronger claim, which should strike us as unconvincing: if irrational laws or practices are not real, do we merely imagine them?

not count. Ideality abstracts from, yet also potentially shapes our understanding of the world. The world from which ideality abstracts is existence. The world that ideality shapes is actuality. When we understand
the world to be ideality we feel at home in it by an act of theory; we
bracket out certain facts in the world, attributing them to mere existence.[41] Hegel has us act as if they did not count. But Hegel's critics will
say they count enormously. For Marx, "that the rational is real is contra-
dicted by the irrational reality which at every point shows itself to be the
opposite of what it asserts."[42] But, I am arguing, Hegel's dialectic lets him
leave open the possibility of judging that irrationalities pervade a society
to such an extent that they cannot be bracketed. Hegel would not ask the
German Jew to act as if "that little fact" of death camps didn't count,
because the practices and institutions of Nazi Germany were evil through
and through; in no way did the free will of its members come into existence in this state. *If* ideality is immanent in existence, then Hegel has us
reconcile ourselves to a less than ideal existence by persevering in the face
of some facts.

We have already seen what this process is like, with our example of
being in love. Our beloved exists as a flawed human being—he is not
always happy or caring or healthy or beautiful or giving. Our ideal picture of him is of having all these qualities. The ideal is only a picture,
something he can never be, but which he can approach. When we commit
ourselves to him, we accept the moments when he is not as we would like
him to be. When his flaws come out, and tempt us to leave him, we might
reflect that this is not really him, but a momentary lapse; he is human,
and humans are subject to all sorts of contingencies, but within him is the
ideal we love—and upon this reflection we might choose to stay committed.

Hegel's distinction between actuality and existence silences the criticism that he thinks all decrees and actions in the world are rational. Yet
it still leaves us wondering about the relation between ideality and existence, between theory and practice. At what point are nonideal features
of existence so pervasive that they defy being bracketed by the theorist?
At what point should we criticize the theorist who gets us to feel at home
when we are not by changing our consciousness of the world? At what
point does the world resist being determined by consciousness, so that
feeling at home in it is not being at home, but being deluded?

Hegel is torn between wanting to reconcile us to our world and yet
wanting to be critical. This tension in his political philosophy mirrors a

---

[41] Hegel goes on to say these facts are not real (see previous note), though we need not
follow him on this point. In any case, what is real is not the issue, except to ontologists. The
real issue is whether these facts count.

[42] Marx, *Early Writings*, ed. T. Bottomore (New York: McGraw Hill, 1963), p. 127.

tension in his ontology: Hegel is torn also between the view that consciousness determines the world and the view that thought is an abstraction from the world, so that what is real shapes our consciousness of it. On the one hand, we are free by an act of theory, by understanding the world we live in to be ideal, to accord with what Hegel calls the Concept: "It is only according to the Concept that humans are free because then they exist in rational relations."[43] "It is quite impossible that anything which philosophy has proved to be non-real should occur truly in experience."[44] On the other hand, the Concept is not merely the product of consciousness, but it inheres in the world: "the movement of the Concept towards its concretization as Idea—the dialectic—inheres in the thing: reason is in nature to be unfolded, apart from us subjects—we do nothing but bring into consciousness the working out of reason."[45]

Hegel has wrongly been understood to stand consistently on one side of the line between idealist and realist, speculative armchair philosopher and practical theorist, reconciler and critic. We have seen that Marx says, as a point in favor of his own doctrine, that Hegel only interprets, that he does not change the world. Many present-day commentators take the same position. To Yermiahu Yovel, Hegel remains in his armchair and gets us to be at home not by action but by thought:

> Hegel puts ... the principle of speculative theoretical comprehension on a higher level than life and action. The climax in realizing rationality lies not in the domain of substantive life, not even in the domain of praxis and the state, but in pure speculative knowledge. In contrast to Kant before him, and to Marx after him, who had given priority to praxis, Hegel adheres to the Aristotelian idea of the priority of speculation, even though he makes historical praxis a necessary prerequisite for attaining the speculative goal.[46]

---

[43] Rph V, 3:242,19–30.

[44] NL 118.

[45] PR 31 Rem. It is the moving from the one hand to the other that constitutes the "dialectic of experience" that is the subject of Hegel's *Phenomenology*. At first consciousness seems to be a mirror of nature, observing an object; but then it discovers that really what it knows is the being-for-consciousness of this object. What it really knows is not some essence, but its own perspective of this object. What is "true" here is the being-for-consciousness of the thing: "What first appeared as the object sinks for consciousness to the level of its way of knowing the object" (PhdG 87). The dialectical relation (or blurring) between thought and being is crucial, too, to Hegel's conception of history. Hegel resists sharply dichotomizing events "out there" and our narration or understanding of them: "History combines in our language the objective as well as the subjective side. It means both . . . the events and the narration of events. (It means both *Geschehen* and *Geschichte*.)" (RH 75; cited in George Dennis O'Brien, *Hegel on Reason and History*, p. 13, note 9).

[46] Yirmiahu Yovel, "Hegel's Dictum That the Rational Is Actual and the Actual Is Rational," p. 121. Bernard Yack takes a similar view of Hegel. See my criticism of his argument in sec. 3.1.

Following Yovel's line, we might say that Hegel achieves climax alone, by intellectual masturbation, while Marx achieves it by intercourse, by having theory "penetrate deeply into the virgin soil of the people."[47]

Nicolas Haines understands Hegel to be an apolitical "owl," merely a spectator: "The preface to the *Rechtsphilosophie* leaves the philosopher with little more than an end-of-the-day twilight, owl-like role, hard to distinguish, in terms of effectiveness, from that which the 20th century positivists preferred."[48] In Haines's view, Hegel's conception of philosophy precluded him from taking any practical role as social critic: "As with poetry and prophecy so with social criticism—[Hegel], like others of our own time, has a notion of philosophy as interpreting and understanding these activities [such as the Wartburgfest] without in any sense participating in them."[49]

In a sense both Yovel and Haines are right to suggest Hegel does not participate politically, if we understand participation as going out to throw rocks at government buildings. But surely we can distinguish protest from criticism, and surely Hegel conceives his theoretical activity as critical, as an activity practical in some sense. Haines goes on to suggest that Hegel scorns judgments that transcend an age, and that "by proposing to combine the actual with the ideal, Hegel dissolved a tension essential to criticism."[50] But Hegel does not try to dissolve the tension between ideals and how the world is; he lives with it. Hegel does not crudely identify ideality with how things are. Rather, he insists we derive our ideals from the existing world, and measure up that world to our ideals, by a back and forth process that allows us to adjust our ideals in light of the facts, and with our ideals to persevere in the face of some facts, until we are at home in the world.

Hegel's dictum expresses the strategy he uses, of immanent criticism. The dialectic of the immanent critic works like this: on the one hand, practices have a history and they change for whatever reasons, and our conception of them reflects this past history and evolution. Our conception of the practice is shaped by the practice. On the other hand, our conception of the practice shapes the practice. Practices evolve because we intentionally shape and reform them, perhaps on the basis of our theoretical conception of their purpose, but also because of unintended factors.[51] In the latter case, there may be good reasons why a practice

---

[47] Cf. Karl Marx, *Critique*, p. 65 (182), cited earlier in this chapter.

[48] Nicolas Haines, "Politics and Protest: Hegel and Social Criticism," p. 419.

[49] Ibid., p. 421.

[50] Ibid., pp. 422–423.

[51] Things are even more complicated. Not only do practices and institutions change historically for various intended and unintended reasons, but so do the concepts and ideals we use to practice and criticize practices. For example, suppose a society equates justice with

changes. Our conception of the practice may no longer fit the "new" practice, and if the reasons it had changed are good enough, we might want a new conception of the practice. But if a practice changes in a way that makes it inconsistent with our present conception of it, but for no good reasons, we might want to reform the practice by bringing it back in line with our conception of how it should be.

Earlier we considered the example of a woman who faces a choice: stay committed to her husband or commit adultery. The example may have seemed quaint to those who do not think adultery need constitute a violation of a marriage commitment. Practices change, and as they do, what counts as the ideal changes as well. Our society has become more sexually permissive, and changing sexual attitudes may have led to a changed conception of marriage, of what the marriage commitment requires, just as our changing attitudes about gender have brought about a change in the practice of courtesy: it is no longer clearly an instance of courtesy when a man holds open a door for a woman; it even seems that, were a man to do this, we would think he was being not courteous but arrogant.[52]

"The actual becomes rational" describes one movement in the dialectic: a practice changes for good reasons, and so our conception of it changes; we come to understand the evolved practice as rational. "The rational becomes actual" describes the other movement: our conception of the practice is used to reform the practice when it has changed for no good reason. Hegel is an immanent critic who engages in this back and forth dialectical process. As we have seen in previous chapters and will see again shortly, Hegel criticizes the world when it fails to live up to ideality. But also Hegel is aware that ideals must sometimes change to accommodate a changing world. Consider Hegel's account of the institution of marriage. In Hegel's view, marriage is essentially an ethical institution; its purpose is to bind what is different, this is its "concept."[53] Through marriage we experience what it means to be committed; once married we are "stuck" with each other, through thick and thin. Mar-

---

vengeance and understands punishment as retribution and retribution as vengeance. Just punishment, in this society, will be punishment that successfully avenges. Now suppose the society comes to disavow acts of vengeance, perhaps as a result of a religious transformation of the sort that occurred in the West through the teachings of Christ. This society may no longer equate justice with vengeance, and it may consequently redefine retribution. In this society, the practice of punishment will likely change as a consequence of a change in ideals, in its definition of justice.

[52] On this example of courtesy, see Ronald Dworkin, *Law's Empire*, pp. 48–49. The examples of marriage and courtesy are different. With the latter I consider the issue: Is this an instance of marriage (i.e., homosexual marriage)? Of courtesy (i.e., men holding doors open for women)? With the former I consider the issue: Is this a requirement of ideal marriage (i.e., that one does not commit adultery)? Of ideal courtesy (i.e., that one is sincere)?

[53] PR 168 Rem, Bem.

riage engenders the sense of obligation that Hegel thinks we need to learn to be good citizens of the state. When we marry, we experience what it is to be in a commitment, and what it is to live ethically—we are on the path to the consciousness of our freedom. Hegel defends arranged marriages because they emphasize the ethical character of the practice.[54] Yet Hegel concedes that in his day romantic love had become an important feature of marriage, a feature arranged marriages tend to ignore. Rather than blinding himself to this fact, Hegel adjusts his account of the ideal marriage: we should no longer view marriage as based purely on ethical commitment and not at all on love.[55] Hegel, acknowledging a changing world, reconceptualizes marriage, arguing that partners should be in love with each other, and if they are not, then there is reason to break the commitment.[56]

Hegel is known as an idealist, but that is a misleading label, given his willingness to adjust his ideals in light of the facts. Indeed, Hegel seems less of an idealist than some contemporary theorists. R. A. Duff, for example, gives an ideal account of legal punishment and notes that this ideal account diverges radically from "the actual character of our legal institutions."[57] But Duff sticks to his ideal nevertheless: "To show that it is hard or even impossible to attain the ideal is not to show that that ideal has no claim on our attention, or should play no part in our actions."[58] In Duff's view, that actuality differs so much from ideality just condemns all the more "our actual institutions for failing to live up to the ideals and values by which they ought to be, and purport to be, informed."[59] Duff is prepared to compromise our ideals for practical reasons:

[54] Ibid., 162 Z.

[55] Ibid., 161. This point is missed by Peter Steinberger in his insightful account of Hegel's view of marriage in chapter 5 of his *Logic and Politics: Hegel's Philosophy of Right*. Steinberger says that for Hegel marriage is "a matter not of romance but of reason," and that Hegel thinks marriage "can subsist and thrive in the absence of sensuousness and romance" (p. 164; cf. pp. 176–177). But this is to ignore Hegel's more complex interpretation of the practice.

[56] See PR 161–163, 168 (and Remarks and Additions). One other example where Hegel adjusts his account of ideality in light of the facts is in his discussion of inheritance in one of his lecture courses. Hegel notes that part of "modernity" is that family ties become less important and friendships deepen. (For our purposes, it does not matter whether Hegel is right about this.) Consequently, Hegel makes a qualification to his claim elsewhere that positive laws denying inheritance to family members are unethical. The "spiritual friendships" we find in civil society can now serve as a functional substitute for family ties, and Hegel therefore thinks it appropriate for property to be willed to someone who "belongs to my family in spirit" (Rph V, 3:557–561).

[57] R. A. Duff, *Trials and Punishments*, p. 11.

[58] Ibid., p. 73, my emphasis.

[59] Ibid., p. 142; cf. pp. 291–299.

Should we insist on trying to live now as if we were already living in . . . an ideal society, despite the disastrous consequences of doing so; or should we, recognising our present imperfections, be prepared to compromise our ideals now in the hope that we can thus begin to build Jerusalem? It may be tempting to insist that Jerusalem cannot be built from foundations which deny or betray its most basic values: but can we hope to begin building it without compromising these values?[60]

Duff is willing to compromise his ideals ("I would act unjustly to prevent the heavens falling"),[61] but not to reassess them. Forced to choose between the ideal and the actual, Duff chooses the ideal: "Such a radical gap between the ideal and the actual does not, I would insist, show the ideal to be misguided or inadequate; it rather reminds us of the radical imperfection of our existing social and legal structures."[62] That is (perhaps refreshing) idealism. Hegel does not go so far. Hegel is willing to engage in the other movement of the dialectic, of readjusting ideals in light of the facts.

We have seen how several commentators misconstrue Hegel's dictum that the actual is rational and the rational is actual to mean that Hegel is in principle uncritical, seeking passive consolation in the existing. This reading is understandable, since Hegel, as immanent critic, himself tends to emphasize his commitment to the materials at hand. In his preface to the *Philosophy of Right* Hegel writes, "to comprehend [*begreifen*] what is, this is the task of philosophy. . . . To recognize reason as the rose in the cross of the present and thereby to enjoy the present, this is the rational insight which reconciles us to the actual."[63] Here Hegel certainly sounds uncritical, concerned only with feeling at home by a theoretical act of reconciliation. In an earlier work on the German Constitution Hegel says much the same thing: he says his purpose as theorist is to promote the understanding of what is, and therefore a calmer outlook and a moderate endurance (*Ertragen*) of it, to recognize that "it is as it must be, that is, it is not contingent or accidental." Once we do this we recognize "that

---

[60] Ibid., p. 192.

[61] Ibid., p. 298.

[62] Ibid., p. 293.

[63] PR Preface, pp. 11–13. Given my account of his distinction between "actuality" and "existence," we might think that Hegel must have meant "existent" in this quote. But I think Hegel could have meant "actual," although our confusion is understandable, since even with our distinction his famous dictum remains somewhat muddled. We must remember that Hegel distinguishes "rational" (what I am also calling "ideal") and "actual." Actuality approaches ideality: ideality is its standard. Actuality does not always live up to ideality, because it inheres in the sphere of existence. If we recognize ideality in existence, we will commit ourselves to an existence shorn of its irrationalities—to actuality.

it is as it should be."[64] Here Hegel appears to recommend passivity and reconciliation. Yet Hegel was critical of the Germany about which he wrote, saying that it was a state in thought only, a *Gedankenstaat*, a state in words not deeds, a state in theory only.[65] To comprehend does not mean merely to legitimate whatever exists, to see its necessity; there is another side to Hegel that insists that "to hold to a constitution, institutions and laws no longer matching the ethos, needs and opinion of the people, and from which spirit has fled, is to be blind."[66] In perhaps the most famous line of the *Philosophy of Right* Hegel writes, "the owl of Minerva spreads its wings only with the falling of the dusk." One of Hegel's students revised this line to read, "the owl of Minerva gives way, then, to the call of a new-breaking day." The student visited Hegel one day and showed his teacher the daring revision. The student recounts how when he read the new version Hegel grinned and gave permission for the critical passage to be published.[67] Hegel is ambivalent: on the one hand he insists we find reason in the present, but on the other hand he refuses to commit himself blindly to whatever exists. This ambivalence is present within Hegel even in the early works, and it remains with him throughout his life. It culminates in Hegel's strategy of immanent criticism, a strategy that insists both on commitment to the present world and also on a willingness to criticize that world.

As immanent critic, Hegel invokes a standard by which he criticizes existing practices, a standard that is immanent in our practices but nevertheless separable from them. Hegel does not hold that a law or practice is justified *because* it exists.[68] One objective of Hegel's philosophy of right

---

[64] "Die Verfassung Deutschlands" ("The German Constitution"), in *Frühe Schriften* (Hegel, *Werke*, vol. 1), pp. 462–464. The essay was written between 1800 and 1802.

[65] Ibid., pp. 504–505, 472.

[66] "Über die neuesten innern Verhältnisse Württemburg" ("On the Recent Domestic Affairs of Wurtemberg"), in *Frühe Schriften* (Hegel, *Werke*, vol. 1), p. 269. This essay was written in 1798.

[67] In Karl-Heinz Ilting, "Der exoterische und der esoterische Hegel," pp. 62–63. Ilting notes that the version of the student (Michelet) is similar to a passage in Hegel's own Berlin inaugural address, and he argues that the source of Hegel's philosophy of action lies in his esoteric side. Hegel is a mole.

[68] Though he has been understood by some to hold just this view. A. A. Piontkowski writes, "In the third part of the *Philosophy of Right* Hegel tries to show that the form of punishment always fits the level of development of the state, and with this actually justifies the existing Prussian *Landrecht*, this codebook of patriarchal despotism that in its complete compass mirrors the principles of feudal society" (*Hegels Lehre über Staat und Recht*, p. 166; cf. p. 266). Ossip Flechtheim makes Hegel out to be a legal positivist in the tradition of Hobbes, holding to the "identification of law with justice" ("Hegel and the Problem of Punishment," p. 308; cf. p. 294). And there are still those who argue that Hegel's political philosophy could be used to justify the law of any modern state, even that of Nazi Germany (see Ernst Topitsch, *Die Sozialphilosophie Hegels*, esp. p. 131, note 3).

is to oppose precisely this view, put forth in Hegel's day by the historicist or "positive" school of law:

> In the positive science of right, right is what is; in the philosophy of right, right is only what is rational as measured by the concept.[69]

> When someone says to a legal scholar, this or that law does not accord with the concept, the scholar probably answers: "My dear Sir, you don't understand," and explains by showing that it is right, because it is from this or that Kaiser, or was the product of this praetor, that Senate counsel, taken up in this legal code. . . . But this only adduces how this law came into the sphere of existence . . . but to reason from the concept requires a different understanding.[70] Just because something is a positive or ancient right does not make it in and for itself [*an und für sich*] right. Positive right can contain something unholy. Slavery can be legal though it is absolutely wrong.[71]

Hegel does not even expect to find a state in which all of the laws are rational: "The content of positive right can be either rational or, as is usual, a mixture of rational law and arbitrary, capricious and contingent propositions that derive in part from the power of, in part from the lack of skill of lawgivers, in part from imperfect conditions of a society or a desire to meet the needs of the moment, leaving aside the connection to the whole."[72]

There are many other passages in the lectures rejecting the claim that laws or practices are rational by virtue of their existence.[73] For example, Hegel makes clear that not all states are good, not all habits are rational: "Man can become accustomed to the very worst [*das Schlechteste*], can by habit be a slave, a serf and so forth."[74] "Custom [*Sitte*] can have either a good or a bad content."[75] Not only aren't all states rational; Hegel even suggests we are rather fortunate if we live in a state that is rational: "the citizen is brought up in a state, and the greatest thing is for him to live in a rational state."[76] Hegel dispels the notion that the modern state is a divine and infallible agent:

> The state makes laws and has the right and the power to do this. The state is the will of existing human beings of an earlier or the present time, it is human

---

[69] Rph VI, 4:81.
[70] Ibid., 4:538,19–539,9.
[71] Rph I, 10,169–171.
[72] Ibid., 5,11–20.
[73] These passages, found in the lectures, have for the most part been unavailable in English.
[74] Rph VI, 4:534,15–16.
[75] Ibid., 4:407,6–8.
[76] Rph V, 3:272,1–4.

will; I am also a human being, and also have a will and intelligence. Others can err; their authority is no greater than mine. With this form of reflection we come to the demand of my subjective will that I should understand and be convinced that what the laws take as right should exist.[77]

Hegel made clear his position not only in his lectures, but also in his published works: there can be irrational posited law. The *Philosophy of Right* is replete with criticism of existing property law,[78] inheritance practices,[79] and numerous other practices that have existed, such as polygamy,[80] the salability of offices,[81] and the Romans' treatment of children.[82] Elsewhere Hegel criticizes Sparta's practice of communal eating,[83] India's caste system,[84] slavery,[85] and feudal serfdom and the institutions of tithes and dues.[86] Hegel thinks some of these institutions are or were relatively justified: slavery is acceptable for those who have yet to be civilized;[87] the caste system may well be appropriate for the spirit of the Indian people. In passages from his own handwritten marginal notes to his copy of the *Philosophy of Right* and the lectures, Hegel makes the distinction between "correctness" (*Richtigkeit*) and "truth" (*Wahrheit*): he says that slavery can be correct and even necessary for a certain historical epoch, but from the standpoint of the concept of freedom, slavery is wrong, is an "untrue appearance."[88] Another institution Hegel regards as relatively but not absolutely justified is democracy. Hegel thinks democracy was justified in ancient Greece, which lacked subjectivity, but that in the modern world, with its emphasis on individuality, democracy would not endure.[89] But even in the cases where Hegel justifies aspects of a premodern society, such as the Indian caste system, slavery, or Athenian democracy, the reason he gives for why these practices or institutions are relatively justified is not that they exist, but that they are "correct" (though "untrue").

---

[77] Rph VI, 4:351,25–352,7. See Rph II, 1:234; 1:238,11–12; Rph VI, 4:89; 4:399,14–16.
[78] PR 62–64.
[79] Ibid., 178 Rem, 179 Rem.
[80] Ibid., 167.
[81] Ibid., 277.
[82] Ibid., 175 Rem.
[83] PH 321(263).
[84] Ibid., 183–185(146–147).
[85] Ibid., 129(99); PR 7, 21, 57.
[86] PH 529–530(448).
[87] Ibid., 124–125(95–96); 128–129(98–99); Rph V, 3:227,6–11.
[88] Hegel distinguishes the correct from the true in PR 57 Bem. In a passage from the lectures he says, "Slavery is wrong, but necessary for certain epochs, though it is an untrue appearance [*Erscheinung*]" (Rph V, 3:227,6–11).
[89] See PH 307–310(251–253).

There is a Burkean side to Hegel that tries to get us to be at home in a less than ideal actuality: "One must acknowledge that the positive law has tremendous authority, the authority of a thousand years, of all mankind. The whole of mankind has worked up the law and it is not so easy to judge this work of spirit, or to want to be more clever than this world spirit."[90] But Hegel, unlike Burke, thinks we are obligated to obey posited law not because we owe it to our fathers, but because the law is rational. As Charles Taylor writes, "the moral drawn by Burke was that men should remain within the spirit of their 'positive' institutions, there is no higher rationality by which these can be judged. While for Hegel the aim of philosophy is to discover the universal rationality in these institutions."[91] For Hegel, "legitimacy comes from rational principles grounding law, not from tradition or custom."[92] Hegel insists that there is this standard of rationality, and though we might find it elusive, this standard presents us with the possibility, even the responsibility, of criticism. Hegel does not propose that we uncritically accept whatever exists, that we feel at home even when we are not.

Hegel's criticism of particular laws he regards as irrational largely deflects the charge of some commentators that Hegel accommodates himself to the status quo, that he is an archconservative. If to be conservative is never to criticize the laws of one's society, Hegel is not conservative. But as immanent critic, Hegel *is* committed to the ideals immanent in the practices we already have, and we may see this commitment as resulting in another sort of conservatism, a conservatism characterized by an unwillingness to reject the ideals and principles immanent in our existing practices. Whether we think Hegel is conservative in this sense depends on whether we think Hegel is ever willing to be a radical critic (an issue on which I shall offer my own conclusions in section 6.4).

Hegel's commitment to the ideals immanent in the practices that already constitute our existing ethical life has led to another charge, distinct from the charge of conservatism. Hegel, by deferring to whatever ideals or standards prevail in a given ethical community, is said to be a relativist. W. H. Walsh writes that "all Hegel could properly find to say against a moral system which diverged markedly from that which prevailed in his own time would be that the ways of proceeding it advocated were impractical. If it turned out to be viable after all, Hegel would have no rational ground on which to object to it."[93] Hegel claims a practice or law is justified, not because it exists, but because it is rational; however, for Hegel, we do not determine that it is rational by appealing to external or

---

[90] Rph VI, 4:83.
[91] Charles Taylor, *Hegel*, p. 423.
[92] PH 417(345).
[93] W. H. Walsh, *Hegelian Ethics*, p. 11; cf. p. 47.

transcendent standards. To what standard of rationality does Hegel appeal, then? In chapter 4 we saw that he invokes a substantive conception of rationality: a particular practice or law is rational, in Hegel's view, if it fits together with an entire set of social practices and institutions that we can understand to be a coherent whole, our ethical substance. "It is in being so connected that the various laws acquire their true meaning and therewith their justification."[94] Hegel looks at the laws, practices, and institutions he sees around him and arrives at an interpretation that sees each "as a subordinate moment in a whole, interconnected with all the other features which make up the character of a nation and an epoch."[95] Once we recognize how they fit together we can then say that each particular law, practice, or institution of this ethical system is rational; it is part of an ethical life that constitutes our identity and substance. Hegel is clearly no relativist when judging right *within* a society. He maintains that societies have a "spirit," a living ethos that provides the standards by which we can criticize the actual practices of that society; for example, we can criticize laws that have "no truth in the present ethical life," that have become relics.[96] Hegel is accused of relativism, rather, because he seems unwilling to criticize an ethical system so long as that system is coherent. Hegel is accused of being a relativist when judging *among* societies—he is accused of being a cultural or historical relativist. This is Walsh's claim.

Hegel avoids cultural or historical relativism by appealing to his teleological conception of history, which sees all states prior to the postfeudal bourgeois rational-legal modern state as inferior, as states whose members were not entirely free.[97] He insists that a rational ethical life, which provides freedom to its participants, requires certain practices, laws, and institutions, those discussed in the *Philosophy of Right*.[98] For Hegel, their mere consistency with other legally established institutions does not justify these practices.[99] The "absolutely valid justification" of these practices is derived "from the Concept."[100] Hegel gives a metaphysical significance to the Concept, and in this sense Taylor is correct in saying that Hegel has a standard of a "higher rationality" by which he judges. Hegel avoids both ethical and historical relativism by appealing to a metaphys-

[94] PR 3 Rem, p. 16.

[95] Ibid.; see my discussion of Hegel's concept of "rationality" in sec. 4.3.

[96] NL 129–131.

[97] Hegel was not an epistemological relativist either, as he had a conception of "absolute knowledge."

[98] It is partly on this basis that Hegel would, I think, criticize Nazi Germany, which failed to recognize each individual as having an abstract right to his or her person and property, and to recognize the claims of *Moralität*.

[99] PR 3 Rem, p. 17.

[100] Ibid., pp. 16–17.

ics of the Concept, which he invokes to justify the practices and institutions of the modern states he sees around him.[101] If we reject the metaphysics, then to appropriate Hegel we need to reinterpret Concept as "concept." A practice justified by *its* concept (as opposed to *the* Concept) is justified by the principle(s) Hegel's interpretation of the practice declares to be immanent in that practice. This justification has no ground apart from the plausibility of the interpretation of our practice on which it is based. In this reading, Hegel offers an account that fits our laws, practices, and institutions into a coherent whole, an ethical life in which we can understand ourselves to be at home and free, an ethical life that constitutes our identity, our substance. Hegel himself seems to have believed that laws are justified not *merely* by being so connected in an integral whole, but because they accord with the metaphysical Concept. Our revised version of Hegel's philosophy, in refusing to take this further step, is no longer immune to the charges of relativism, as Hegel thought his version to be. But insofar as a postmodern commitment to nonfoundationalism commands us to reject Hegel's metaphysics, this is a charge we must be willing to face. In the next section I shall pursue the nonmetaphysical, nonfoundational revision of Hegel.

6.3   Hegel and the Activity of Justifying Practices

Hegel wants to be both reconciler and critic, idealist and realist, philosopher and practical theorist. He believes we can be at home by an act of thought, of interpretation, yet acknowledges that there are limits to our ability to reshape reality by thinking. Interpretation has ontological status, in part determines what is real; yet interpretations can be inadequate to the world. By an act of theory we can understand actuality to be ideality; but sometimes existence resists being transformed into what it is not.

What is the line separating those facts that unmask ideality as a myth from facts that are mere contingencies, part of existence but not really real, not really counting? Can we know? What sort of question is this, and what standards are available to us as we seek its answer?

Hegel has us put our commitments to the test. Any commitment our East Oakland convict might have to his state is being put to the test as he sits in jail and thinks about the injustice of his punishment: Should the state be a commitment of his? Are the facts of his life in the state consis-

---

[101] In detailing the institutions of the rational modern state, Hegel borrows from at least three existing states: England, France, and Prussia. Hegel's Prussia did not have juries, yet Hegel regards juries as a rational institution.

tent with Hegel's account of the state as an ideal commitment?[102] The
wife contemplating adultery puts to the test her commitment to her husband: Is this still a commitment? Is her marriage an ethical bond with the
meaning Hegel claims such bonds have? Must we understand adultery as
violating the commitment?

Justifying our commitments is a peculiar activity, because, unlike some
other sorts of justification, in this one there are no standards to which we
can decisively appeal, standards that reduce our role to a mere applier of
rules.[103] Whether we are justified in keeping our commitments, whether
we conclude that we are at home and free in them, depends not only on
certain facts, but on who we are, on how we can feel, on what our commitments are. This is why it is so hard to determine that line that deline-
ates when existence is so bad that we cannot claim it contains an essentially rational actuality.

Whether we feel at home in the world depends in part on who we are,
on our conception of the world and its practices, and on facts about our
commitments. Consider the woman thinking about committing adultery.
There must be enough facts about her marriage to substantiate the claim
that it is essentially an ideal commitment of the sort Hegel describes,
enough facts to warrant persevering in the commitment even given some
other facts that fly in the face of the ideal, for example, that the couple
fight a lot, or that they do not share each other's interests. Which facts
make plausible the claim that the marriage is essentially an ideal commit-

---

[102] We might ask, "What commitment?" "When did this man commit himself to the
state—*is* he even committed?" These questions do eventually get raised in the process of
reflection that we undertake when we test our commitments. Hegel asks us to assume as a
starting point that we belong in the modern state, that we are free only in it; he has reasons
for thinking this is a plausible assumption, reasons we explored in chapter 4, having to do
with the Aristotelian notion that our community is our ethical substance, something into
which we are born and which shapes who we are. While the East Oakland man probably is
excluded from the state, and rightly protests the workings of a machine that in fact op-
presses him, he still is part of the ethical life of his community and shares in (some of) its
values. Even in our worst ghettos there is a shared sense of right and respect for a morality
imprinted in the law. Recently when a "posse" of East Harlem youth went "wilding" in
Central Park, committing acts of random violence on women and children, the *New York
Times* reported: "The East Harlem community itself is appalled by the attacks. Even many
criminals believe the rampaging youths violated a moral code that forbids attacking and
beating a child, an old person or a woman. That may be why three of the youths who were
arrested in the case were attacked by other inmates at detention centers, experts say" (May
2, 1989, p. 85). One sociologist noted how "everyone condemns it. Not even in joking have
I heard people justify it. . . . Even those who are criminals think criminals should be punished . . . there is a strong ethic of protecting women" (ibid.). Even our man sitting in a jail
in East Oakland probably speaks the language and shares in (some of) the values of his
community.

[103] On the distinction between justifying a practice and justifying an action of a practice,
see my *Punishment: Theory and Practice*, ch. 1, sec. 2.

ment? I think there is no decisive answer. An answer emerges only when her commitment is put to the test; she must grapple for herself in a process of dialectical reflection.

The process of dialectical reflection is double-reflexive. How we view the commitment ideally, the theory we have of it, shapes our judgment of our actual commitment, of what we think it requires; but also, how we view our actual commitment, what in fact is required for and gained from it, shapes how we interpret its ideals. It is his making these connections between ideality and existence that distinguishes Hegel from Kierkegaard. Hegel insists that we face the facts, rather than evade them by a spiritual withdrawal from the world of the sort taken by Kierkegaard's knight of faith.

If there is no decisive answer to questions that test our commitments, is there nothing we can say about where a rational person will wind up after dialectical reflection? Is there no argument of which we can say it compels us to be committed, so that we would be making a mistake by doing otherwise? In a way Hegel will persuade us to be committed to the actuality he construes as ideality, to be at home in our world, if we already feel at home: Hegel will persuade whom he will persuade. But this is hardly an exciting or praiseworthy accomplishment. Surely Hegel does more.

Hegel hopes to get us to see our true commitments in a certain way, to see that they *are* our commitments. In the same way that, in Hegel's view, a proof of God's existence should "elevate us to God,"[104] so should Hegel's theory of our commitments bring us back to them. The theory Hegel offers is meant not merely to persuade those whom it will persuade, but to change us so that we will be persuaded: "Spiritual movement, the movement of our own selves and our will, ought to be there in the demonstration."[105] Hegel's conception of our commitments might lead us to an understanding of them and what they require that we use to guide our will, to act anew.

But can we be compelled by argument to arrive at a new understanding that would lead us back to our commitment? I think not. The standards we have when justifying our commitments fall short of the standards available in foundationalist justifications. Foundationalist justifications are proofs that compel. But, I have suggested, in the justificatory activity where we reflect on our commitments, foundationalist justifications are of no avail.[106] The activity consists in a process of reflection, a back and

---

[104] PRel 168–169.

[105] Ibid.

[106] For an argument that justification in political theory cannot be foundational, see Don Herzog, *Without Foundations: Justification in Political Theory*. Herzog distinguishes foundationalists, such as Hobbes, Locke, and the utilitarians, from contextualists, such as Hume

forth dialectic between on the one hand an ideal account, which Hegel expounds with language suggesting he gives a foundational justification, language I think we should criticize, and on the other hand the facts of our commitments. We take ideality to task on the basis of the facts we confront, but also we weigh the importance of the facts in light of ideality. If Hegel's conviction is plausible, that ideality is immanent in existence, then upon our reflection we may well arrive at a point where we remain or become committed, and feel free in our commitment.[107]

We can understand Hegel as practical in the sense that he means to educate and thereby to change us.[108] Hegel claims that his ideal account is further justified by a metaphysical conception, and so one sense in which Hegel is an educator is as logician, teaching how the dialectical process unfolds in history and has culminated in the modern state and its commitments.[109] But we can understand Hegel as an educator in another sense. Hegel provides a coherent account of a panoply of commitments that sees them as an integral whole. He calls us to reflect on our commitments: "If asked in earnest whether we wanted that the whole not be present, we would be driven to come to consciousness that the state alone

and Smith. Contextualists "justify an institution by showing that it is better than the available alternatives" (p. 24). Herzog writes that, "successful foundational justifications are philosophers' pet unicorns; we have yet to see one. Contextual justifications provide a preponderance of good reasons, so they are good enough to qualify as justifications, even if they do not deliver the certainty that foundational arguments might" (p. 225).

For an argument, or, more accurately, reflections that can be construed as an argument, that foundational justifications are a myth not merely in political theory, but even in mathematics or logic, see Ludwig Wittgenstein, *On Certainty*, ed. G. E. M. Anscombe and G. H. von Wright, especially remarks 46–47, 110, 192, 204, 219–220, 232, 262, 323–327, 358–359, 447–448, 455, 477, 498, 609–612, 651ff., and 669.

[107] John Rawls's idea of "reflective equilibrium" might be a useful term with which to describe the process we undergo when we engage in the peculiar justificatory activity of testing our commitments. See John Rawls, *A Theory of Justice*, pp. 20ff., and in particular: "A conception of justice cannot be deduced from self-evident premises or conditions on principles; instead, its justification is a matter of the mutual support of many considerations, of everything fitting together into one coherent view" (p. 21). Also, "justification rests upon the entire conception and how it fits in with and organizes our considered judgments in reflective equilibrium" (p. 579).

[108] Cf. Steven B. Smith, *Hegel's Critique of Liberalism*, p. 140: "the *Philosophy of Right* ultimately reveals Hegel's overall commitment to the ideals of the *Rechtsstaat*. His purpose in publishing it was, I believe, to help foster and create a public-minded ruling class, a sort of ideal civil service, fully committed to the values of civility, impartiality, and honorable conduct. The need to put his lectures in textbook form was part of what he hoped would be a long-term educational project which would begin in the universities and spread out from there."

[109] Cf. Otto Pöggeler, Introduction to Rph I, p. xxxviii: "Hegel presupposes that history has led to rational institutions which are to be comprehended systematically as necessarily linked together, as the concretization of the good."

is the basis of our existence and must be maintained."[110] Hegel "teaches" us about the interconnections among our various commitments.[111] Walsh captures well the sort of argument I take Hegel to be educating us about:

> The man who wonders what obligation he has to pay his debts . . . need no longer be told an unconvincing story about the categorical imperative requiring him to do so, but can be shown instead the way in which the honouring of such obligations is a condition of the whole complex system of credit, without which advanced economic life would be impossible. The rule which is brought forward in a case of this sort gains in authority from the simple fact that it is widely observed; its force is enhanced again by its connecting with a wide range of human wants and purposes.[112]

Hegel means to educate, but not everyone. He writes for a limited audience. "Religion is for everyone. It is not philosophy, which is not for everyone."[113] Hegel thinks that only some will have philosophical insight, will "know" that the state satisfies their interests (if it does), while others will be committed to the state on the basis not of insight, but of national pride and patriotic sentiments.[114] We can be committed (but not free) without having theoretical knowledge or insight, just as "everyone eats and drinks without knowing anatomy."[115] For Hegel, philosophical insight into the rationality of our commitments is best, "but absent this, religious disposition can provide the bond."[116] Hegel is resigned to the fact that some, perhaps most, will merely feel at home. Perhaps those lacking philosophical insight do not merely feel at home but are at home. Perhaps they lack the reflection, or capacity to abstract, requisite to alienate oneself from one's home. They lack the philosophical insight not only to get back home, but to leave home in the first place. They never feel stuck or chained. Hegel would say such people are not genuinely free, just as the Athenians living in "the happy state" were not truly free in their ignorant state of bliss. For Hegel, real freedom is being able to leave home, being troubled, feeling alienated, yet choosing home after all.

---

[110] Rph V, 3:724,13–21.

[111] In this book I have focused primarily on Hegel's theory of legal punishment. I have limited my discussion of Hegel's views on other practices and institutions and how they all fit together. To see how Hegel links our practices into a coherent whole, one needs to read the entire *Philosophy of Right.*

[112] W. H. Walsh, *Hegelian Ethics*, p. 47.

[113] PRel 106.

[114] Rph VI, 4:642,7–13.

[115] Ibid., 4:642,28.

[116] PR 270 Z, p. 284.

6.4   Immanent vs. Radical Criticism

Hegel calls on us to reflect on our commitments: "We are confident that the state must subsist and that in it alone can particular interests be secured. But habit blinds us to that on which our whole existence depends. When we walk the streets at night in safety, it does not strike us that this might be otherwise. This habit of feeling safe has become second nature, and we do not reflect on just how this is due solely to the working of special institutions."[117] But in some places we are too scared to walk the streets at night; there is no habit of feeling safe. When facts contradict ideality, we might not be confident that the state must subsist, or share in the conviction that the actual is rational. Hegel wants us to stay committed to our state and its practices. His strategy as a theorist is immanent criticism, and this strategy is defensible only if the world in which we live contains ideality within it. The radical critic may well challenge the immanent critic, arguing that our social practices are bad, root and branch. The radical critic might argue that to abstract out from society some ideal account, to erect a facade that makes pleasing to the sight a less than perfect building, is to neglect the building's rotten foundations: inevitably the building will crumble, facade and all. Does Hegel's strategy of immanent criticism, which insists that we find ideality by abstracting from what exists, from the materials at hand, prevent him from ever being a radical critic?

Most Hegel scholars believe that Hegel in principle rejects radical criticism. Yet, as we have seen, Hegel holds that "if my free will does not come into existence in the state, I have no corresponding duty to the state,"[118] and he suggests there is a right to resist state authority if the state denies to some the means of their existence.[119] One reason Hegel is not regarded as a radical critic may be that these passages have only recently been made available, and only in the German. It is tempting from these passages to take Hegel as a Marxist, a radical. Ilting and others suggest that such passages, never published by Hegel but only spoken in lecture, "off the record," reveal the true Hegel, who felt forced to conceal himself from the Prussian powers that be for fear of losing his status and salary as a university professor.[120] But such a reading, which reads Marx back into Hegel, is suspect, not because it relies on a few scattered passages, but because it ignores the very heart of Hegel's political philoso-

---

[117] Ibid., 268 Z.

[118] Rph VI, 4:154,12–21.

[119] Cf. sec. 5.3.

[120] See Karl-Heinz Ilting, "Zur Genese der Hegelschen Rechtsphilosophie," and his "Der exoterische und der esoterische Hegel."

phy. As immanent critic, Hegel is committed to the materials at hand, to finding the positive in the existing: "Uneducated people delight in argumentation and fault-finding, because it is easy enough to find fault, though hard to see the good and its inner necessity. The novice always finds fault, but the educated sees the positive merit in everything."[121] Of course, Hegel is an immanent *critic*: finding the positive merit in everything does not mean ignoring what is bad (just as to feel at home does not mean that we never have to clean, repair, or even remodel our home). Rather, only by finding the positive can we come to a standard by which we can criticize what is bad.

Hegel insists that we first must try to comprehend the existing so that we may feel and be at home in it. It is what we have; it has shaped us. Hegel insists that we not pretend to look beyond the present "with the eyes of superior wisdom" but admit that it is in the present that we find whatever we have of "the substance which is immanent and the eternal which is present."[122] Just like Marx later, Hegel criticizes utopian theorists, who attempt "to construct a state as it ought to be."[123] Hegel is not Burke: if we cannot find rational principles immanent in our practices, we are not obligated to continue to live with them. But this possibility of breaking radically with existing commitments goes counter to Hegel's strategy as a whole, and to his metaphysical justification of the institutions of the modern state as the latest and final instantiation of *Geist*. Hegel is not *committed* to radical criticism.

As an immanent critic, Hegel criticizes our actual practice of legal punishment by calling us back to its ideal, that we punish to vindicate right, that we punish for justice. There are some who will not think we can realize this ideal. There are others who do not think we should try. One hears the voice of Nietzsche rejecting justice as an ideal and calling us away from the practice: "Let us stop thinking so much about punishment, reproaching, and improving others. . . . Let us not contend in a direct fight—and that is what all reproaching, punishing, and attempts to improve others amount to. Let us rather raise ourselves that much higher."[124] For Nietzsche, elevating justice as an ideal is but creating a myth, and claiming it is *our* ideal is perpetuating a costly self-deception: "But have you ever asked yourselves sufficiently how much the erection of every ideal on earth has cost? How much reality has had to be misunderstood and slandered, how many lies had to be sanctified, how many

---

[121] PR 268 Z, my translation.

[122] PR Preface, p. 10.

[123] Ibid., p. 11.

[124] Friedrich Nietzsche, *The Gay Science*, sec. 276. Cf. my discussion of Nietzsche and radical criticism of punishment in *Punishment: Theory and Practice*, ch. 2.

consciences disturbed, how much 'God' sacrificed every time?"[125] Nietzsche tells us that "if a temple is to be erected *a temple must be destroyed*: that is the law."[126] Nietzsche tears down our buildings, leaving us homeless. Hegel gets us to be at home in the dwelling we have. Not by deluding us, or getting us blindly to accept what is, but by commanding us to reflect, to put our commitments to the test, to call us back to our true commitments.

We began this chapter by discussing a single and homeless man living on the margin of society, sitting in jail, being told by the Berkeley Hegelian that he is free in his punishment. Our Hegelian, an immanent critic, assumes that the practice of legal punishment, and the society practicing it, are just. When our practices are bad, root and branch, then we adopt Hegel's strategy of immanent criticism only at great cost. The advantage of immanent criticism—commitment to the materials at hand, to working from within our practices—is no advantage if our practices are evil through and through. If our society is such that the homeless man's free will does not come into existence in it—if he is oppressed, excluded, marginalized, stepped on, exploited—then he might be, and should be, unconvinced by any principles deriving from practices he regards as externally imposed by the enemy. But before this man takes the route of withdrawal from and revolution against society, Hegel has him consider whether the problem lies not in our ideals, but in society's failure to live up to them.

[125] Nietzsche, *On the Genealogy of Morals*, 2:24.
[126] Ibid., Nietzsche's emphasis.

Bibliography

Arato, Andrew. "A Reconstruction of Hegel's Theory of Civil Society." *Cardozo Law Review* 10, no. 5 (1989): pp. 1363–1388.

Arendt, Hannah. *On Revolution*. New York: Viking Press, 1963.

Aristophanes. *The Clouds*. Trans. William Arrowsmith. New York: New American Library, 1962.

Aristotle. *Nichomachean Ethics*. Trans. J. A. K. Thomson. Harmondsworth, Eng.: Penguin, 1955.

———. *Politics*. Ed. Stephen Everson. Cambridge: Cambridge University Press, 1988.

Arnolds, Edward, and Norman Garland. "The Defense of Necessity in Criminal Law." *Journal of Criminal Law and Criminology* 65, no. 3 (1974): pp. 289–301.

Avineri, Shlomo. *Hegel's Theory of the Modern State*. Cambridge: Cambridge University Press, 1972.

Barber, Benjamin. *Strong Democracy: Participatory Politics for a New Age*. Berkeley: University of California Press, 1984.

Bell, Daniel. *The Cultural Contradictions of Capitalism*. New York: Basic Books, 1978.

Benn, C. K. "An Approach to the Problems of Punishment." *Philosophy* 33 (October 1958): pp. 325–341.

Bentham, Jeremy. *An Introduction to the Principles of Morals and Legislation*. New York: Hafner Press, 1948.

Bockelmann, Paul. *Hegels Notstandslehre*. Berlin: Walter de Gruyter and Co., 1935.

Böning, Peter. *Die Lehre vom Unrechtsbewußtsein in der Rechtsphilosophie Hegels*. Frankfurter Kriminalwissenschaftlich Studien, vol. 1, no. 1. Frankfurt: Peter Lang, 1978.

Bok, Sissela. *A Strategy for Peace*. New York: Pantheon, 1989.

Bottomore, T. B., ed. *Marx's Early Writings*. New York: McGraw Hill, 1963.

Brubaker, Stanley. "Can Liberals Punish?" *American Political Science Review* 82, no. 3 (1988): pp. 821–836.

Cooper, David. "Hegel's Theory of Punishment." In *Hegel's Political Philosophy*, edited by Z. A. Pelczynski, pp. 151–167.

Davidson, Donald. "Actions, Reasons, and Causes." In *Essays on Actions and Events*, pp. 3–20. New York: Oxford University Press, 1980.

Davies, Thomas. "A Hard Look at What We Know About the Costs of the Exclusionary Rule: The NIJ Study and Other Studies of Lost Arrests." *Research Journal* 1983, no. 3 (Summer 1983): pp. 611–692.

Dix, George, and Michael Sharlot. *Criminal Law: Cases and Materials*. 3rd ed. St. Paul: West Publishing Co., 1987.

Dolinko, David. "Some Thoughts About Retributivism." *Ethics* 101, no. 3 (April 1991): pp. 537–559.

Duff, R. A. *Trials and Punishments*. Cambridge: Cambridge University Press, 1986.

Dworkin, Ronald. *Law's Empire*. Cambridge, Mass.: Harvard University Press, 1986.

Dyde, S. W. "Hegel on Crime and Punishment." *Philosophical Review* 7, no. 1 (1898): pp. 62–71.

———. "Hegel's Conception of Freedom." *Philosophical Review* 3 (1894): pp. 655–671.

Elster, Jon. *Ulysses and the Sirens: Studies in Rationality and Irrationality*. Cambridge: Cambridge University Press, 1979.

Ewing, A. C. *The Morality of Punishment*. London: Kegan Paul, 1929.

Faris, Elsworth. "The Origin of Punishment." *International Journal of Ethics* 24, no. 1 (October 1914): pp. 54–67.

Feeley, Malcolm. *The Process Is the Punishment: Handling Cases in a Lower Criminal Court*. New York: Russell Sage Foundation, 1979.

Feinberg, Joel. *Doing and Deserving: Essays in the Theory of Responsibility*. Princeton, N.J.: Princeton University Press, 1970.

———. *The Moral Limits of the Criminal Law*. 4 volumes. New York: Oxford University Press, 1984–1988.

Findlay, J. N. *The Philosophy of Hegel*. New York: Collier Books, 1958.

Flechtheim, Ossip. "Die Funktion der Strafe in der Rechtstheorie Hegels." In *Von Hegel zu Kelsen*, pp. 9–20. Berlin: Duncker und Humblot, 1963.

———. "Hegel and the Problem of Punishment." *Journal of the History of Ideas* 8 (1947): pp. 293–308.

———. *Hegels Strafrechtstheorie*. Berlin: Duncker und Humblot, 1975.

Foucault, Michel, ed. *I, Pierre Riviere*. New York: Penguin, 1975.

Franklin, Mitchell. "The Contribution of Hegel, Beccaria, Holbach and Livingston to General Theory of Criminal Responsibility." In *Philosophical Perspectives on Punishment*, edited by Edward H. Madden, Rollo Handy, and Marvin Farber, pp. 94–125. Springfield, Ill.: Charles Thomas, 1968.

Gallie, W. B. "Essentially Contested Concepts." In *Philosophy and the Historical Understanding*, pp. 157–191. London: Chatto and Windus, 1964.

Gutmann, Amy. "Communitarian Critics of Liberalism." *Philosophy and Public Affairs* 14, no. 3 (Summer 1985): pp. 308–321.

Haines, Nicolas. "Politics and Protest: Hegel and Social Criticism." *Political Science Quarterly* 86, no. 3 (September 1971): pp. 406–428.

Hampton, Jean. "The Retributive Ideal." In *Forgiveness and Mercy*, by Jeffrie Murphy and Jean Hampton, pp. 111–161. Cambridge: Cambridge University Press, 1988.

Harris, H. S. *Hegel's Development: Toward the Sunlight, 1770–1801*. Oxford: Clarendon Press, 1972.

Hart, Henry M., Jr. "The Aims of the Criminal Law." *Law and Contemporary Problems* 23 (Summer 1958): pp. 401–441.

Hartmann, Klaus. "Review of Ilting's Edition of *Rechtsphilosophie*." *Modern Law and Society* 9, no. 1 (1976): pp. 21–26.

Hawkins, D. J. B. "Punishment and Moral Responsibility." In *Theories of Punishment*, edited by Stanley Grupp, pp. 13–18. Bloomington: Indiana University Press, 1971.

Haym, Rudolf. *Hegel und seine Zeit*. Berlin: Rudolph Gaertner, 1857.

Hegel, G. W. F. *Early Theological Writings*. Trans. T. M. Knox. Chicago: University of Chicago Press, 1948.

———. *Encyclopaedia of the Philosophical Sciences (1830)*. 3 volumes. Trans. William Wallace. Oxford: Oxford University Press, 1971.

———. *Enzyklopädie der philosophischen Wissenschaften*. Frankfurt am Main: Suhrkamp, 1986.

———. *Grundlinien der Philosophie des Rechts*. Frankfurt am Main: Suhrkamp, 1976.

———. *Hegel: The Letters*. Trans. Clark Butler and Christiane Seiler. Bloomington: Indiana University Press, 1984.

———. *Hegel's Political Writings*. Trans. T. M. Knox. London: Oxford University Press, 1964.

———. *Jenaer Realphilosophie*. Ed. J. Hoffmeister. Hamburg: Felix Meiner, 1969.

———. *Lectures on the History of Philosophy*. Trans. E. S. Haldane. London: Kegan Paul, 1892.

———. *Lectures on the Philosophy of Religion*. Ed. Peter C. Hodgson. Berkeley: University of California Press, 1988.

———. *Natural Law: The Scientific Way of Treating Natural Law, Its Place in Moral Philosophy, and Its Relation to the Positive Sciences of Law*. Trans. T. M. Knox. Philadelphia: University of Pennsylvania Press, 1975.

———. *Phenomenology of Spirit*. Trans. A. V. Miller. Oxford: Oxford University Press, 1977.

———. *Philosophie des Rechts: Die Vorlesung von 1819/20 in einer Nachschrift*. Ed. Dieter Henrich. Frankfurt am Main: Suhrkamp, 1983.

———. *Philosophische Propädeutik*. In *Werke in zwanzig Bänden*, vol. 4. Frankfurt am Main: Suhrkamp, 1970.

———. *Philosophy of History*. Trans. J. Sibree. New York: Dover, 1956.

———. *Philosophy of Right*. Trans. T. M. Knox. Oxford: Oxford University Press, 1952.

———. *Reason in History*. Trans. Robert Hartman. Indianapolis: Bobbs-Merrill, 1953.

———. *Science of Logic*. Trans. A. V. Miller. Atlantic Highlands, N.J.: Humanities Press International, 1969.

———. "System der Sittlichkeit." In *Jenaer Schriften*, edited by Gerd Irrlitz. Berlin: Akademie-Verlag, 1972.

———. *Vorlesungen über Naturrecht und Staatswissenschaft*. Ed. Claudia Becker et al.; with introduction by Otto Pöggeler. Hamburg: Felix Meiner Verlag, 1983.

Hegel, G. W. F. *Vorlesungen über Rechtsphilosophie (1818–1831)*. 4 volumes. Ed. Karl-Heinz Ilting. Stuttgart-Bad-Canstatt: Friedrich Fromann, 1973.

———. *Werke in zwanzig Bänden*. 20 volumes. Ed. Eva Moldenhauer and Karl Michel. Frankfurt am Main: Suhrkamp, 1986.

Henrich, Dieter. "The Contemporary Relevance of Hegel's Aesthetics." Trans. Michael J. Inwood. In *Hegel*, edited by Michael J. Inwood, pp. 199–207.

———. "Hegels Theorie über den Zufall." In *Hegel im Kontext*, edited by Dieter Henrich, pp. 157–186. Frankfurt am Main: Suhrkamp, 1967.

———. "Vernunft in Verwirklichung." Introduction, in G. W. F. Hegel, *Philosophie des Rechts: Die Vorlesung von 1819/20 in einer Nachschrift*, edited by Dieter Henrich, pp. 9–39.

Herman, Judith, and Lisa Hirschman. "Father-Daughter Incest." In *The Signs Reader*, edited by Elizabeth Abel and Emily K. Abel, pp. 257–278. Chicago: University of Chicago Press, 1983.

Herzog, Don. *Without Foundations: Justification in Political Theory*. Ithaca: Cornell University Press, 1985.

Hinchman, Lewis P. "Hegel's Theory of Crime and Punishment." *Review of Politics* 44 (1982): pp. 523–545.

Hobbes, Thomas. *Leviathan*. London: J. M. Dent, 1973.

Hoffmeister, Johannes, ed. *Dokumente zu Hegels Entwicklung*. Stuttgart: Friedrich Fromman, 1936.

D'Hondt, Jacques. *Hegel in His Time*. Trans. John Burbridge et al. Peterborough, Ont.: Broadview Press, 1988.

Hook, Sidney. "Hegel Rehabilitated?" *Encounter* 24 (January 1965): pp. 53–58.

Horstmann, Rolf-Peter. "Ist Hegels *Rechtsphilosophie* das Produkt der Politischen Anpassung eines Liberalen?" *Hegel-Studien* 9 (1974): pp. 241–252.

———. "Review of Ilting." *Hegel-Studien* 11 (1976): pp. 21–27.

Huysmans, J. K. *Against the Grain (A Rebours)*. New York: Dover, 1969.

Hyland, Richard. "Hegel: A User's Manual." *Cardozo Law Review* 10, no. 6 (April 1989): pp. 1735–1832.

Ilting, Karl-Heinz. "Der exoterische und der esoterische Hegel (1824–1831)." Introduction, in G. W. F. Hegel, *Vorlesungen über Rechtsphilosophie (1818–1831)*, edited by Karl-Heinz Ilting, vol. 4, pp. 45–66.

———. "Einleitung: Die 'Rechtsphilosophie' von 1820 und Hegels Vorlesungen über Rechtsphilosophie." Introduction, in G. W. F. Hegel, *Vorlesungen über Rechtsphilosophie (1818–1831)*, edited by Karl-Heinz Ilting, vol. 1, pp. 23–126.

———. "Zur Genese der Hegelschen Rechtsphilosophie." *Philosophische Rundschau* 3, no. 4 (1983): pp. 161–209.

Ingersoll, David, and Richard Matthews. *The Philosophic Roots of Modern Ideology*. 2nd ed. Englewood Cliffs, N.J.: Prentice-Hall, 1991.

Inwood, Michael J., ed. *Hegel*. London: Oxford University Press, 1985.

Kadish, Sanford. *Blame and Punishment*. New York: Macmillan, 1987.

Kalven, Harry, and Hans Zeisel. *The American Jury*. Boston: Little Brown, 1966.

Kant, Immanuel. *Groundwork of the Metaphysic of Morals*. Trans. H. J. Paton. New York: Harper and Row, 1964.

————. *Metaphysik der Sitten.* In *Werke in Sechs Bänden,* vol. 4, edited by Wilhelm Weischedel. Darmstadt: Wissenschaftliche Buchgesselschaft, 1963.

Kaufmann, Walter. *Hegel: Reinterpretation, Texts, and Commentary.* Garden City, N.Y.: Doubleday, 1965.

Kierkegaard, Søren. *The Concept of Irony.* Trans. Lee Capel. Bloomington: Indiana University Press, 1971.

————. *Fear and Trembling.* Trans. Howard V. Hong and Edna H. Hong. Princeton, N.J.: Princeton University Press, 1983.

Kimmerle, Heinz. "Die Widersprüche des Verhältnisses von esoterischer und exoterischer Philosophie in Hegels Systemkonzeptionen." In *Esoterik und Exoterik der Philosophie,* edited by Helmut Holzhey and Walther Zimmerli, pp. 139–157. Basel: Schawe and Co., 1977.

Kundera, Milan. *The Book of Laughter and Forgetting.* Trans. Michael Henry Heim. New York: Penguin, 1980.

Lamb, David. *Hegel and Modern Philosophy.* London: Croom Helm, 1987.

Larenz, Karl. "Hegels Dialektik des Willens und das Problem der Juristischen Persönlichkeit." *Logos* 20, no. 2 (1931): pp. 196–242.

————. *Hegels Zurechnungslehre und der Begriff der objektiven Zurechnung.* Darmstadt: Scientia Verlag Aalen, 1970, reprint of 1927 edition.

Lasson, Georg. "Einleitung." In *Grundlinien der Philosophie des Rechts,* edited by Georg Lasson, pp. vii–xciii. Leipzig: Felix Meiner, 1921.

Lenin, V. I. *The State and Revolution.* Peking: Foreign Language Press, 1976.

Liebruck, Bruno. "Recht, Moralität und Sittlichkeit bei Hegel." In *Materialen zu Hegels Rechtsphilosophie,* edited by Manfred Riedel, vol. 2, pp. 13–50.

Locke, John. *Second Treatise of Government.* Ed. C. B. Macpherson. Indianapolis: Hackett Publishing, 1980.

Machiavelli, Niccolò. *The Discourses.* London: Penguin, 1970.

Maier, Hans. "Einige Historische Vorbemerkungen zu Hegels Politischer Philosophie." *Hegel-Studien,* supplemental vol. 9 (1973): pp. 151–165.

Marx, Karl. *Critique of Hegel's "Philosophy of Right."* Trans. Annette Jolin and Joseph O'Malley. Cambridge: Cambridge University Press, 1970.

Marx, Karl, and Friedrich Engels. *Marx-Engels Gesamtausgabe* (MEGA). Berlin: Dietz, 1975–.

McTaggart, J. M. E. "Punishment." In *Studies in Hegelian Cosmology,* pp. 129–150. Cambridge: Cambridge University Press, 1901.

Menninger, Karl. *The Crime of Punishment.* New York: Viking Press, 1966.

Mill, John Stuart. *On Liberty.* Ed. Gertrude Himmelfarb. Harmondsworth, Eng.: Penguin, 1985.

Mitias, Michael. "Another Look at Hegel's Concept of Punishment." *Hegel-Studien* 13 (1978): pp. 175–185.

Morris, Herbert. "Persons and Punishment." *Monist* 52 (October 1968): pp. 475–501.

Morris, Norval, and Thomas Buckle. "The Humanitarian Theory of Punishment." In *Theories of Punishment,* edited by Stanley Grupp, pp. 309–316. Bloomington: Indiana University Press, 1971.

Nardulli, Peter F. "The Societal Cost of the Exclusionary Rule: An Empirical Assessment." *Research Journal* 1983, no. 3 (Summer 1983): pp. 585–610.

Nicholson, Peter. "Hegel on Crime." *History of Political Thought* 3, no. 1 (Spring 1982): pp. 103–121.

Nicolin, Günther, ed. *Hegel in Berichten seiner Zeitgenossen.* Hamburg: Felix Meiner, 1970.

Nietzsche, Friedrich. *The Gay Science.* Trans. Walter Kaufmann. New York: Penguin, 1978.

———. *On the Genealogy of Morals and Ecce Homo.* Trans. Walter Kaufmann. New York: Random House, 1967.

Nozick, Robert. *Anarchy, State, and Utopia.* New York: Basic Books, 1974.

———. *Philosophical Explanations.* Cambridge, Mass.: Harvard University Press, 1981.

O'Brien, George Dennis. *Hegel on Reason and History.* Chicago: University of Chicago Press, 1975.

Pare, David. "Hegel's Concept of Punishment." *Gnosis* 2 (1981): pp. 65–76.

Parkinson, G. H. R. "Hegel's Concept of Freedom." In *Hegel,* edited by Michael Inwood, pp. 153–173.

Pashukanis, Evgeny B. *Law and Marxism.* Trans. Barbara Einhorn. London: Ink Links, 1978.

Pelczynski, Z. A., ed. *Hegel's Political Philosophy: Problems and Perspectives.* Cambridge: Cambridge University Press, 1971.

———, ed. *The State and Civil Society.* Cambridge: Cambridge University Press, 1984.

Petry, Michael J. "Hegel and 'The Morning Chronicle.' " *Hegel-Studien* 11 (1976): pp. 11–80.

Piontkowski, Andrej Andreevic. *Hegels Lehre über Staat und Recht und Seine Strafrechtstheorie.* Trans. from the Russian by Anna Neuland. Berlin: VEB Deutscher Zentralverlag, 1960.

Pitkin, Hanna. *The Concept of Representation.* Berkeley: University of California Press, 1967.

———. *Wittgenstein and Justice.* Berkeley: University of California Press, 1972.

Plant, Raymond. *Hegel.* Bloomington: Indiana University Press, 1973.

Pöggeler, Otto. "Hegel der Verfasser des ältesten Systemprogramms der deutschen Idealismus." *Hegel-Studien,* supplemental vol. 4 (1969): pp. 17–32.

Posner, Richard. "An Economic Theory of the Criminal Law." *Columbia Law Review* 85 (October 1985): pp. 1193–1231.

Primoratz, Igor. *Banquos-Geist: Hegels Theorie der Strafe.* Bonn: Bouvier Verlag Herbert Grundmann, 1986.

Radbruch, Gustav. *Der Handlungsbegriff in seiner Bedeutung für das Strafrecht.* Berlin: J. Guttentag, 1903.

———. "Die Überzeugungsverbrecher." *Zeitschrift für die gesamte Strafrechtswissenschaft* 44 (1924): pp. 34–38.

Rawls, John. *A Theory of Justice.* Cambridge, Mass.: Harvard University Press, 1971.

————. "Two Concepts of Rules." In *Contemporary Utilitarianism*, edited by Michael D. Bayles, pp. 59–98. Gloucester, Mass.: Peter Smith, 1978.

Reyburn, Hugh A. *The Ethical Theory of Hegel*. Oxford: Oxford University Press, 1921.

Riedel, Manfred, ed. *Materialen zu Hegels Rechtsphilosophie*. 2 volumes. Frankfurt am Main: Suhrkamp, 1974–1975.

————. *Studien zu Hegels Rechtsphilosophie*. Frankfurt am Main: Suhrkamp, 1969.

Riley, Patrick. *Will and Political Legitimacy*. Cambridge, Mass.: Harvard University Press, 1982.

Ritter, Joachim. *Hegel and the French Revolution*. Trans. Richard Dien Winfield. Cambridge, Mass.: MIT Press, 1982.

Rosen, Stanley. *G. W. F. Hegel: An Introduction to the Science of Wisdom*. New Haven: Yale University Press, 1974.

Rosenblum, Nancy, ed. *Liberalism and the Moral Life*. Cambridge, Mass.: Harvard University Press, 1989.

Rottleuthner, Hubert R. "Die Substantialisierung des Formalrechts." In *Aktualität und Folgen der Philosophie Hegels*, edited by Oscar Negt, pp. 211–264. Frankfurt am Main: Suhrkamp, 1970.

Rousseau, Jean-Jacques. *The Social Contract*. Ed. Sir Ernest Barker. New York: Oxford University Press, 1960.

Sabine, George. *A History of Political Theory*. New York: Henry Holt, 1937.

Sandel, Michael. *Liberalism and the Limits of Justice*. Cambridge: Cambridge University Press, 1982.

Sayers, Sean. "The Actual is the Rational." In *Hegel and Modern Philosophy*, edited by David Lamb, pp. 143–160. London: Croom Helm, 1987.

Scanlon, Thomas. "Promises and Practices." *Philosophy and Public Affairs* 19, no. 3 (Summer 1990): pp. 199–226.

Schafer, Stephen. *The Political Criminal*. New York: Free Press, 1974.

Schild, Wolfgang. "Die Aktualität des Hegelschen Strafbegriffes." In *Philosophische Elemente der Tradition des Politischen Denkens*, edited by Erich Heintel, pp. 199–233. Vienna: R. Oldenbourg, 1979.

————. "Der Strafrechtsdogmatische Begriff der Zurechnung in der Rechtsphilosophie Hegels." *Zeitschrift für Philosophische Forschung* 35 (1981): pp. 445–476.

Schnädelbach, Herbert. "Zum Verhältnis von Logik und Gesellschaftstheorie bei Hegel." In *Aktualität und Folgen der Philosophie Hegels*, edited by Oscar Negt, pp. 58–80. Frankfurt am Main: Suhrkamp, 1970.

Seelmann, Kurt. "Hegels Straftheorie in seinen *Grundlinien der Philosophie des Rechts*." *Juristische Schulung* 10 (1979): pp. 687–691.

Skinner, Quentin. "Meaning and Understanding in the History of Ideas." In *Meaning and Context: Quentin Skinner and His Critics*, edited by James Tully, pp. 29–67. Cambridge, Eng.: Polity Press, 1988.

Smith, Steven B. "Hegelianism and the Three Crises of Rationality." *Social Research* 56, no. 4 (Winter 1989): pp. 943–973.

Smith, Steven B. *Hegel's Critique of Liberalism: Rights in Context*. Chicago: University of Chicago Press, 1989.

———. "Hegel's Idea of a Critical Theory." *Political Theory* 15, no. 1 (February 1987): pp. 99–126.

Solomon, Robert C. *In the Spirit of Hegel*. New York: Oxford University Press, 1983.

Der Spiegel. "Recht zur Revolution." No. 52 (1983): pp. 130–132.

———. "Sprache der Revolution." No. 13 (1973): pp. 144–145.

Steinberger, Peter J. "Hegel on Crime and Punishment." *American Political Science Review* 77 (1983): pp. 858–870.

———. *Logic and Politics: Hegel's Philosophy of Right*. New Haven: Yale University Press, 1988.

Stern, David. "The Immanence of Thought: Hegel's Critique of Foundationalism." *Owl of Minerva* 22, no. 1 (Fall 1990): pp. 19–34.

Stillman, Peter G. "Hegel's Critique of Liberal Theories of Rights." *American Political Science Review* 68, no. 3 (September 1974): pp. 1086–1092.

———. "Hegel's Idea of Punishment." *Journal of the History of Philosophy* 14, no. 2 (April 1976): pp. 169–182.

Strauss, Leo. *Persecution and the Art of Writing*. Glencoe, Ill.: Free Press, 1952.

Taylor, Charles. *Hegel*. Cambridge: Cambridge University Press, 1975.

Taylor, Mark. *Journeys to Selfhood: Hegel and Kierkegaard*. Berkeley: University of California Press, 1980.

Topitsch, Ernst. *Die Sozialphilosophie Hegels als Heilslehre und Herrschaftsideologie*. Munich: R. Piper and Co., 1981.

Tucker, Robert C., ed. *The Marx-Engels Reader*. 2nd ed. New York: W. W. Norton, 1978.

Tunick, Mark. "Hegel's Justification of Hereditary Monarchy." *History of Political Thought*, forthcoming.

———. "The Justification of Legal Punishment: Hegel's *Rechtsphilosophie* as Practical Theory." Doctoral dissertation, University of California, Berkeley, 1990.

———. *Punishment: Theory and Practice*. Berkeley: University of California Press, 1992.

Turk, Austin. *Political Criminality*. Beverly Hills: Sage Publications, 1982.

Vlastos, Gregory. "Socrates on Acrasia." *Phoenix* 23 (1969): pp. 71–88.

Waldron, Jeremy. *The Right to Private Property*. Oxford: Oxford University Press, 1988.

Walsh, W. H. *Hegelian Ethics*. New York: Macmillan, 1969.

Walzer, Michael. *The Company of Critics*. New York: Basic Books, 1988.

———. *Interpretation and Social Criticism*. Cambridge, Mass.: Harvard University Press, 1987.

Wasserstrom, Richard. "Strict Liability in the Criminal Law." *Stanford Law Review* 12 (July 1960): pp. 731–745.

Waszek, Norbert. "Hegels Schottische Bettler." *Hegel-Studien* 19 (1984): pp. 311–316.

———. "A Stage in the Development of Hegel's Theory of the Modern State." *Hegel-Studien* 20 (1985): pp. 163–172.

Wiedmann, Franz. *Hegel: An Illustrated Biography*. Trans. Joachim Neugroschel. New York: Western Publishing Co., 1968.

Winch, Peter. *The Idea of a Social Science*. London: Routledge and Kegan Paul, 1958.

Wittgenstein, Ludwig. *The Blue and Brown Books*. New York: Harper and Row, 1965.

———. *On Certainty*. Ed. G. E. M. Anscombe and G. H. von Wright. New York: Harper and Row, 1972.

———. *Philosophical Grammar*. Berkeley: University of California Press, 1978.

———. "Remarks on Frazer's Golden Bough." In *Wittgenstein: Sources and Perspectives*, edited by C. G. Luckhardt, pp. 61–81. Ithaca: Cornell University Press, 1979.

Wootton, Lady Barbara. "Diminished Responsibility: A Layman's View." *Law Quarterly Review* 76 (1960): pp. 224–239.

———. *Social Science and Social Pathology*. London: George Allen and Unwin, 1967.

Yack, Bernard. *The Longing for Total Revolution*. Princeton, N.J.: Princeton University Press, 1986.

Yovel, Yirmiahu. "Hegel's Dictum That the Rational Is Actual and the Actual Is Rational." In *Konzepte der Dialektik*, edited by Werner Becker and Wilhelm K. Essler, pp. 111–131. Frankfurt: Vittorio Klostermann, 1981.

Index

Abraham, 146
abstract (*abstrahieren*), 39–41. *See also* freedom: abstract
abstract freedom. *See* freedom: abstract
abstract right, 12n.38, 49n.57, 94, 110–13, 114, 120n.58, 129n.114
accountability, of criminal, 124–31
acrasia, 56n.90
action (*Handlung*), 126–28
actual is rational, vii, 8–10, 152–67
actuality (vs. ideality), 144–47, 148, 150–52, 155–56, 160–61, 167, 169–70. *See also* actual is rational; existence
Adorno, Theodor, 153
adultery, 112, 142–45, 159, 168–69
Agamemnon, 106n.134
alcoholic, 42, 56, 74
Alexander, 20
Antigone, 96
Arato, Andrew, 153
Arendt, Hannah, 119n.51, 145n.4
Aristophanes, 20
Aristotelianism. *See* Hegel: Aristotelianism of
Aristotle, 85, 86
Athenians, 70, 73, 101, 155n.39, 171. *See also* Greeks
authority, of state to punish. *See* political crime
Avineri, Shlomo, 94n.81

Banquos-Geist, 34, 76, 78, 81
Barber, Benjamin, 16–17
beautiful soul, 47
Beccaria, Cesare, 136
Becker, Claudia, 6
Befriedigung, 16, 51, 51n.74, 72n.17
begriefen, 45, 51, 98, 148–50, 161
being-at-home, 82–83, 91; vs. feeling-at-home, 105, 142, 144–45, 147–48, 148n.13, 150–52, 156, 165, 171. *See also* theory: relation to practice
Bentham, Jeremy, 25, 110
Bildung, 53, 97, 100, 103, 106n.134, 129n.114

Böning, Peter, 125n.88, 129n.114
Bourgeois, Philippe, 144n.3
bulimia, 56, 74
Burke, Edmund, 104, 107, 165, 173

capital punishment, viii, 124, 134, 136–37
capitalism, 118
Carlsbad censorship decrees, 7, 8, 9, 153–54
Carove, Friedrich Wilhelm, 7n.17
categorical imperative, 31–33, 171
Charlemagne, 97
China, 135
civil society, 88, 114, 119, 140, 160n.56; vs. state, 106–7
clutching: defined, 109, 109n.1, 113; Hegel on, 113–20. *See also* political crime
commitment, 47–51, 54–56, 59, 63, 84, 143–47, 150, 151, 159–60, 167–74; internal, 66–68; levels of, 48–50, 59. *See also* freedom: as commitment
common law, 18
communitarian, Hegel as, 100, 105n.130
community. *See* ethical substance
Concept (*Begriff*), 12–14, 19, 155n.37, 157, 166–67; vs. concept, 12, 14, 17, 167
concrete, 111n.7
confessions, 120n.59, 121–22
conscience, 38, 78; moral right of, 111
constitution, 96
content, 47, 51, 55–60, 66, 72, 111. *See also* commitment
contingency. *See Zufälligkeit*
contract, 18n.73, 49; state not based on, 49, 98, 100, 136
conviction, ethics of, 17, 67–70
Cooper, David, 33–34n.49, 133–34
correctness, vs. truth, 155n.39, 164
courtesy, 159
crime: concept of, 25, 119; vs. fraud, 26–28; Hegel's account of, 25–29, 97–98, 111–12; necessity of, 33; vs. nonmalicious wrong, 26, 27
criminal law, vs. civil law, 25, 28n.27, 134

death penalty. *See* capital punishment

deed (*Tat*). 126–28

democracy, Hegel on, 164

Des Esseintes, 40n.15, 44, 45

determinate negation, 13, 88

determination of guilt: Hegel on, 120–31; issues raised by, viii, 124–25; as subpractice, 109, 120. *See also* accountability, of criminal

de Wette, Professor W. M. L., 9, 10, 69

d'Hondt, Jacques, 9n.23, 68–69

dialectic, 156, 169; in Hegel's metaphysics, 13, 157; of immanent critic, 22, 150, 158–61; between theory and practice, 152. *See also* actual is rational

Dickens, Charles, 40

Dinocrates, 20

discretion, judicial, 131

divorce, 49

Dostoyevski, Fyodor, 56n.91

due process, 120–24

Duff, R. A., 160–61

Duncan v. Louisiana, 122n.70

Dworkin, Ronald, 159n.52

East Oakland convict, 142–45, 167–68, 174

education. See *Bildung*

Egyptians, 112, 112n.17

ethical life. See *Sittlichkeit*

ethical substance, 32, 77, 79, 80–91, 93–107, 112, 166–67; Greek polis as, 81–84, 91; jury's verdict as expressing, 122–23; modern state as, 93–95, 99–107, 115; Rome's lack of, 106n.134

Eumenides, 34, 76, 81

Ewing, A. C., x n.15

exclusionary rule, 24, 121, 138

excuse, vs. justification, 119–20

existence, vs. actuality, 154–56, 161n.63, 163

existentialist argument, Hegel's. *See* justification: existentialist

extraordinary punishment, 122

false consciousness. *See* being-at-home: vs. feeling-at-home

Feinberg, Joel, 109n.1, 110n.5

Feuerbach, Ludwig, 12

Fichte, Johann Gottlieb, 113

Flechtheim, Ossip, 30n.25, 33nn.46 and 47, 81, 134, 136, 153, 162n.68

foundationalism, 3, 3n.4, 169–70; Hegel's, 12, 12n.40, 14, 16–17, 22, 71, 86, 101–2, 170; modern rejection of, 103, 167

founder, 96–97

fraud, vs. crime, 26–28

freedom, 13, 37–75, 102, 157, 171; abstract, 39–47, 54–55; as being-at-home (*bei sich*), 50–51, 59–60, 73, 75, 154; as commitment, 47–48, 50–51, 54, 59, 62–63, 66–67, 72–74, 143–45; connection with right, 36n.62, 37, 37n.2, 64, 72, 76, 93, 98–99, 108, 110–11, 116; as rational freedom, 53–54, 59–60; role of, in Hegel's philosophy, 37–38; subjective or inner, 40–43, 44–45, 66–67, 147. *See also* being-at-home; justification: connected with freedom; legal punishment: as making the criminal free; rationality: Hegel's standard of; will

French Revolution, 9, 10, 46, 93

Fries, Jacob, 10, 68–69

Gans, Edward, 8

Geist. See Spirit

Genealogy, 19. *See also* justification: historical

German idealism, 47

God, in Hegel's philosophy, 3, 12, 86, 169

Greeks, 81–84, 89–90, 99, 106n.134, 118, 127–28, 137, 164. *See also* Athenians; ethical substance: Greek polis as; Sparta

Griesheim, Karl Gustav Julius von, 7, 8

guilt. *See* determination of guilt

Haines, Nicholas, 69n.133, 158

Hampton, Jean, 25n.5, 28n.19

happiness, Hegel's criticism of, 57n.92, 61–63, 64–65

Hartmann, Klaus, 10n.30

Haym, Rudolf, x n.17, 8, 152

Hegel, G. W. F.: Aristotelianism of, 87, 89, 91, 157, 168n.102; conservatism of, alleged, vii, xi n.17, 8–10, 93, 114, 152–53, 161, 162n.68, 165; as critical of practices, xi, 9, 45, 70, 100–102, 104, 105, 136n.156, 156, 158, 159–65, 173–74; early vs. late, 43–44, 44nn.30 and 32, 76–77, 86–87, 90–94, 99, 107, 116,

162; as educator, 170–71; exoteric vs. esoteric, 7–11, 154–55, 155n.38, 162n.67, 172; idealism of, vii, 153, 161; irrelevance of, alleged, vii, viii, x; vs. Kant, 32, 66, 157; as lecturer, 5, 6–7; as legal interpretivist, x, 17–20; limits of the theory of punishment of, viii n.7, 109–10, 112–13, 121–22, 134–35, 137–38; vs. Marx, 118–19, 148–52, 156, 158; metaphysics of, viii, 3–4, 12–14, 16–17, 85–86, 89, 99, 101–4, 166–67, 170, 173; obscurity of, ix–x, 3, 4–5, 11–12, 26, 77, 79, 87; ontology of, 13–14, 85–86, 144, 155–57, 167; philosophy of history of, 3, 14–16, 42, 101–2, 157n.45, 166; vs. Plato, 22; and radical criticism, 151–52, 165, 172–73; rehabilitated version of, 4, 14, 17, 86, 102–4, 167; vs. utilitarianism, 35, 61–62, 80, 122, 173; vs. utopianism, 20–21, 67. See also freedom; immanent criticism; legal punishment; rationalism; relativism; retributivism; revolution; state; teleology; theory

Works: Aesthetics, 5, 43; Älteste Systemprogramm, 92; Encyclopaedia, 5, 14–15, 154–55; "English Reform Bill," 117–18; Frankfurt fragments, 116, 137; "German Constitution," 161–62; History of Philosophy, 5, 149; Jenaer Realphilosophie, 87, 131n.128; Natural Law, 32, 41; Phenomenology, 5, 12n.40, 78–87, 89–91, 93, 97, 99, 126, 147, 157n.45; Philosophy of History, 5, 16, 94–95, 106n.134; Philosophy of Religion, 5, 44, 46n.42, 95; Philosophy of Right, 5–11, 48–50, 111–12, 129n.114, 153–54; Propädeutik, 5, 31, 94, 98; Science of Logic, 5, 26, 28, 29, 155; "System der Sittlichkeit," 83, 87. See also lecture notes of Rechtsphilosophie

Henrich, Dieter, 6, 7, 10, 44n.30, 92–93, 116–18, 141n.166, 154
Herder, Johann Gottfried, 90
Herzog, Don, 3n.4, 169–70n.106
historical justification. See under justification
historicist school, Hegel's criticism of, 162–63. See also Savigny, F. C. von
Hobbes, Thomas, 25n.8, 78n.5, 169n.106

Hölderlin, Friedrich, 92
Homeyer, Carl Gustav, 7
Hook, Sidney, vii n.3, 153
Horstmann, Rolf-Peter, 10, 11
Hotho, Gustav Heinrich, 6n.14, 8
Huysman, J. K., 40n.15

Idea, 12, 13, 14, 15, 69, 72, 85, 92, 157
ideality. See actuality
Ilting, Karl-Heinz, 5, 6, 8n.19, 162n.67, 172. See also Hegel: exoteric vs. esoteric
immanent criticism, 20–22, 109, 150–51; of Hegel, 115–16, 119, 122–24; as Hegel's strategy, vii, xi, 14, 20–23, 54, 89, 101, 108–9, 138–39, 151–52, 158–65, 172–74; Marx and, 151n.23; vs. radical criticism, 23, 138–39, 172–74; of war, 89. See also actual is rational; dialectic: of immanent critic; Hegel: as critical of practices; theory: Hegel's application of, to the practice of punishment
incest laws, 51–54
India, 135, 155n.39, 164
infliction of punishment: Hegel on, 133–37; as subpractice, 109
inheritance, Hegel on, 160n.56, 164
insanity defense, 124, 129–31
intent. See accountability
intention (Absicht), 126–28
international law, 101
interpretation, Hegel's political philosophy as, 14–20, 22, 145, 151, 166–67. See also Hegel: as legal interpretivist

Jews, 135, 156
judicial discretion, 131
jury trials, justification of, 120, 122–23
justification: connected with freedom, 53–54, 60, 91, 98–99, 100; defense in criminal law, 119–20; existentialist, 104; historical, 18–20, 162–63; objective, x, 3–4, 35, 60, 100; as objective and subjective, 72–74; of practices as a whole, 102–3, 104, 167–70; relative vs. absolute, 112n.17, 164; subjective, 35, 61–72, 115. See also legal punishment: justification of; rationality: Hegel's standard of
justified disobedience, Hegel's theory of. See political crime

Kant, vii, 31–32, 33; on perpetual peace, 88; theory of punishment of, ix, x. *See also* Hegel: vs. Kant
Kierkegaard, Søren, 46, 146–47, 150, 152, 169
Knox, T. M., 57n.92, 58n.94
Kotzebue, Friedrich, 9, 69, 69n.131
Kundera, Milan, 54n.84

Lamb, David, 136–37
Larenz, Karl, 41n.22, 57n.92, 58n.93, 73n.151
Lasson, Georg, 6n.12, 22n.96
law, 95, 96–97; form vs. substance of, 17–18, 121, 131; international, 101; natural, 51–52, 53, 72, 95–96. *See also* second nature
lawmaking: Hegel on, 95, 110–13; as subpractice, 109, 110
laws of nature, vs. laws of right, 95–96
lecture notes of *Rechtsphilosophie*, 5–11, 123n.75, 154–55, 163, 172; authenticity of, 5–7, 10–11; discrepancies of, with *Philosophy of Right*, 8–10, 19n.85
legal interpretivist. *See under* Hegel
legal punishment: as criminal's right, ix, 35–36, 37, 74; Hegel's justification of, ix, 14, 34–36, 64, 76, 80, 87–88, 99–100, 108–10, 134; justification of, viii, 24; as making the criminal free, ix, 36, 37, 38, 73–75, 116, 128, 142; practical issues of, viii, 24, 108–9. *See also* punishment
legitimacy, of state punishment. *See* clutching
Lenin, V. I., 151n.23
Leo, John, 105n.130
lex talionis, 133
liberalism, Hegel and, 10, 10n.25, 11, 60, 68–69, 88, 91, 98, 100, 106n.134, 113. *See also* contract: state not based on; Locke, John; Mill, J. S.
limits, of Hegel's philosophy. *See* Hegel: limits of the theory of punishment of
Locke, John, 64, 76n.3, 88, 169n.106

Machiavelli, Niccolò, 20, 96–97
Maier, Hans, 94n.81
marriage, 12n.39, 14, 49–50, 54, 143–44, 159–60

Marx, Karl: critic of Hegel, viii, xi n.17, 148, 157. *See also* Hegel, vs. Marx
master-slave, 45–46, 97n.104, 141
Menninger, Karl, 24nn.1 and 3, 102n.120, 172–73
mens rea, 124–25. *See also* accountability
metaphysics: vs. politics, 14, 16–17, 67. *See also* Hegel, metaphysics of
Metternich, Klemens von, 9
Mill, J. S., 42n.25, 60n.104, 111, 111n.14
Miller, A. V., 37n.1
Mitias, Michael, 31n.28
mole, Hegel as, 10
monarchy, 8–10
monasteries, 19
Montesquieu, 90, 93
Moralität, 111n.7, 115, 126, 166n.98
The Morning Chronicle, 18n.74, 121, 123
Morris, Herbert, 25n.5, 28n.19

Napoleon, 9, 87
Napoleonic code, 18
natural law. *See* law: natural
Nazi Germany, 100, 101, 102, 156, 166n.98
necessity, right of, 118, 119–20, 138n.164, 140–41
negation of the negation: punishment as, x, 34–35, 88, 134–35; war as, 88
negative freedom, 46–47. *See also* freedom: abstract
negative infinite judgment, 26, 28–29, 30, 140, 141n.166
negligence, 128–29
New Hegelians, xi n.17
Nicholson, Peter, 26n.9, 112n.15
Nietzsche, Friedrich, 3n.4, 173–74
nonfoundationalism. *See* foundationalism
nonmalicious (or civil) wrong, vs. crime, 26, 27
Nozick, Robert, 24n.2, 103–4n.127

Oedipus, 53, 127–28
ontology. *See under* Hegel
original intent theory, 18–19, 19n.79
owl of Minerva, 162

Pare, David, 64, 137
Parfit, Derek, 130
Parkinson, G. H. R., 41n.22, 57n.92, 62–63n.114

particularity. *See* will: particular
Pashukanis, Evgeny, 149, 151
patriotism, 88, 171
Payne v. Tennessee, 132–33
Pelczynski, Z. A., 4
phrenology, 126
physiognomy, 126
pietism, 67–70, 72
Piontkowski, A. A., xi n.17, 125, 125nn.87 and 89, 162n.68
Pitkin, Hanna, 11n.32, 21n.90
Plato, 22
plea-bargaining, viii, 24, 109; Hegel on, 123–24
Pöggeler, Otto, 92n.72, 170n.109
police, 113–14
police power, 129n.114
political crime, 113, 113n.20, 114–20, 140–41
political protest, Hegel on, 68–70, 158
politics, 147. *See also* metaphysics; rational politics
positive infinite judgment, 26, 27
Posner, Richard, 25, 110
poverty, 116–17, 118–20, 140–41
Primoratz, Igor, 11, 28n.18, 31, 78n.9, 131n.128, 133–34, 136
property, 21–22, 26, 28, 32, 33, 48–49, 49n.57, 98, 164. *See also* abstract right; inheritance
punishment, defined, 133–34. *See also* infliction of punishment; legal punishment; retributivism; utilitarianism: as theory of punishment
purpose (*Vorsatz*), 126–28

rabble, 116–17, 118, 140–41. *See also* poverty
radical criticism, 148–49, 150–52. *See also* Hegel: and radical criticism; immanent criticism
Raskolnikov, 115
rational politics, 17, 68–71
rationalism, Hegel's, 3, 17–20, 33, 67–71, 92–93, 99, 163, 165. *See also* actual is rational
rationality: of criminal, imputed, 30–31, 33, 128–31, 142; Hegel's standard of, 19, 23, 32, 49n.67, 59n.99, 99, 102–3, 155n.39, 165–67
Rawls, John, 170n.107

Recht, translation of, 37n.1
Recht-an-sich, 28, 28n.14, 34, 64, 77, 80, 94–95, 97–101, 120; translation of, 77n.4, 120n.58
Rechtsphilosophie, 5, 6–8, 11, 77
recognition, 97–98
Rehnquist, Chief Justice William, 132
relativism, Hegel and, 21n.89, 101, 112, 112n.17, 136, 165–67
restitution, vs. punishment, 134
retributivism, ix, 14, 25, 34–35, 110, 124–25, 131; Hegel's, 14, 34–35, 110, 116, 137. *See also* legal punishment: Hegel's justification of
revenge, 158–59n.51; Hegel's criticism of, 64–65, 79, 79nn.10 and 11, 115, 133
revolution, Hegel on, 116–19, 120
Reyburn, Hugh, 15, 94n.81, 136
right, 37, 37n.2, 76–77, 105, 110–11; of intention, 128–29; language of, 93; origin of, 95–98; to punish, 76, 76n.3, 77–81, 94; to work, 119. *See also* abstract right; freedom: connection with right; necessity; *Recht*; *Recht-an-sich*; subjectivity: right of
Riley, Patrick, 57n.92
Riviere, Pierre, 74–75
Robin Hood, 115
romanticism, German, 17
Rome, Hegel on, 90, 106, 106n.134, 164
Rosen, Stanley, 4
Rosenzweig, Franz, 8
Rousseau, J. J., 30, 36; and Hegel, 92, 93

Sabine, George, 37–38, 71
Sand, Karl Ludwig, 9, 68–69
satisfaction. See *Befriedigung*
Savigny, F. C. von, 18–19. *See also* historicist school
Sayers, Sean, 152–53
Scanlon, Thomas, 32n.37
Schelling, Friedrich, 4, 87, 92
Schild, Wolfgang, 11n.35, 62n.113
Schiller, Friedrich, 92
Schleiermacher, Friedrich, 9, 10
search and seizure, 113–14. *See also* exclusionary rule
second nature, 32, 53–54, 73, 95
Seelman, Kurt, 97
self-consciousness, 13, 42, 72, 81–84, 90. *See also* spirit; subjectivity

sentencing, viii; Hegel on, 131–33; as subpractice, 109
serfdom. *See* slavery
7-Eleven, 58–59
show, 16, 26, 29, 152
simple negative judgment, 26, 27
Sitte, 82, 98, 135, 163. *See also* second nature
Sittlichkeit (ethical life), 28, 32, 65, 66, 73,
  77, 87. 111n.7, 128, 167. *See also* ethical substance
Skimpole, Harold, 40
Skinner, Quentin, vii n.1
slavery, 18, 41–42, 42n.25, 101, 116, 163,
  164
Smith, Steven, 17n.72, 21n.90, 22, 33n.48,
  57n.92, 90, 93n.76, 97, 102–3,
  170n.108
smoker, 30
Socrates, 47, 70, 72, 84, 101, 146; Aristophanes', 20; Kierkegaard's, 46
Solomon, Robert, 4–5, 12n.36, 17n.71, 86
Souter, Justice David, 132
Sparta, 164
Der Spiegel, 116
spirit (*Geist*), 10, 12n.38, 13, 14, 72, 79,
  81–87, 89–91, 93, 99–102, 154, 173; as
  parochial or universal, 90–91, 99, 100–
  102; of world, 15, 16, 101
state: vs. civil society, 106–7; Hegel's theory of, 50, 65, 67, 72–73, 118, 163–64,
  170–72; Hegel's use of the word, 94,
  94n.81, 105, 119; as power that punishes, 76, 77–80. *See also* contract: state
  not based on; ethical substance: modern
  state as
Steinberger, Peter, 129–30, 134, 160n.55
Stern, David, 12n.40
Stoic freedom. *See* freedom: subjective or
  inner
Stoicism, 106n.134, 146, 147
Strauss, David, 8
strict liability. *See* accountability
subjectivity, 66, 83–84, 135, 164; right of,
  71–72, 115, 122, 123, 127, 131. *See also*
  freedom: subjective or inner; justification: subjective
substance, 16. *See also* ethical substance
suicide, 39, 41, 46

Taylor, Charles, 13n.49, 17n.71, 47n.55,
  85–86, 90, 165, 166

teleology, Hegel's, 14–15, 16, 67, 91, 99,
  102, 166
Ten Commandments, 112
testimony, 121
theory: Hegel's application of, to the practice of punishment, viii–ix, 24, 108–10,
  128–32, 134–35; and practice, Hegel on,
  40–42, 45, 51, 150; relation to practice,
  20, 143–45, 148–52, 156. *See also* begreifen; immanent criticism
Thompson, Bartholomew, 18, 121
Topitsch, Ernst, xi n.17, 162n.68
torture, Hegel's criticism of, 120n.59
treason, 111
Tunick, Mark, viii n. 5, 3n.4, 21n.91,
  48n.56, 71n.141, 109nn.1 and 2,
  111n.7, 124n.80, 168n.103, 173n.124

Understanding (*Verstand*), 12, 19, 61, 88,
  153
universal. *See* state: Hegel's theory of; will:
  universal
utilitarianism, 62n.113; as theory of punishment, ix, 25, 110, 124–25. *See also*
  under Hegel
utopianism. *See under* Hegel

victim-impact evidence, 132–33
Volksgeist, 96, 97

Waldron, Jeremy, 21–22, 47n.55
Wallace, William, 77n.4, 120n.58
Walsh, W. H., 165–66, 171
Walzer, Michael, 21n.90
Wannenmann, Peter, 7
war, Hegel on, 83, 88–90, 99
Wartburgfest, 68, 69, 158
Wasserstrom, Richard, 125n.85
welfare, 114, 118–19
will (*Wille*), 38, 97, 127–28, 131–32; arbitrary, 33, 34, 40n.14, 48–49, 50, 55,
  56–60, 63, 140; common (*gemeinsam*),
  49; free, 39n.6, 47, 50–51, 55, 72–74,
  115; general, 30, 36; immediate (or natural), 55, 56, 57n.92, 58n.94, 61, 142;
  particular, 26–30, 33, 34, 35, 36, 47, 65,
  66, 106–7, 118; split (of criminal), 29–
  33, 35, 122, 128, 142; universal, 26–30,
  33, 49, 64, 88, 116, 134. *See also* freedom
Willkür. See will: arbitrary; *Zufälligkeit*

wish, 30
Wittgenstein, Ludwig, 11n.32, 55n.86,
    170n.106

Yack, Bernard, 43–45, 54, 93n.77,
    157n.46

Yovel, Yirmiahu, 157–58

Zeno, 149–50
Zufälligkeit (contingency), 15, 16, 22, 33,
    57–59, 62–65, 127, 163, 167. *See also*
    existence